Celebratin

Gordon MacLellan

www.capallbann.co.uk

Celebrating Nature

ISBN - 186163 168 5
ISBN 13 - 9781861631688

Cover design by HR Design
Cover photograph Tall Tree Puppet from project at Alyn Waters Country Park, Wrexham. Photo G. MacLellan

Published by:

Capall Bann Publishing
Auton Farm
Milverton
Somerset
TA4 1NE

Acknowledgements

It is often hard to know where activities first begin. We meet ideas, passing thoughts, and whole activities with other people and find that our own ideas evolve with the encounter.

The activities in Celebrating Nature are all ones that we use in Creeping Toad projects but where their starting points were, by now, is anyone's guess.

So I would like to thank and acknowledge the inspiration that has come to me through work with these people and places

Paula Bowman
Cate Clark
Josie Coggins
Angie da Silva (for introducing me to bottle flowers)
that wonderful person on a training course who introduced us all to bottle fish
Alida Gersie
Malcolm Green
In Pursuit of Love and Passion (people, workshops and the whole celebration)
Lesley Martin
Mid-Pennine Arts
the Stone and Water Team

the hills, streams and dales of Derbyshire
Kimmeridge Bay, Dorset
Kilmartin Glen, Argyll

gorillas and toads everywhere and always

Special thanks to

Cheshire County Council Countryside Management Service, Teggs Nose Country Park and the staff and children of Hollin Hey Primary School for use of the Stone Poem words that we grew together

Scottish Natural Heritage and RSPB for the Biodiversity inspiration

Contents

Using this book

Celebrating Nature is a manual to guide you through a process for creating celebrations with groups of people. As such it is a place for ideas and activities but not for rules or definitive statements.

There are no rules in this game, only suggested paths to follow. As project organisers, our role is to help our groups find their own paths to celebration and I hope that *Celebrating Nature* will offer you some signposts for the route and vehicles to ease the journey.

Celebrating Nature takes you through a celebratory process, offering a variety of activities for different stages of that adventure. You might just plunge in and out of this book, clutching at activities as you need them but to understand the entire process, try reading the whole book first.

Age groups?

Most of this book is written as if for use with young people of perhaps 8-12 years of age. Most of the activities will work across age groups. Those Junior School years are good starting points for laying out ideas: if you are working with younger, older or more mixed groups look at the techniques and ideas involved and adapt accordingly. To be honest, I find I need to shift things remarkably little to accommodate other groups. Hold onto a balance between imagination, freedom and effective processes. Have fun.

Finding activities

Within *Celebrating Nature*, activities are indexed by their names but try reading through first rather than just picking names from the index! My earlier book *Talking to the Earth* (Capall Bann 1995, ISBN 1-898307-43-1) is very much a companion volume to *Celebrating Nature*. It is another collection of similar, but different, environmental exploration, art and discovery ideas. In writing *Celebrating Nature* I have tried to avoid overlap of activities with *Talking* but it has happened in a few places but only where the activities felt very necessary and valuable to the process of celebration described here.

Disclaimer

In this book activites and the processes by which they might be followed are described as best I can. No matter how good, or poor, my directions might be, you remain responsible for your own way of delivering activites, managing groups and sourcing materials. I have tried to be clear about all these, but it is up to you to test, try and refine activities to suit yourself, your groups and your situations.

Creeping Toad

I suppose I should explain the repeated "Toad" references that surface through this book. I work as "Creeping Toad": an environmental arts and education consultant who "works with groups to find ways of celebrating the places where people live, work and play". I spend my time fexploring the principles that lie behind this book. Out of a working background that has included zoology and teaching, countryside ranger work and heritage interpretation, I have grown into this role where my ecological and educational experience fuse with the art, story and drama that have run alongside the more formal work all through my life.

Projects mentioned here are generally Creeping Toad ones and all these activities are ones that have been used in Toad projects and "field tested" as it were.

You can find out more about Toad work at :
www.creepingtoad.org.uk.

celebrate
(selibRayt) v/t and i perform (solemn function); consecrate the Eucharist; observe solemnly; commemorate (a festival, anniversary);
extol; (coll) have a gay time
Penguin English Dictionary

celebration
an occasion of wonder and delight
Creeping Toad

It seems much better to me to approach the world around us, to face the challenge and need for environmental, technological and social change from a place of wonder and delight than one of guilt and despair. So much of the news about our relationship with the world around us is grim that environmental campaigns seem designed to induce fear, anger and grief more than anything else. Environmentalists are easily painted as doom-mongers and killjoys or promoting action that is either too extreme to countenance or too simplistic to make a difference or, simply, pushing a dogmatic, politic agenda.

Without dismissing the horror of what we are doing to the world around us and the life we share this planet with, I think it is just as valuable, if not more so, to approach environmental change from a place of wonder. We need to remind ourselves that we live in; that we are part of, a world that is, quite simply, amazing: glorious, spectacular and, as far as we know, unique. We are part of that world, part of that wonder and glory and spectacle. *Celebrating Nature* sets out to offer readers activities that we can all use to remind ourselves:

of our connection to this world

of the wonder and delight of it

of our freedom as individuals to have our own personal, unique experience of it all to tell our own stories of ourselves and this world

of life in a world worthy of celebration

1

Because.....

Why "celebrate"? Why perpetrate some action based on excitement, delight and joy in this time of worry, fear and anger?

Because...

We live in a world worthy of celebration: a world of wonder and delight, a place of glory and marvels and

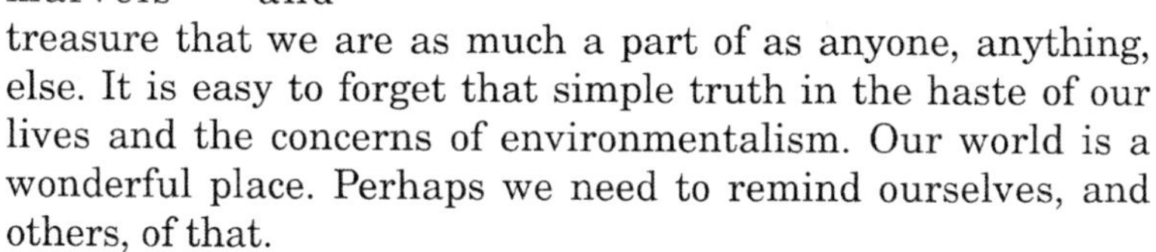

treasure that we are as much a part of as anyone, anything, else. It is easy to forget that simple truth in the haste of our lives and the concerns of environmentalism. Our world is a wonderful place. Perhaps we need to remind ourselves, and others, of that.

Creating a celebration is a collaborative process: this book is a manual to help you create your own celebrations. As such you might be reading it as someone who is liable to leading groups in the process, but make no mistake about this: you will not own the final product. Effective celebrations grow out of their participants. A celebratory process should feed imaginations and encourage new ideas. Our role as leaders (or whatever you may want to call yourself) is to help people embark upon that process, guiding, teaching, arguing, holding the pattern of it together. Just how much flexibility there can be within your celebration will depend upon time, confidence (your own as much as the group's!), experience and more. Through this book we'll explore that whole process.

Creating a celebration teaches new skills: all sorts of skills from straightforward "how to make" ones: masks, puppets, drystone walls, lanterns, baskets to perhaps more unexpected one as poets, storytellers, dancers, producers, planners.

Celebrations engender confidence and reflection: and out of those skills come confidence in self. People, hopefully, find that they can break some of those old inhibitions. Discard those old damning words "I can't paint, or draw, or dance, or sing, or design, or plan..." See now all the things that we can do! And in the process, we look at ideas for encouraging stillness, for giving people time to think and feel, and reflect, recognising their feelings and offer folk the opportunity to express them. This does not mean that we are expected to become therapists. We are working with creative ideas and communication, using these to give people avenues for exploring and feeling in a supportive space, but, on the whole, we are not there to provide in-depth one-to-one counselling. Do not, however, let the risk of strong emotions discourage you: it is not irresponsible to give people the courage to feel.

Celebrations encourage people and groups to cooperate: and as our celebratory adventure continues we may well work with different groups, drawing them into the whole planning process, getting groups to meet, share ideas, admire each other's work, find ways of using each other's material. This all begins to sound like "wonderstuff" with celebrations ready to change the world. It is easy both to talk celebrations up into spectacular processes that revolutionise individuals and communities: panacea for all a community's ills, or to be completely cynical and see it all as wishy-washy, ineffective, New-Age drivel. Of course, in truth, celebrations fall somewhere between the two. An effective celebration can be a powerful occasion in the life of an individual or a community. We may try to find ways of establishing a legacy of celebrations (see: A Place in Time for Dreaming). We need to remember we are just a moment, hopefully, a treasure seized out of the bustle of other lives. Our celebration may come and go but it will leave new skills and new confidence in its wake. We plant seeds and hope

Celebrations foster a sense of belonging and ownership: the ideas presented in this book are very much bound to an exploration of place. At the heart of most of my work as Creeping Toad is that sense of an adventure (I use that word a lot!) into the relationships between people, place and wildlife. Similar activities could be applied to more conceptual rather than place-based work, but for me seeing that sense of "I know this place now" growing in people is very important. There is a feeling of belonging inherent in much of this, in the stories, the poems, the dances of tall trees, that hopes to encourage a sense of the value in being a part of things.....and out of that, hopefully, a readiness to speak, to act on behalf of that place and the wider world.

We can find all sorts of opportunities to have a celebration. Celebrations might provide light relief in a more serious campaign, a fire for the imagination at the launch of another or a rite of passage in the completion of a third. There aren't really any rules about "when" you should celebrate. A celebration might be part of a larger campaign or simply be a celebration in its own right. A birthday party might be seen as part of the ongoing campaign of a person's life but it is also as much a stand-alone celebration of a moment in that person's life.

Celebrations are adventures: a celebration depends, in the end, upon place and people. As we said above, we might work with lots of creative media, growing celebrations with puppets and processions and wild dances but we should never forget that celebrations depend upon their people. To create a celebration is to take a group on an adventure. Like a good old-fashioned story, it will have a beginning, a middle and an end. There will be doubt and the monsters of uncertainty to face. We may rest by the muddy swamps of local ponds and seek counsel from wise frogs, or run with the harvest mice of excitement across the fields. We may be blessed by the wild witches of inspiration. Our group of heroes will grow, change and, hopefully, become even more adventurous. It is the characters that make the story and we need to make sure we do not lose the process of the unfolding story in our desire, as organisers and leaders, for a glamorous, dramatic denouement.

Essentially, if we need to look at justifying celebratory work we can argue for celebrations as agents of community and individual growth and empowerment. Celebrations can work across social boundaries of experience, age and outlook and bring in new skills, confidence and perspectives. Celebrations involve people in the landscape around them, in their local places. And let's face it, they are fun. If the celebratory process gets caught up in itself, losing the sense of adventure, if the commitment of our participants starts to wane, if we lose the sense of rewarding activity (and the fun does not need always to be all singing and shouting) - if it is no longer fun, then we need to review activities.

Celebrations encourage people to see themselves in new ways: as thinking, feeling, creative people. People with the strength to think for themselves, to expect to be heard. An effective celebration can be one of the steps that start to change the world.

Simplicity

I am very aware that this book feels full of things. Things to make. Things to do. The idea of "celebration" can easily disappear under the weight of activities we might pursue. So, relax, step back and feel your way into things. There are so many possibilities, they almost defy description. You might set out with an activity you want to work with. Perhaps you have a vision of a company masked as woodland animals, speaking. Or maybe it is lanterns, winter-lights winding down a hill and through the town. Or maybe it isn't an activity but a thought or a storyline and you have no particular vision of how it will be explored: a dream to unfold with a group, or not even a dream, but a moment for a group to dream for themselves and unfurl that story as they see fit.

All are valuable. All can be viable. Seeds for a celebration.

Relax. Step back. Sift through the locust swarms of possibilities and choose activities that set imaginations going, that give people confidence to think and speak and act for themselves. *Celebrating Nature* is a book of possibilities. Choose what you need. Use what your group want for that occasion and let the rest lie. Their time may come.

Often just one basic idea is enough to let a whole celebration flow.

Relax. Step back. Trust your group. Be still.

2

A shape for celebrations

"***celebration:** an occasion of wonder and delight*" (*Creeping Toad*)

There are no real rules about celebrations, about the ups and downs, the shoulds and should nots of wonder and delight. But in a situation like ours, where we are looking at ways of growing a celebration in a workshop, or series of workshops, with groups, it helps to have some starting points to build upon.

Our celebration needs a certain structure. This need not be a strait-jacket that defines and determines everything that happens. At its most effective, a celebration's structure should provide a strong foundation upon which a group can build their own unique moment

My working definition of "celebration" is "an occasion of wonder and delight". The "wonder' and "delight" components may vary in the mix so that perhaps a funeral may be seen as a celebration with wonder shading into awe and a smaller seasoning of delight while a birthday party has lots of delight while the wonder has perhaps been submerged under the cake candles. But you might take one of those real "rites of passage" birthdays: 13, 18, 21, 40, 50, 67 (and why not?) and find that your party-goers are very ready add more wonder to

The Stone waited for a thousand centuries
as wind and rock and the first rains
slowly ground volcanic peaks to sand

The Stone waited as the sea came in.

The Stone speaks:

I remember a holiday that lasted 5 million years

Sunbathing among the coral.
I remember a world of green and blue water
Of yellow animals and shining fish.
Shells, jellyfish, sharks and ammonites,
All spirals and tentacles

I listened to the singing of the waves,
The swaying of the coral
I wrapped myself in seaweed
Cold, clammy, slimy seaweed
Clinging to my smooth skin

I remember water as still as death
A shallow sea, a gentle wave,
The long, slow drift of
shells and bones and fine coral dust
Building up around me.

Centimetres become metres.
Dust and shells become stone
Limestone lies over the land

celebrating stones and geology: extract from *A Stone Poem*, by Hollinhey Primary School, Life of Stone Project at Teggs Nose Country Park the mix. As the organiser of the celebration, you may simply need to provide the opportunity to pause and reflect, to offer hopes and dreams for the birthday-person's future, to embrace a moment of wonder among all the delight.

Planning a celebration need not be a "serious adult thing", young people are just as ready to stop, to plan, to mix wonder with the delight, to offset grief with smiles, to reflect, to disarm fear with strength drawn from tree-roots and the long-slow continuity of stone.

With "an occasion of wonder and delight" in mind, just about anything can become a celebration (try approaching the washing-up, the laundry, cleaning the house as celebrations), but this book is about creating occasions of wonder and delight that celebrate the world around us. Into what other places you take these ideas and these activities is up to you.

When planning a celebration we can think of the whole adventure as having three main components:

> **process:** the ideas and activities that will take us from nowhere through to our final celebration
>
> **dynamics:** managing the groups we are working with
>
> **celebration:** the main event itself

And, of course, there are also:

> **people:** the adventurers who accompany us through the process and maybe other participants who join us only for the final celebration

Process

In devising a celebration, we need to look at:

inspiration: gathering first ideas, encouraging consultation and participation, developing a storyline that will hold it all together. whizz!, bang! excitement!

investigation: gathering information along themes suggested by inspiration, ooo, find out more, find out more!

development: turning ideas and information gathered into exciting things to celebrate with

The Celebration Itself: of course there might be more than one

reflection and recovery: appreciating achievement, thinking ahead

These stages more or less set the shape of this book

Dynamics

We might call ourselves leaders, teachers, facilitators, but whatever title we use, or don't use, we need to recognise that the groups and individuals we work with will turn to us for support as we develop our celebration. So it might help us to think about

consultation: presenting ideas, listening to responses and moving on from that

participation: finding ways to allow everyone to be involved as far as they choose to be

creativity and freedom: designing activities and processes that offer people ways of doing things but allowing them space to experiment and achieve for themselves within a wider structure

fear and panic: yes, we all have those, recognising these and finding ways of letting them go, creating safe spaces where our participants can have confidence in us and grow in confidence in themselves so that they know they can achieve what they set out to do

leading activities: operating as workshop leaders with grace, humour, strength and style that allows the previous ideas to operate

Ways of dealing with these issues are built into the activities described through out this book and while we will come back to them and how they affect the development of our celebration, we will not spend a lot of time dissecting them.

Celebration

There is a shape that can be found in celebrations: a certain structure that guides people through the celebration, giving them information and opportunities to act and making sure (as far as we can) that everyone knows what is happening. Similar structures can be found repeated all over the world, seeming to operate across time, culture and continents. Sometimes a celebration will seem radically different in its structure from what we might think of as logical. Then it may turn out that elements of a similar basic form can be discerned, but with sections of that basic structure no longer expressed as everyone knows the flow of what is happening: shortcuts available where everyone knows the emotional route of the event.

In planning a celebration, or in talking the process through with a group, often using a birthday party as a model is helpful. We might sift a celebration into a set of stages:

preparation: anticipation builds, people get ready, talk about what is happening
Party: invitations are issued, presents bought, getting ready, dressing up,

arriving: getting there, making the most of people's arrival
Party: anticipation and excitement, the journey is part of the anticipation, is the house decorated outside? being greeted at the door, feeling welcomed

claiming the space: creating a special place for the occasion, marking out the boundaries of the celebratory space, the enchantment arena, whatever (sometimes boundaries are about people rather than about defining the space
Party: walking around, admiring decorations, greeting everyone else

declaration: a simple statement of why we are here, what is this gathering for
Party: loud "welcome to X's birthday party"

contributions: inviting contributions from different members of the company: maybe encounters with strange animal puppets, parading with lanterns, walking through woodlands full of magical sculptures: building tension and excitement
Party: games, presents

climax: all this activity usually builds to a particular special moment, may be loud and spectacular but might be graceful and silent
Party: is the Birthday Tea the climax?

review: time to relax a bit before it is all over, time to appreciate each other and our own achievements, maybe share food and drink
Party: quiet games after supper?

release: formal closing, thanks and farewell. End the magic
Party: collecting coats, having a piece of cake, a balloon, a gift, to take home, carrying the specialness away with you

Experienced workshop leaders will probably be sitting here reading this saying "O, we do that already". Good! So we should! I try to approach each workshop I lead as a celebration, whether it is formally designated a "celebratory" one or not. I plan workshops as experiences in themselves and use that sort of structure to shape the sessions: simplified for shorter sessions, but trying to work with that sense of order and progression.

In creating a big celebration at the end of a project, we can approach the whole process and each workshop as expressions of that structure: a sort of fractal structure with the same format recurring in larger or smaller reflections of itself. A quiet familiarity with that structure can help groups when they come to plan the bigger final event; you don't need to take them through the idea of a structure every time you meet, but come a planning session, we could talk about how we started our sessions, together, what did we do to "claim a space", what did we do to reflect and so on.

We do not need to lay all this structure stuff on too thick or heavy. Keep it graceful and simple. Don't be trapped by the structure, but do use it. It is very easy to grow too confident and think "O we all know why we are here and where we can do things, so let's get rid of that bit and this bit and those other bits as well". But the structure helps. It helps all of us: experienced celebrants, participants, newcomers, whoever. It helps hold our concentration, keeps us focussed on where the event is going, and why, and gives us spaces where everyone can be involved. A celebration is rarely a detached performance with an audience and a set of performers. In a celebration the "audience" are more likely to find that they have suddenly become part of the performance. Involvement and participation, are vital

And one basic structure does not mean that all your celebrations will be the same. This structure is only a skeleton: the flesh, blood, skin and passion of your celebration will come from the participants. Zebras, horses and donkeys all share very similar skeletons but are quite different animals...in fact zebras, antelopes, camels, mice and lions all have remarkably similar skeletons and no one would dream of getting them mixed up. Or, at least, I hope not.....

So get a large piece of paper to scribble on and think about what your celebration might look like. But before you get too carried away, we need to let the first ideas, the inspirations, themes and storylines start to germinate

STAGES IN A CELEBRATION

Stage	**Quality**	**Possible activities**
arrival	anticipation	meeting points, greetings, procession
	claiming the anticipation	raising flags, marking boundaries
	space	opening doors
declaration	understanding	formal invitation, story telling, poetry
	intention	speech
contributions	building	sequence of small acts: drama, installations,
excitement		stories, other performances
climax	achievement!	culmination of storyline
	review	wind down sharing stories, food, "thank you's" appreciation admiring each other's achievements
	release	sense of reverse of Claiming Space?,
Closing Moment	completion	process back to meeting point. Final thank yous. Remember to say good bye

A pattern for a workshop

While most of *Celebrating Nature* will look as if it works with groups on a longer time scale, the same celebratory ideas can be built into shorter workshops. Even in a longer project, it is still worth thinking of each workshop as a celebration in its own right, even if they all contribute, eventually to a main possibly final celebration. So, in a 2 hour workshop we might think about a structure that breaks down as:

preparation and and arriving: meet your group, welcome them

claiming space: where are we. where will we be working, where are toilets, etc (time elapsed: 5 minutes ?)

declaration: an invitation: what are we here to do? (8 minutes)

contributions: first ideas: what do the group already know about your theme - or what might they guess? (12 minutes)

first actions: a quick "getting ready to be artists/ adventurers/whatever" activity: maybe animals by numbers, getting ready for adventure or tree exercises (20 mins)

ready to go exploring? what are we looking for?

outside: exploring and investigating (50 - 60 mins)

drawing ideas together: what have we found? what have we seen? (65 mins)

make things: if appropriate: quick puppets, perhaps, instant stories (90 mins)

celebrate: present a few finished ideas to each other (110mins)

review: pause to remind ourselves of what we have discovered and congratulate group

release: thank the place we have been working in, thank the group for being such good artists, remind them to take their stories/ new friends, away with them (120 mins)

Of course, things rarely work that smoothly or to timing that precise, but it is always good to have a plan in mind, at least at the start of the session.

3

A place in time for dreaming

Giving celebrations a context

The ideas we explore in a celebration need structure just as much as the activities we use. We need an idea, an image, a storyline that will inspire our groups and a wider audience and give a sense of purpose and direction to our work

In looking for the thought behind a celebration, we can instantly trip ourselves up over terminology. So:

Themes

"what we want to find out about". The overall concept we are exploring, a subject title as it were, perhaps "trees and woodland wildlife". Within a broad theme we might identify a number of topics: specific knowledge points that we hope people will learn and take away with them. With that tree example, we might go for: "1. Being able to identify 6 different sorts of trees. 2. Appreciate the diversity of life that a tree can support......" But is "appreciation" a factual "topic"? As soon as we start talking about values, ideas and skills, we might prefer to switch terms and talk about Aims - general personal and social concepts to be explored and Objectives: specific development goals that we hope to reach. Of course most projects have both "knowledge" and "appreciation" goals, so we may well end up with sets of both Topics and Objectives. No matter how convoluted our discussion becomes here about what is an aim, an objective, a theme or a topic, it is worth bearing in mind that many people will miss our delicately balanced nuances. A useful challenge for us is to distil our theme down to a single, simple sentence: a few words that encompass the essence of what we are setting out to do.

If we are brought in as an external group to lead a celebration for an organisation, these areas might already be decided and be delivered to us as the Brief we are expected to work to. We might add to this list, drawing upon our own experience of what our work brings to people, but essentially, think of Themes and Topics and Aims and Objectives as "what we hope people will know or have achieved by the end of our project":

"What we need to know" often sounds rather staid: a set of not very inspiring points about knowing, understanding and using. The challenge for the celebration leader is to find a way of inspiring that theme: to find an idea that will help us explore the theme, achieve the objectives, often without consciously addressing those points at all. We need a Storyline: a horse that our imaginations can jump onto and go galloping off on into the woods of our themes and topics.

Storylines

A storyline (or scenario or plot if you prefer) in my work is often presented as a challenge or an invitation. It is an imaginative opening that encourages our participants to enter the celebratory process with excitement, enthusiasm and maybe a degree of uncertainty, a feeling of "can we really do this?". Often that is accompanied by another line saying "this person leading all this is completely potty".

How a storyline is delivered can range in complexity from a simple statement to a full blown story, depending upon the workshop time and number of people involved. A useful rule, however, is that no matter how intricate the way you introduce people to the storyline, once again, as with the Theme, the essence of it should be able to be distilled into a single sentence.

So our tree example from earlier might give us:

> **a simple, if improbable, invitation:** to go home with a forest/ your personal tree/ your favourite woodland animal on your own head (half-day workshop)
>
> **a challenge:** to uncover the adventures of some of these trees and to tell these stories (whole day workshop)
>
> **open-ended story:** once upon a time, in a wood, something strange happened.......and we are going to become the investigators, the detectives, the storymakers who can find and reveal the stories the trees want to tell (week long project)

Storylines for longer projects can be much more open-ended. Within a short workshop, we need a clear target: "take a peat bog back to school to hang from your classroom ceiling", but where we will work together for longer we can grow our storyline as we go. We do need a strong starting point, and an approximate target but I like to leave exactly what that end point is like up to the imaginations of the group. We will return to ways of managing that process throughout *Celebrating Nature*.

Storyline Summary

Look for a storyline that:

is simple: can be summed up in a single sentence

is flexible/open-ended: can accommodate the ideas of the group

offers challenges or adventures: offers people new experiences either physically or creatively

is appropriate to the site you are working on: so that your storyline will encourage people to explore that environment sensitive to its sources: if you draw upon material from other cultures, for example, make sure it is because this offers us a different way of meeting our world, not because "these funny people away over there do something that we can all laugh at"

How much to prepare?

In many projects, particularly with short workshops, we probably need to set Theme and Storyline in advance. It would be nice to have a very open situation where people can come in and shape everything in the short time they are with you, but this needs confidence, not just your own but within the group as well. A group's confidence in themselves and in us takes time to grow and part of that lies in their feeling of security with us. In short sessions, I go for presenting a strong, supportive idea that allows the group to flex the muscles of their imaginations and find that within the short time we are together they have accomplished the unexpected and then maybe next time with me, or with someone else, they'll remember that confidence and it will come bubbling up and out again. Of course, you might meet the group who have gone through all that with someone else and are up and ready for lots of creative freedom from the first moments they meet you. If there is a good length of time with a group, however, we may well be able to establish the Theme and Storyline of our work and a final celebration collectively. We shall look at that in Big Adventures below.

In short workshops, then, we may know Theme and Storyline and will use that storyline to set everyone's imaginations in motion. We will also have a whole set of activities on hand that could carry us from initial invitation to that final "forest on your head" moment. Ideally, as we enter our first activities with the group, they themselves will identify some of the planned "topics" as "things we need to find out".

what sort of trees do grow in our woods

how old are they?

how do you know one sort of tree from another?

what do people do in our woods

and what do the trees think about this

what animals live here....and so on

Trust in your group. You may need to fire in a few leading questions to help get things going, but even a few minutes altogether or a bit longer in small groups can establish targets that the group accept and own as their own rather than some set of questions given to them by you, "the teacher".

Often in this process, completely new ideas appear and you may have to let your plans evolve. Sometimes you will be able to accommodate new ideas and changes of direction, sometimes it will not be possible and you may need to say, "Sorry, I don't think we can do that..."(Find wolves, find elephants, stick pins in hunters, have all been proposed) Make sure that you do not simply say "no" to everything that was not on your original topic and activity lists.

As you get going with your group, you will have that set of activities you had in mind to do but do try to hold onto your flexibility. You may need to abandon timetables as a group become completely absorbed in one activity and are getting so much out of it that maybe you need to just run with that and feed little bits of others into it rather than halting it and moving firmly on to the next in your careful sequence. Or perhaps you find that people really want to make puppets where you had planned for masks and you need to decide which is more important: your plans or the groups' imaginative progress. Maybe you will need to improvise quickly around what puppets we can make with a set of mask resources....

Using stories

Working with a storyline is not necessarily to work with "a story". A story is often a closed circle: it begins, the action unfolds and it ends. A storyline needs to hold a strong element of "what happened next" being open to debate. You may tell a story and leave the ending for the group to work out for themselves during the day. You may tell a story just to set in motion a way of thinking or looking at the world (Boggart Questing is always popular). You may tell a story and set to find out what happened next to its characters... what did happen when the rats, lizards and mice of Cinderella's entourage didn't turn back into their original forms? We might do any of these things but I would always be wary of telling a story then simply doing activities that act out the story again: where is the challenge and open-endedness in something where you know how the adventure ends?

Bigger adventures

You might have the delicious opportunity to work with a group for more than a single workshop or a couple of days.

Perhaps your community group, afterschool club, playscheme, youth group or junior naturalist tribe want to do work on a weekly or monthly basis over a longer period of time to create something special. This could allow a much greater degree of decision-making by the group themselves in what they could do to create a celebration, either for themselves or for a wider company. Rather than going straight in as The Artist or whatever who is in charge and making all the decisions, it might be much more frightening but in the end, hopefully, more rewarding to go in and simply work around a set of questions: "in our neighbourhood what would we like to share with other people/would we like to celebrate". You might suggest a few activities first. Maybe tell some stories and get the company to devise new stories about their neighbourhood or make miniature models of favourite places, or work in a wood to build "the ideal den"....but move on into some of the following activities at an early stage with the company so they can start making those decisions and owning the celebratory process.

Activities like Calendars below are ideal for even longer term work: you might build a group calendar for their single event with you but when you have gone elsewhere, their calendar and their experience of how they made a celebration will remain and just perhaps spark another activity later.

Overall, storylines need to inspire. They are the spark that lights the fire of our groups. They need to offer richness without prescribing it. The best storylines launch a journey and let the group decide where the journey ends up. And as leaders we need to be ready to let things go, to recognise the moments when the storyline changes because the group as a whole are moving in a different direction. Hopefully they will be finding a more exciting way of exploring our Themes, Topics, Aims and Objectives, and then we need to let go of our precious ideas about how brilliant our storyline was. It may not be needed any more. On the other hand, you might need to find the compromise that brings people back a bit closer to Themes and Aims, within their new storyline. Finally you may find groups who need you to give them a lot of support, who will want to follow your storyline through to its conclusion and on this first encounter are very reticent about pushing their own ideas forward.

The activities following here are generally more suited to longer projects. If you are planning for a shorter workshops or series of workshops the quicker activities outlined in Bumblebees might be for you.

Organising inspiration

A few activities that you might use with a group, or just on your own or with the workshop team rather than participants.

The timings given below are unpredictable. Sitting quietly in a classroom or visitor centre we might stick to the times given, but going outside and exploring the site using these activities as guidelines might take much more time but be more rewarding in the long term.

Starting

Time: 5 minutes
Materials: pencils or felt pens, lots of strips of paper maybe 20 cm long and 3 - 5 cm wide (enough for 5 or 6 each at least)
Organisation: pairs or groups of 3 or 4

Issue a few strips of paper to everyone and invite them to write down(or draw) the features of the site that are most important to them. This might come from a question "How would you describe this place to other people: what things do you think someone else should know?". Essentially, we are trying to get people to start thinking about the resources we have on site and scraps of paper and the freedom to write or draw helps, Sometimes music helps as well...you could even do it like Musical Chairs: stop scribbling when the music stops, here are some extra bits of paper, now when the music starts again could you think about....some other aspect of the site.

Keep it brief, the aim is to get people thinking. Then armed with those bits of paper we might move onto one of the following

Inspiration grid

Time: 20 minutes
Materials: blank grids on A3 paper (the group could draw them if need be) felt pens
Organisation: groups of 3 or 4

It is very easy to fall into familiar patterns when looking at a new site or a new theme. I tend to gravitate towards ponds, stones and trees and it is useful to go through a disciplined process of really looking at what a site or theme has to offer. You might complete a grid like the one illustrated. This essentially catalogues what resources a site offers. It does not especially touch activities yet. A group might enter this "cold" or you might have done Starting above or some of the quick ideas in Bumblebees .

On the grid, groups might stick down their Starting scraps and, or scribble thoughts around:

Place: what plants and animals live here

what can be seen at this time/season

any distinctive physical features

Inspiration grid

Any useful stories? about birds + flowers bluebells & fairies hawthorn, may, black-thorn songs – people / birds Fernseed + invisibility!	**Place:** animals, plants, landscape features first flowers + leaves migrants return birds nesting bumblebees may-bugs, may flies birdsong, catkins bluebells
Title Woods in Spring date May venue, etc	
May Day Beltane National Wildlife week (late May) Dawn Chorus Day (early May) Beating the Bounds **Calenders:** anything relevant to this time	used to collect flowers – "fernseed" May Songs dog walking picnics **People:** past and present

People: how do people use this site now

historical use?

historical use of these plants and animals?

current management (producing anything we could use?)

local characters

Calendar: date and season: traditional local festivals we could use other festivals: Easter, Chinese New Year, Diwali

modern initiatives: Apple Day, Tree Dressing Day, World Environment Day, Seed-gathering Sunday

Stories: any stories told about our site?

about our theme?

also think about:

ghosts (always popular, you could always invent new ones with your group)
local characters

big myths: the stories everyone might know: Robin Hood, King Arthur (people might arrive with a lot of very established preconceptions about what a Robin Hood day, for example, should contain)

little stories: curious tales of boggarts and spirits of stream and wood and stone

Modern Myths: visiting aliens can be very useful

Often just trying to work out what we have got to work with will give us a storyline to work with, linking note from several boxes.

Lots of flowers and butterflies in a meadow where people picnic already might set us off on a wildflower picnic where you arrive as your favourite flower with attendant insects and indulge in flower-racing, butterfly show-jumping, snail leaping.....no, not using real animals

I find grids useful for organising my thoughts about a site and can be good for groups to really get to grips with what they have to work with. Most people, however, arrive at a project with some ideas of activities they might like to do, so an Exploded Spider, which is also often a faster process might be a better bet

Exploded Spider Diagram

Take a "spider diagram" and enthuse it a bit
Time: 20 minutes
Materials: A2 or A3 sheets of paper, chunky felt pens
Organisation: groups of 3 or 4 people

Radiate:
a) centre: our starting point: theme or site
b) side box: things we know: dates, money, time available
c) first joint of spider's legs: things about the theme/site: maybe choose 10 most exciting things you can think of
d) second joint: activities that might explore the first knee
e) web: threads of storyline that unite this and this and this leg

making Spring books
exploring activities
'spring stories'
"Wonderful woods"
WOODS IN SPRING
trees
stories
wild food?
make paper with flower + leaf patterns
flowers
just enjoy them!
nests
"Can you make one?" sculpture with natural materials
returning birds
stories - old
new stories + poems about journeys
Dawn Chorus Day
adaptation - masks
puppets

An 'Exploded Spider' Diagram showing 2 tiers of ideas

Pooling ideas

Time: 15 minutes or more
Materials: A2 sheet where everyone can see it, chunky felt pens
Organisation: whole company attending on one activity: you may do the writing or find a scribe

With both of the above activities there will probably come a time when you have to pull the results from a number of groups into a single whole

Try doing a big version of whichever form you have used and invite each group to propose their favourite storyline and, or their favourite two or three ideas or legs

Encourage supportive discussion: could we make this idea work? can we find the right materials to make that really effective? would we really find elephants under the stones in the school wildlife area (that happened)? how could we do that?

Out of this start to distil some questions about our storyline. If we are doing this, what sort of information do we need to find out about our site? What can we go out and find out on site? Is there anything we need to ask someone else about? Anything we need to go and research?

Calendars

Time: 30 minutes for the paper version, a whole hour or more if you go on to make a calendar
Materials: scraps of paper (A6 and smaller), sheets of A2 paper (eg flipchart pad), pens
Organisation: groups of 3 - 5
One of my favourite activities to almost fall into storylines is to build new calendars with a group. This takes time and can be a whole workshop in itself and as such is not always

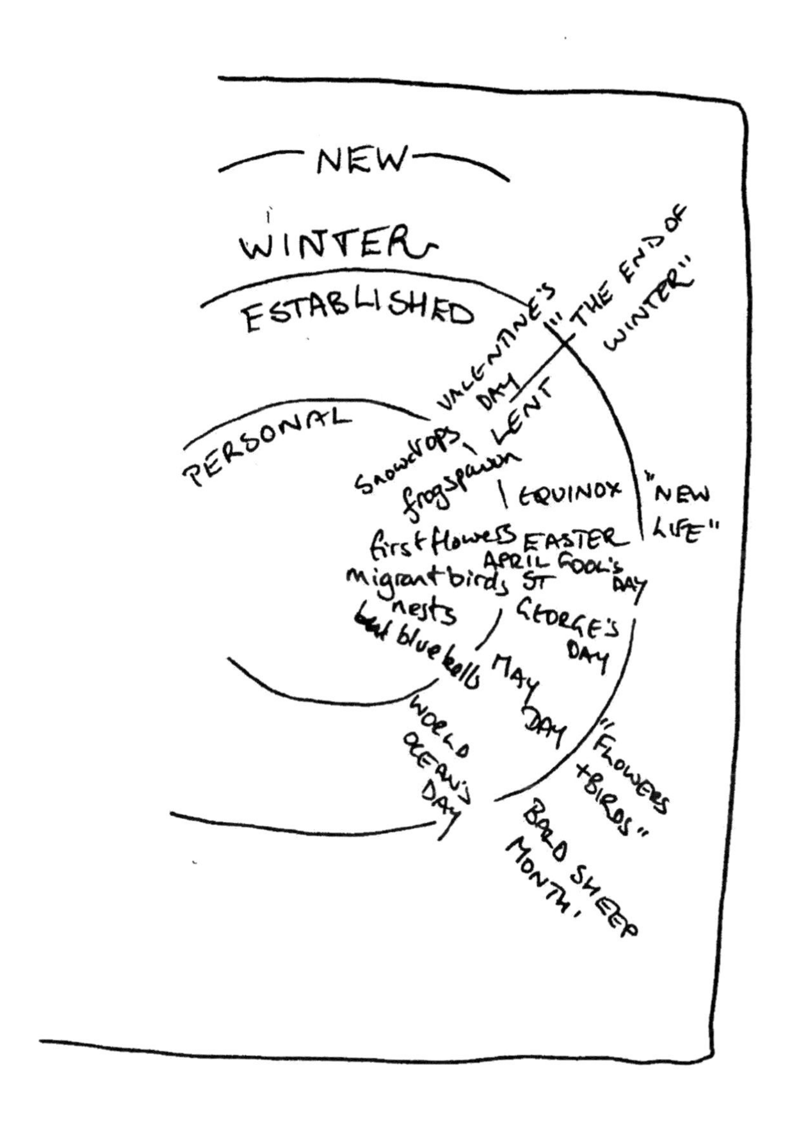
NEW
WINTER
ESTABLISHED
PERSONAL
VALENTINE'S DAY
"THE END OF WINTER"
LENT
snowdrops
frogspawn
EQUINOX
"NEW LIFE"
first flowers
EASTER
APRIL FOOL'S DAY
migrant birds
ST GEORGE'S DAY
nests
bluebells
MAY DAY
WORLD OCEAN'S DAY
"FLOWERS + BIRDS"
BARD SHEEP MONTH'

appropriate, but where you can work it, the results can be a real gem.

Working on large bits of paper in groups although you could do it individually or just with a friend:

1) Discussion first: what are the things you look for in the world around you during the year? What are the things you notice that make you say "O, spring is coming": what are your environmental landmarks. I think everyone has these but often we do not think of them as reflections of the natural world. Landmarks might be things like "light enough to play football in the street" or "warm enough for barbecues". Try not to be too precious and expect migrating swallows and flower spikes. Write a few of your own landmarks onto scraps of paper

2) Draw three concentric circles and divide them up to give a year: by months? by seasons? by school holidays? I generally go for a rough division by seasons. Months can get too precise.

3) Innermost circle: **personal landmarks** position your personal landmarks on their scraps of paper. Jiggle them around to fit them into a series round the year and maybe start to add some more as conversations develop. Leaders could suggest things like: collecting conkers, noticing lambs in fields, feeding birds, breaking ice on puddles, seeing the first frogspawn.

4) Second circle: **established festivals**: what regular celebrations do you and your family or school or community pursue? This might include public holidays and wider traditional days: Easter, Eid, Harvest festival, Cup Final, Hallowe'en, Christmas; family or school specials: end of term party, summer picnics, the annual school Play. Very personal things also creep in: "my birthday", "the day our dog died". That is OK for now. Mark all these on the second circle of your year

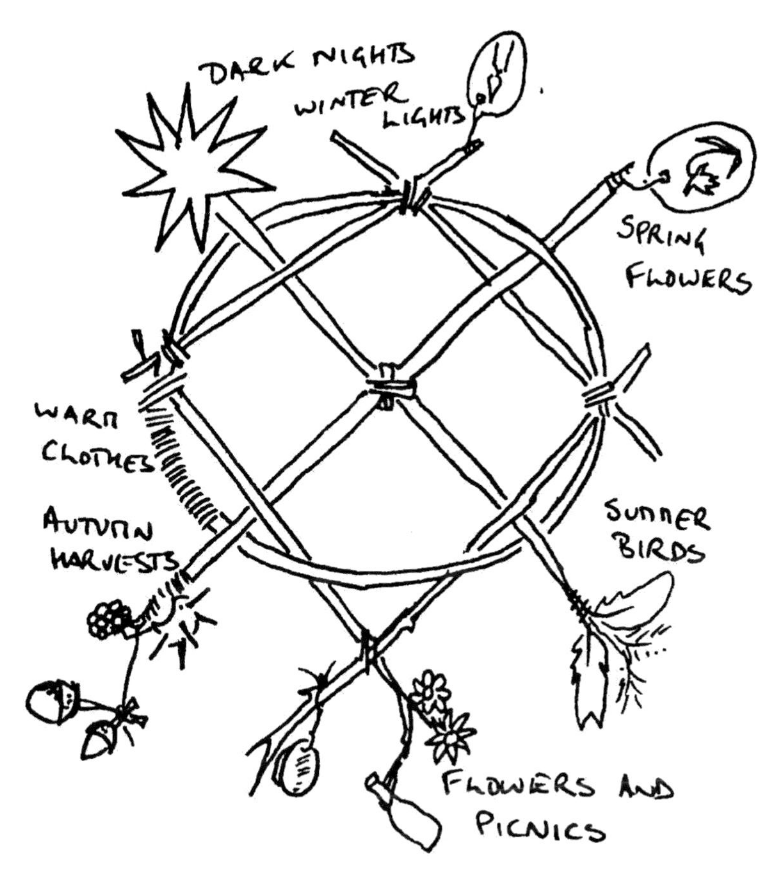

5) Outermost circle: **the new calendar**: looking at the innermost circle again, choose perhaps 4, 6 or 8 moments that everyone in your group can agree as being really special. Do they coincide with any of the established festivals in the second circle? Enter this in the third circle as new festivals. The new festivals might involve a change of orientation in an existing one but more often call for brand new celebrations, with new names and storylines that often grow straight out of the discussions that brought us to that moment.

How much input from us as leaders?

Sometimes people find it a struggle to think of any "environmental landmarks" and it can be helpful to talk through things they might notice to help them on their way. Think about the neighbourhood: trees in parks and gardens, ponds, the school grounds. Or things that people do that take them outside: holiday trips and so on.

Results

First flowers are often important, as are the arrival of swallows, seeing ducklings in the park, collecting conkers. Conker Day could be more meaningful for children than Harvest Festival which these days can mean bringing in a tin or a packet of pasta from home with little connection to "harvests". But Conker Day: now there is a harvest that is anticipated, a resource that is guarded and is already celebrated! First Frost and Heavy Snow days are hard to pin down but significant. "Kicking Dead Leaves" and "Smashing Ice" are seasons rather than individual celebrations.

Groups may get carried away and redesign everything: Bald Sheep Month and Grockle Season came out of Derbyshire work ("Grockles" are tourists).

You might reinforce public (Circle 2) and personal (Circle 1) calendars, recognising that some things we all celebrate while others like birthdays and funerals are more personal. Some of those initial landmarks remain personal but that does not mean they are not important. I have found very few people who celebrate their sighting of the first frogspawn of the year, but I always do! The personal celebrations could be picked up with some of the activities in Personal Moments later

This might end here, giving us a theme and perhaps a storyline for the celebration we approach now and leaving the group with a legacy of ideas to work with in the future. Or you might now build the new group calendar: perhaps a wheel of willow decorated with coloured wool spokes for different festivals and festooned with drawings or models of the landmarks that led to the different festivals.

Balancing Acts

Planning and leading a workshop can perhaps best be seen as a sort of circus act: a juggler with too many clubs, spinning too many plates. As we have discussed above, we may enter a workshop with our set of proposed activities but to run a participatory workshop we need to have the freedom and confidence in ourselves to respond to the ideas and needs of our groups. So, we end up holding...

> a balance between our own plans for activities we want to use and any suggestions our group made in that first session. With experience you get used to shifting quickly and making the, often small, adaptations needed to revise activity presentation so it ties in more closely with group plans
>
> a balance between freedom and restraint: set physical boundaries for the group that give a maximum safe amount of space to roam
>
> a balance within the choice of activities: providing a range that varies from freeform to more disciplined exercises
>
> a balance in group dynamics: so that at different times people might work on their own, with a friend, in small groups and as a whole company

This may sound petty, but it is worth remembering that people do learn in different ways and enjoy different sorts of experience. We may never please "all the people, all the time" but in reviewing our planned activities and trying to make sure we provide a range of freedom, form and dynamic then hopefully most people will get something out of our expedition. Setting clear physical boundaries to a working space may give some people a boundary to work against (there will always be someone who challenges your limits in so many ways) and with others it will give security and confidence.

4.

Bumblebees

Activities to get your group buzzing

I often feel that those first 5 or 10 minutes with a group will set the flavour of everything else we do together. In those first few minutes we need to recruit the group as excited adventurers in our celebratory expedition and involve them in the development of the whole event - or just make sure they are involved in our workshop.

So, we need to:

welcome everyone

introduce ourselves: get the group to introduce themselves? up to you, names may take a lot of time (and I always forget them) and might be better a little later on, if at all

opening parameters: say where toilets are, where coats and bags will be safe, where to get drinks of water: essentially point out the things that make the group feel welcome and confident about this place they are in.

Keep this information minimal: if more detail is needed, add it later. Too much information just now ends up sounding tedious; I know it may be essential but get an activity or two behind you before you launch into lots of rules. Keep physical boundaries of where to go until you are about to set off exploring

set the scene -- what are we going to do: offer the invitation, issue the challenge - either now or in a few minutes after the next section below

All the above can take just a couple of minutes, and then we might:

establish what the group know already: invite the group to tell you: about the site, what animals or plants might be there (do they know? or are they hoping? both are fine) what adventures might people have had here in the past. The terms here depend upon the invitation issued above, essentially encourage people to tell you things which you can then use in setting up some of the activities below

get physical : try some of the following

Animals by numbers

Time: 10 minutes
Materials: none
Organisation: varies, see below

First: call out an animal and a number of people, maybe 'a Squirrel made of 3 people' then folk will have the time it takes for you to count from 10 down to 0 to find two other people to work with and make themselves into a single squirrel. When you get to 0, shout 'freeze' and then, whatever state the animal is in, freeze and we can see how many different sorts of squirrels are around us.

Do this, and when everyone freezes say something quickly about the variety of animals in front of you: lots of variety, some large, some small, O good ears, lovely tail, one that has been trodden on by elephants (say it with warmth and a smile).

Then: another animal!

But now the numbers change so folk will need to find other people to work with. And every time we do this, we'll change the size of the group. Sometimes the Maths will not work and everyone else will be making Hedgehogs out of 4 people and someone will be left on their own. If that happens, cheat! and make a bigger hedgehog of 5. Or maybe make a very small baby hedgehog with someone else who has been left over. Or lie down and be the slug that a hedgehog is about to eat

Keep going. Keep the numbers changing and wherever possible use the animals that the group gave to you back in those opening conversations. I don't think people register this consciously but it does show that you were listening to them and have taken their information on board.

Last one: a couple of big animals using everyone: 2 snakes, a centipede, the fattest caterpillar you can manage. Or go for something usually seen as inanimate: tree, stone, piece of architecture, (groups of 4 or 5 are best) and then move into Hand Faces, below.

Of course, you do not have to do "animals" by numbers. Use whatever is appropriate to your storyline: we have done gardens (flowers, habitats and animals), rivers, seas, bits of houses and castles, geological formations (caves made of 6 people, mountains made of 10)......

Geological sessions reveal another development. Ask the group to make one thing and then move on to the next stage in its history or life cycle. So a mountain range may avalanche into pebbles (processes in a game like this are unlikely to be quiet and gradual), a volcano will inevitably erupt, but a dinosaur may be fossilised, a cave inhabited and painted, a stone built into a house.

Hand faces

Time: 5 - 10 minutes, variation: add another 10 - 20 minutes
Materials: none although the variation calls for large sheets of cloth and clothes pegs
Organisation: groups of 4 or 5

Picking up the last figure from Animals by numbers, your group might have turned themselves into a wonderful forest of trees, lumpy, rooty, straight and elegant....

"In our woodland we sort of notice the trees but often we don't really think about them. We can forget that some of them are old, very old, that they might have been growing here for a hundred or two hundred years and if they could talk....What stories would they tell? What would they be like? Would we find some friendly old Grandpa of a tree who really liked people having picnics under his branches, or some Wise Grandmother who was tickled by squirrels running up and down her trunk. Or would we find some grumpy old codger who just wanted to drop branches on anyone who sat underneath their branches....Give your tree a face."

Use hands to make a face. Demonstrate with a volunteer.... Start with one person making two large circles with their hands, holding these close together to make eyes. Then around these you could demonstrate:

curved hands above the eyes for eyebrows

various mutations of mouth, teeth and tongue

wiggly ears

pointing fingers as pupils in the eyes

So use all the hands in your group to make a face: keep the face to the front of the tree, so that it can look out and about when you have made it (original construction with branches and roots, etc will probably disappear: you need all the hands you can get). Avoid building your face on top of some participant's real face.

Encourage the group to think about the character of the face they are making.

Finally, take a few moments to get each face to turn and look at everyone else and say something about that tree: age, behaviour, secret desires (these are often there waiting to come out almost as soon as a face has been settled upon).

Wild applause.

Variation: you might take a little longer and invite the faces to play with language, sounds, rather than words, and have them speaking in tree, stone or some other appropriate tongue.

You can also try throwing a large sheet of cloth over the group, using clothes pegs to stop it sliding off, and arranging the cloth so that only the hand-face is visible. Then ask the different trees (everything now generally looks like great lumps of stone or mud) to wander around and have a chat with each other. Doing this out of doors can be great fun: these strange beings can wander around a field, sniffing flowers, exercising their dogs, practising their "sneaking up on picnics" skills.....Come out of this activity and take time for each group to record something about their new "friend" .

Hand animals

Time: 5 - 10 minutes
Materials: none
Organisation: company sitting all together

Very young children who do not know you or the other people in the group, might find Animals by numbers rather intimidating, so here is a gentler alternative that still uses the information they gave us back at the beginning of the session.

Sit with hands relaxed on your knees.

Turn your hands into different animals:

slug: clenched fist with 2 fingers extended, whole arm slides

snail: as slug but second hand curls into a shell into which your snail can retreat (count "1, 2, 3...whoops!") and then cautiously slide out again

spider: hold hands up, palms out, thumbs together. Then flip them forwards, holding thumbs up as "eyes" and letting fingers droop as 8 legs. Run your spider around your lap, up to your shoulder, wiggle your legs at someone else beetle: hands up again, tucking thumbs out of the way against your palms. Flip hands forward, pointing index fingers out and forward as antennae and leaving 6 finger-legs for running around. Meet another beetle and say hello by touching antennae

crab: thumb and index fingers of each hand can make claws, holding hands together at base of thumbs. 6 finger-legs are left to scuttle back and forwards on. Try picking things up with your claws and passing things round the circle of crabs

butterfly: hands up, palm facing you, cross arms at wrists, hook thumbs together and flutter fingers with palms uppermost

bird: hook thumbs together and flap hands, palms downwards

Bird and butterfly can now tell a story with your hands flipping back and forwards from one to another as a butterfly flits around the flowers oblivious to the hungry bird flying overhead

centipede or caterpillar: now start joining different people's hands together, use wriggling fingers to go for that elegant "Mexican wave" rhythm of millipede and centipede legs

People will eagerly add their own variations on themes here. Play with it. The animals lend themselves readily to creating stories and you can gradually encourage people to work with strangers to make bigger sculptures or tell more complicated stories.

Again, as with Animals by numbers you can try this with other ideas: rock forms (pebbles, boulders, mountain ranges, volcanoes......gets large and physical quickly), trees, underwater: start with hands and go on to whole movement ideas.

Look at Here is a seed in the New characters chapter.

Tree exercises

Time: 10 minutes, variation: 20 minutes
Materials: none, or CD player for the variation
Organisation: whole company working as individuals but gradually forming into groups

This is another movement activity drawing upon information delivered by the group (and maybe supplemented by yourself). Essentially,we will use relevant imagery to get the group to go through a movement warm-up and stretch, turn, twist, expand, contract, flow and stab in their movements. This sequence here is for trees, it could as easily be Wizard School Wake-up Exercises, Boggart Gymnastics, Tadpoles Circuit Training

Become:

a tall straight ash tree (like that one over there)

an ancient oak, with a huge trunk and heavy spreading branches

a prickly holly

a poplar pointing branches to the sky,

a conker on the ground,

a tree holding onto a birds nest in a storm

a long thin hedge (join up into lines?)

ivy smothering a tree (join up in groups)

Variation: you might add some music (or not) and the trees could:

slowly sway as the tree wakes up

stretch up and out with your branches

slowly, painfully? pull your roots from the ground: feel them coming out

try walking on your root-feet

explore

meet other trees: how do you greet them

notice a person in your woods...what do you do?

root yourself in earth again! be as still as people always think you are!

Just Talk About It

Time: 5 - 10 minutes
Materials: none
Organisation: individuals, pairs, groups of 4

No fancy stuff here, just ask people to think about some occasion in their past when they did something relevant to today and take a minute to describe it to a friend. Their favourite tree perhaps? Favourite animal? Often there will be people who just clam up and have nothing to say. Offer some alternatives: "think about the sort of tree you would really like to see? Something you would like to do? An animal you wish you could meet?"

Pairs can then join up into groups of 4 or 6 and have a few minutes for each member of a pair to tell the rest of the group about the tree, or whatever, they have just heard about. So Person A will tell the group about the tree of her partner, Person B. If possible, it can be rewarding for this telling to be in the third person and be a bit exag-gerated, "I once heard about a girl who climbed this huge tree, climbed it all the way to the top. We know she got to the top 'cause people saw her waving, but she never climbed back down again...."

Walking and talking

Time: 10 minutes
Materials: none
Organisation: individuals

Usually used as the first stage of one of the later activities in this chapter rather than something I use on its own, for some groups this activity really pushes "embarrassment buttons".

Start by looking at our feet, with yourself reflecting something along the lines of, "you know, when we are outside for a walk, we tend to spend a lot of time talking to each other: we might look around a bit, but mostly we look and talk to each other and don't pay a lot of attention to everything else that is going on. Our feet, for example, they are having adventures all the time. They will be walking on things, touching things, kicking things, noticing things while we may not have a clue what's going on. Even when they are all wrapped up in socks and shoes or boots, they will be up to all sorts of mischief....so start by talking to your feet.....where have they been recently? what have they broken, crushed, kicked, felt...the last ice of winter, the difference between tarmac and pavement, dead leaves, fresh mud....have a conversation with your feet."

This is probably best done walking around, but if your group seem very alarmed at the prospect, they could do it sitting down, wiggling their feet in front of them. Get them to say things out loud, shaping an experience into words is very helpful.

After a minute or so on feet, try hands: what have your hands felt, stroked, fondled (?), touched recently? Shape that thing again with your hands in front of you as you walk and talk.

Move on again: you might try noses and smells, ears and hearing but I usually go for eyes and what really special sights have been seen. 3 senses seems to be enough for this activity

Usually, I would ask a group to gather their memories along relevant lines: what trees have your feet met recently, what do you feet remember of riverbanks, the seaside and so on. Sometimes just asking about recent seasonal moments is enough...and if someone says their feet have not encountered anything, you might suggest that maybe this is their head talking and that those feet might have been up to all sorts of things behind your back. Your feet might have been enjoying the differences between road, pavement and carpet. They might have squidged in mud, kicked leaves, slid in dog-muck....until you talk to them, you will never know...

Scribbling

Time: 10 minutes
Materials: sheets of paper torn up into strips and felt pens (I use these a lot!)
Organisation: individuals or groups

Take a few minutes to write down some of the images from Walking and talking on scraps of paper. These might at once be arranged into collaged poems. They might feed into Calendars. We might quickly stick them on stronger card discs and put those on sticks to create word-flowers. We might fold each image up small and hide them in a Treasure Chest.

Clapping Symphony

Time: 10 - 15 minutes, variations: might add 5 or 10 minutes
Materials: none, variations might need some
Organisation: individuals working within whole company

Picking up on Walking and talking, ask people to choose their favourite image out of all those they have reminded themselves of. Go on wandering, saying that image over and again until they can feel a rhythm in the words. Now clap that rhythm. Slowly come into a circle, still clapping. Quiet. Quieter. And stop. (Most groups recognise a lifting hand as louder and lowering hand or clenching fist as a sign to turn down the volume).

"And now we will play a Pond Symphony (or whatever). We are the orchestra and you have just written the music!

If I start, I'll just clap my rhythm a few times - does everyone have a rhythm? does anyone have an extra one, just in case? - no, I don't need to say my words out loud. I'll keep saying them in my head but the only sound I need to make is with my hands

And when I've clapped my rhythm a few times I'll nod to this person here beside me and she can start and when she has done hers a few times, she'll start the person next to her with a nod. And so on round the circle, always watch the person on your right/left to see when to start."

We are passing the cue round the circle, rather than us as leaders doing it all

"So the sound will build up until everyone is clapping. Then keep going! if you get tired, pause at the end of the phrase you are saying in your head and have a rest. Or switch to clicking your tongue, slapping your thighs, stamping your feet..."

Then let it rip.

It can sound chaotic at first but usually a group starts to find a collective pace and the whole set of individual ripples come together into some sort of a stream

To finish, unwind that circle again.

You stop, then nod to the person next to you and they can stop, passing the cue round the circle again until the person who started last is the only one clapping. Then they can stop and we can all laugh in delight!

Hints:

watch the speed of it all: keep your rhythm interesting but not too complex: a rhythm of 6 or so beats is ideal. And use that to act as a constant try not to speed up or slow down(some people always try to go galloping off and it can all fall apart)

with a smaller group, it can be interesting to take it in turns to stand in the middle of the group for a moment and listen to the sound there

again with a smaller group, you might like to go round the group before the mains symphony starts and sample each other's rhythms: hear their words and repeat their clapping.

don't correct other people's clapping! Listen to and respect the way they choose to count their syllables

you don't need to do the whole walking and talking bit, you could ask individuals,pairs or groups to anticipate something "what we hope to find at the bottom of the pond" perhaps and use that to set the rhythms. Sometimes groups working together are easier: we end up with fewer rhythms in our symphony but with a more confident group.

Variations

Conductors, afterwards, get everyone to draw the image they were clapping on a long roll of paper (give them maybe a frantic minute). Appoint perhaps 2 conductors who, armed with pointing sticks set the symphony in motion by pointing at images; when a stick points at your picture, you start. When a conductor touches it again, you stop.

Heftier orchestras: sometimes a group will give up on, or just be very reluctant to join in, the clapping. If you anticipate this have a supply of noise-making things around (generally not instruments) and after a minute or so ask groups to move their rhythm onto: bin-lids, saucepans, sticks, tones, chairs, stools...

Symphonies always takes a long time to explain but is worth the effort. The results are often surprising and exciting for participants and set some useful skills in place. You might return to the idea of words giving rhythms later with masks or puppets: when a "musician" plays "a fox hunting rabbits" our fox puppet can move, in time to his own music, stopping when the music stops, while several rabbit musicians are holding their rabbit colleagues absolutely still before "rabbits eating grass" kicks in as the fox slows down.......

Getting ready for adventures

And finally a quick drama activity that can be just the right thing to get your group ready for anything!

Time: 10 minutes

Equipment: none (or Adventure books)

Organisation: work as whole company, maybe breaking into book groups at end

Before going outside, we will put on our sensible clothes (hats, coats, shoes, boots, etc) but if, to-day, we are being adventurers and story-makers, maybe we should wear other clothes?.....invite suggestions: what should we wear on our heads? - helmets? caps? pointed wizard hats? On our feet? Trousers (how far down our legs do they go? how high up our bodies do they come?). Coats (what are they made of? how do they fasten?). Jumpers? Mime putting on whatever is suggested.

What equipment will we take with us? - we might pack rucsacs with...sandwiches, drinks, magnifying glasses, binoculars, mirrors, books. We might strap on swords, butterfly nets, umbrellas. We might put things in our pockets.....

Let this run: the wilder it gets, the better: encourage imagination and explanations for our choices.

Conclusion: either set off straight away, or take a few minutes to record (drawing or writing) what each group (or individual) was wearing. Encourage purpose here: move from just a list of things to more information about the choices they have made.

Then, ready for adventure, we can set off

Depending upon your planned main activities, you might find other warm-ups in the relevant chapters. Don't get too bogged down in these bumblebee activities. they are intended as moments to excite your group and warm them up physically and imaginatively but not to take over the whole of a session.

Working with younger children

It is easy to underestimate younger children. They might not have the manipulative and physical skills of older people but their imaginations and their senses are as active as anyone else's.

In planning work with under 7s, look for a balance between imagination and achievement where the activities are ones that they can do as much of the work in as possible. So plan activities that, while they might use adults to cut, hold, pin or staple, the creative control of an activity lies as far as possible with the young people.

Suggestions:

start quietly: open sessions with gentle ideas - try hand animals, rather than the noisier animals by numbers - or maybe Here is a seed. Getting ready for adventures will adapt to many scenarios - start sitting down with small movements, then jump up and be more exuberant

explore gently - walk, wander, rummage, story bundles might be helpful

words - perhaps work in groups with one adult with each group as a scribe

try Stillness Poems and kennings

Adventure Books - can shape a whole workshop

Wizards (and Fairies) can likewise set whole sessions in motion

Keep ideas relevant: look for friends, secret places, make new homes, explore physically, don't worry about abstract concepts, work from what we can experience

Water pictures and shining leaves are good (if messy) ways of holding onto experiences

Try: leaf strings (with adults doing the pinning), carrier bag puppets, leggy bugs and boatmen, experimental worms, treasure chests and treasure maps. Taped banners can work remarkably well but keep designs simple and ration colours of paint so we don't get layers and layers of paint piled onto the flag.

Look at the work of the Reggio Emilia schools for some very profound inspiration: *The Hundred Languages of Children*, 1996, ISBN 88-87960-08-9

5

Exploring

Exploring is important. We need to rub our hands over the elephant-skin bark of a beech tree, smell leaf mould, sink fingers into moss sponges, savour sun-warmed stones. We need the freedom to look, to listen, touch and sniff. We need to get grubby. A sense of connection, of wonder, is rooted in a physical, a sensual, experience of the world. We gather a different set of lessons through what our bodies tell us than through what we read or are told and if we are hoping to build a celebration of this place or that concept we need that direct experience of it to root our developing ideas in.

This chapter looks at stepping out of doors and getting our noses down in the grass. If you are working indoors you can still "get down and physical", using drama, movement and rhythm to explore shapes, ideas and processes.

After our initial inspiration, after that telling story or laughing drama, we should be ready to go adventuring. We may be heading out to the wilds, to the park at the end of the street, a school playground or maybe we are indoors and our exploration will be more into knowledge and information than into physical experience. Or yet again on some rain-drenching morning, we bring the pond to the classroom with buckets and aquaria of water, plants and animal-rich sludge.

The challenge now for us as leaders here is to manage that whole set of balances described at the end of Bumblebees. Assuming that we are working outside, at this phase in the development of our celebration, while we need to bear themes and storylines in mind and keep an eye on the development of that storyline, overall, that sense of exploration is probably more important. Even where we cannot offer a lot of physical freedom to roam we can offer imaginative freedom, working with activities that encourage people to look, listen, touch, feel and smell and find creative ways of expressing their discoveries.

Look for absorption. Look for people being swallowed by the environment you are working in.

Do not talk too much. Get people into action.

Covering ground

A couple of useful "travelling" activities.

4-Shout

Time: 10 minutes
Materials: none
Organisation: groups of 4 or 5

Each group hold hands or link elbows, in a line (walk side by side rather than in a column), and counting together take 4 big steps. On '4', stop, close your eyes, open them and name the first thing you see. Don't politely wait for others in your group to say their thing first (everyone names their own observation, not a collective statement), shout them all at once and point (with your toes? knees? noses?) at the item itself! The challenge here lies in naming something different every time you shout .

Leaders can change:

what you point with: start with feet and vary if you will: knees, elbows, noses...

how frequently you shout: every 4 steps, every 3, every 2?

A group can get quite spread out with this activity, so I tend not to call too many changes. Sometimes it fizzles out quite quickly, so watch the group carefully and pull them together when the attention starts to waver.

Then get people talking about what they named and move on to one of the First Impressions activities below.

Animal walking

Time: 10 minutes
Materials: none
Organisation: groups of 4 (ideally need groups that are all the same size)

Start by numbering people in groups (1 - 4, with maybe one person being 1 and 4 or even two people sharing a number in a bigger group).

Whenever you give a signal (ring a bell, blow a whistle?) you will shout a number and that person in the group announces an animal in the style of which all that group must move until you ring the next change. Extra challenge: the group must always stay in touch with each other (move as a line or a lump or a shoal but not as separate individuals).

This activity gets silly very quickly (which is fun), and you may have a whole woodland kingdom crawling across a field towards you with foxes, rabbits, bats and slugs all at the same time.

You may want to set parameters beforehand: "animals that might live here" is a useful one and an earlier discussion about what might live here can give people confidence in what they can call out. Some groups will still wander off into elephants and sharks but that is only a problem if you want it to be. People can also repeat animals if they want to.

Again, watch for the moment the company starts losing its concentration and draw this to a close.

First impressions

Activities to follow up a "travelling" one, perhaps.

Accumulating images

Time: 10 minutes (or more)
Materials: none
Organisation: work with whole company

Play that familiar game of an accumulating list. Starting with a phrase like "When I was an animal, I saw......" and working round the company have everyone add to the list. It might be a single word, it might be an image, repeating everything that had been said before their turn. Use this cooperatively rather than competitively and encourage everyone to join in the chanted recitation.

With images rather than just single words this might develop into a story, as people start speculating about "what they think they just might have seen a bit of when no-one else was watching......."

"Listen to me, I have seen...."

Time: 10 minutes
Materials: none
Organisation: whole company (or break into 2 or 3 groups of 10 or so)

Start standing up and take it in turns to declare, "Listen to me! I have seen...." and add something they noticed, perhaps when playing 4-shout. They might just make an observation: "Listen to me! I have seen a hole under a log" or they might add a possibility: ".....a hole under a log where a mouse might live." When one person has said their piece, they touch someone else, who becomes the next person to speak, then, ideally, sit down and enjoy what other people have to say.

Past, Present and Future

Time: 15 minutes
Materials: none
Organisation: mixed groups of 5 or 6: if you are following up Animal Walking, above, make sure people mix those groups up.

Tell each other instant stories: combining an animal, an observation you made when you were that animal (the present) and adding a past and a future to that observation that might (or might not) be made from the animal's point of view (or might not). You could always not worry about the animal bit and just go for, "I have seen....." giving past, present and future of your chosen item.

So we might hear:
"When I was a rabbit, I saw a leaf that had spent a summer on a tree but has fallen to the ground. I think it tastes horrible but the worms will it eat it soon".

After everyone in their smaller groups have spoken, gather the whole company together and hear maybe one story from each group. Keep all of this brief: we do not need epics here. Use this activity as a way of heightening observation and context skills and reminding everyone that there are stories everywhere and that we can all tell those stories.

After the noise and movement of the above, perhaps a quiet, stilling moment is called for. You might try:

Stillness poems

Time: 15 minutes
Materials: postcard-sized card and a pencil for everyone
Organisation: usually work as a whole company but you might like to set this up and then allow people to slip away in silence and do it themselves

"When we leave here, it is easy to forget the small details of this place but....." Think about your context: as storytellers we need descriptions that will take our listeners to this place, to feel it and hear it, experience it as we do. As puppeteers maybe we need the spell that will wake our puppets up, or their sensations on waking. Or maybe we just need to remember the moment for ourselves........Choose your own reason and your own language. I talk of spells, charms and stories....you might prefer poems.

1. Forget about cards and pencils just now (but give them out so they are ready)

2. Sit in silence (ideally) and count on your fingers: the sounds you can hear.

   Sit in silence and what do you feel: on your face, your hair, under your hands, under your feet, under your bottom.

Sit in silence and take a deep breath: what can you smell?

Sit in silence, turn away from everyone else and open your eyes! What is the most striking thing you see?

3. Now quickly write down that list of hear, feel, smell and see.

4. Turn this into a verse by taking the (usually individual) words, turning them into a phrase, and grouping them into verses marked by an opening line.

I sit in silence and I hear
 the leaves blowing in the breeze
 the rustle of a coat
 the distant rumble of cars
I sit in silence and I feel
 the breeze on my face
 the grass beneath my hands
 the soft earth beneath my feet
I sit in silence and I smell moss and damp earth
I sit in silence and I see a tree whose buds are just bursting

Use the repetition of the key line to build impact and the "seeing" line as a sort of punchline. I think of it as gradually taking listeners (or ourselves) to that place through all our senses until when we open our eyes we are ready to see that last, striking image and to feel that we are really there.

The key phrase can change to suit individuals. "I sit in the garden..." or "In the wood, I hear..." maybe.

We could add another line at the end. This might be about emotions: how do we/I feel sitting here or it could be an identity so the poem becomes the waking-up words of an animal or other character. The earlier lines often become a bit less human then, so we might hear:

> "I sleep and I hear a rabbit under a bush,
> I sleep and I feel the dry grass of my lair,
> I sleep and I smell my cubs and my home,
> I sleep and I smell that rabbit running by,
> I open my eyes and I see my dinner!
> I am a Fox"

End this by encouraging everyone to speak their spell to someone else and close with a couple of spells being told to the whole company

Other quick word activities are given in the Stories chapter. Kennings and Riddles both work well as alternatives to Spells.

Enjoying a wonderful world

By now we are ready, hopefully, to go further: to start exploring materials and making individual connections with the place around us. The following activities come in a leaf-fall of ideas. Pick, choose and adapt to suit your needs.

Leafstrings

Time: 15 - 20 minutes
Materials: none, but work on a site with a mixture of leaf shapes and sizes and where people can find thin, stiff shafts for pins
Organisation: pairs or individuals within a wandering company
Note: you need to know what leaves people can collect on your site and to find a good place for "pins" to suggest that people could try. Look for dry flower stalks, stiff grass stems and slender twigs.

"As we now enter the place where we are going to have adventures, perhaps we should offer a present to the trees of this woodland to encourage them to let us discover their secrets..."

Or...

"Usually when we are out and about as humans, we are noisy and fright-ening to the animals and plants around us, so perhaps this time we need to wear a badge, flag or label so that the natural world will know we are friends and..."

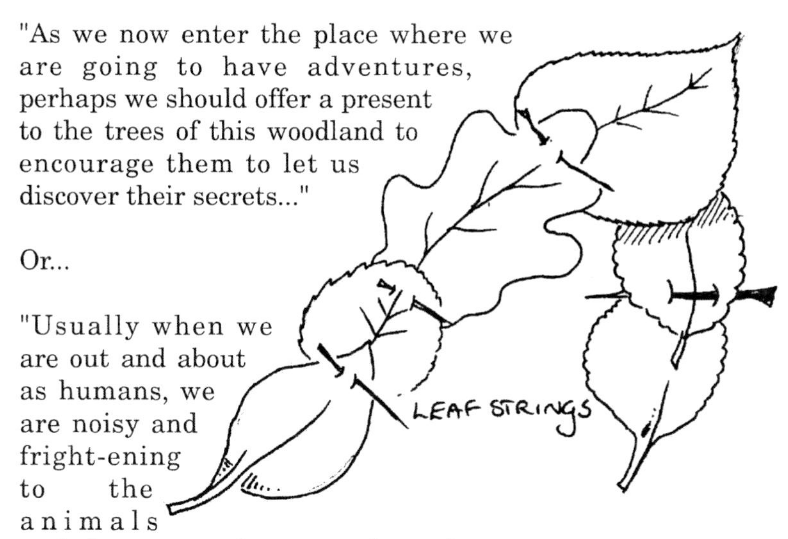

Or...

"Our first bit of making to-day will use nothing but what we can find and I wonder if you could make an animal that has never been seen before..."

Choose your own setting-up speech!

Collect a few leaves (choose large tough ones for the demonstration) and pin these together by aligning their mid-ribs and pinning the leaf blades with a thin but firm twig (dried stalks of last year's yarrow or cow parsley are often good or thorns from a blackthorn). Easier to say than to describe: pin a few leaves together to make a string and invite people to try the same. They might make:

a string of leaves (add to a friend's string and see how long it can become) and hang it in a tree as a decorative gift

a string of leaves as a bracelet or crown for themselves

an animal: good use of different leaves can give heads, wings and tails

a flag: folding one or two leaves round a twig and pinning: wear in a hat band or shoe strap: good for younger groups

Leafstrings can get very out of control and you can quite literally lose a group for ages with it. Decide the time limits for yourself. A good activity for encouraging people to have a good rummage in the undergrowth and find out what is there and an excellent skill to come back to later, perhaps as clothes for a puppet or decoration in a sculpture.

Tree Passports

Time: 15 minutes
Materials: handful of water soluble felt-pens
Organisation: whole company scatters into ones or twos. You might combine this activity with Sticky pictures, below.

"We are young and to the trees around us we live short human lives. But out here in these woods there will be a tree that has been waiting for you for years. A friend you have never met before, a friend who you can sit beside and talk to, who may have secrets to share with you. And we all of us hold a secret key that will help us find that one special tree...."

Draw in three or four of the lines on your palm and look in the branches of the trees around you for this pattern to be repeated. It might be on a large scale among the branches, it

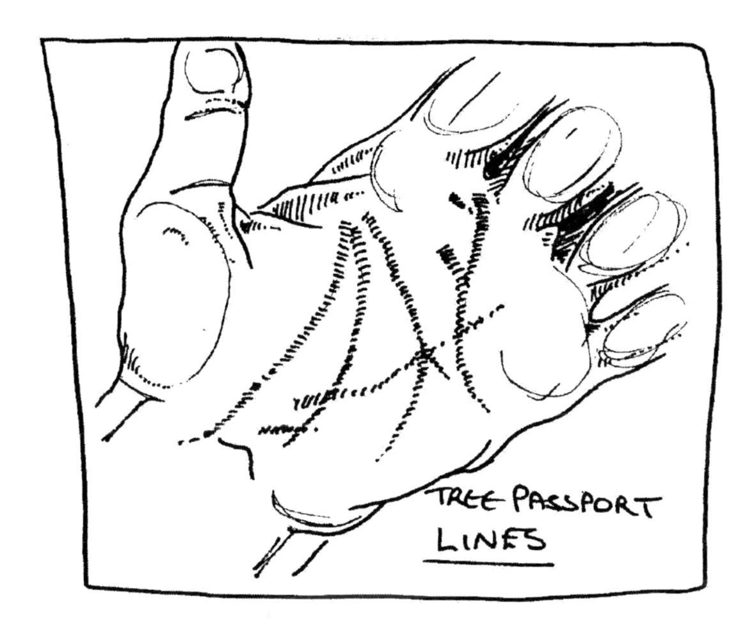

might be found in the smallest twigs at the end of a branch, but somewhere that pattern will be waiting. And the tree that holds your palm pattern is your tree.You may find that you share you tree with a someone else, but trees are large and full of friendship. Trust the tree to accommodate several people.

Problems? If someone can't find their tree, help them. Look up, step back, look small, turn a hand round, turn ourselves round. Sound confident. You'll find the palm-pattern somewhere, usually in a tree that the person already likes the look of.

I usually draw the patterns in myself rather than giving out a lot of pens. People seem to want to feel that the "one who knows about this" has looked at and identified their Tree Passport pattern. This also means that if anyone cannot have pen lines drawn in, for whatever reason, you can share a moment with them and show them their pattern, maybe tracing the lines with a twig so they can be sure of what they are looking for.

While obviously being limited by needing trees to work with (although I have looked for patterns in the walls of quarries and in the cracks of crazy-paving paths) this is a very powerful and exciting activity.

Sticky Pictures

Time: 15 minutes
Materials: postcard sized piece of card with a strip of double-sided tape down the middle
Organisation: maybe collect material with a friend but everyone makes their own picture

Peel off the double-sided tape backing(put the peel in your pocket!) and build a picture on the card using only things you can find. Experiment with stains (leaves, berries, earth) on the bare card. Try drawing with mud and twigs, charcoal and so on. What will or will not stick to the tape?In conjunction with the Passport activity above, we make pictures of our trees. Other themes might be "My Disappearing point", "a home I found". Longer bits of card can become Storyboards, building up stories using the materials we find as we explore.

Other Animal's Eyes

Time: 20 minutes
Materials: a small mirror for everyone. I usually use mirror tiles with bevelled edges, maybe wrapped with gaffer tape for extra protection, or mounted on card.
Organisation: start as a whole company and gradually watch people break into small groups and pairs. Let this process happen as it will

"We are used to looking at the world through human eyes and seeing the world from about this height. But if we are to understand the animals of this place maybe we could look at the world in something of the way they see it. So here I have a new set of eyes for everyone (don't worry, you don't need to take out the old ones!)."

By manouvreing the mirrors, we can see the world from a range of perspectives:

> held at arms length above the head: look up into the mirror and navigate with your eyes "in the sky" like a bird in flight. Swoop and dip from side to side....
>
> airsick? Then bring your bird to rest on a branch and hold the mirror about level with your eyebrows pointing straight down. Become an owl watching the ground for
>
> mouse, hold your mirror level with the end of your nose, facing up. Hold one hand out in front of you so you don't bang into things. Do this one out of bright sunlight: under trees is best. Revel in the green of leaves or the stark shapes of winter trees.
>
> deer or rabbit: hold mirror in front of your face so you are looking straight into your own eyes, then slide it sideways so you can look ahead of you with your ordinary eyes and over your shoulder with the mirror at the same time. Crouch down and walk at deer or rabbit height
>
> squirrel: lean against a tree and hold your mirror against the trunk so you get the stretching perspective a squirrel sees when it runs up a tree
>
> beetle: down on the ground with our mirror held in the grass. Look in the mirror and go trundling through the grass and fallen leaves

I usually go through all of these at the start of a session (maybe trimming down to only 3 forms for some groups) and then let people change from one animal to another as they will rather than collecting everyone back together over and again.

At the end, round the company up and talk: hardest form? easiest? favourite animal? did anyone invent any new animals to try?

Concluding: set all the mirrors on the ground in a circle or a spiral, step back and take a minute to look at the pictures that we can see. Try walking slowly round the mirrors and watch the kaleidoscope change

When we can, we will leave a mirror circle where it is for the rest of the session and use it as a meeting point or as a relaxing point. Then, if anyone wants a break from activities they can come and sit down quietly beside the mirrors and watch the pictures change with the clouds and the wind. If you start finding a lot of people at the mirrors you may need to review your activities.

Follow-up: you might try Sticky pictures or A Spell after a mirror session, with individuals working from their favourite animal's point of view

Being absorbed

After a combination of some of the above activities and some Investigating (next chapter), your group might be ready for a bit of quiet, personal "quality time". Now is the time to send them out on their own (or just maybe in a pair) to simply be there in your working site. You might do this by just inviting them to go exploring, to find somewhere special of their own, a den, a secret place, but for some groups this may prove to be an invitation to run shrieking off into the distance. So you could try something more structured but just as personal. Tree Passports work well here or you could show your group how to Disappear.

You might also try Postcards from Personal Moments.

Disappearing in the woods

Time: up to 20 minutes
Materials: none, but you might combine this with another activity: Sticky Pictures, A Spell, Storyboards, Postcards.
Organisation: usually people work alone or quietly with a friend. It would be up to the leader to set parameters depending upon circumstances. Either because of group or site, we might Disappear in groups up to the last stages when each cluster can radiate out from its adult attendant

Becoming invisible is not about hiding it is about becoming inconspicuous: "Practice not being noticed and you can disappear anywhere".

There are 10 stages to disappearing in the woods (or just about anywhere else!).....

Stage 1: all stand together, back to back at a meeting point. Take 1 big step and make yourself inconspicuous: lie on the ground, lean against a tree, crouch down next to a bush, a boulder, a park bench, a friend and be very still. Stay there for the time it takes to relax and breathe in and breathe out then...

Stage 2: take 2 more steps and make yourself inconspicuous... Stay there for the time it takes to relax and breathe in and breathe out then...

Stage 3: take 3 more steps and...and so on until by Stage 10 there are 10 paces between Stages 9 and 10.

The Disappearing Point: when you get to the end of Stage 10, you will have practiced being relaxed and unremarkable so often that you will just slide into the background and, hopefully, well, disappear. (Sometimes you may need a bit more practice).

The aim is to get people to relax more and more as they go until by Stage 10 they are ready to:

Sit down and breathe quietly, look around, see if anyone or anything is noticing you and perhaps you will have disappeared (or you might need a little more practice!). That place is your Disappearing Point and here are various activities you could do here....

Sometimes your situation may need you to Disappear in pairs, or a small group with attendant adult could all work in the same direction up to Stage 6 or 7 and then radiate out from the adult....

The Disappearing Point can become a focus for all sorts of activities. Make the most of it, value the fact that everyone finds their own place and this gives them a personal connection to the site. You might ask them to:

make a Sticky Picture of the place

think about and write or draw other people, creatures, whatevers that use that place when we are not around (gives good for phrases for poems: "a hedgehog snuffling for worms", ‘a fox pauses at midnight", "toadstools push up through the dead leaves")

write a Spell

other poem forms you could try: "I am...." (Talking to the Earth) or "These roots of mine...."

bring something back from your disappearing point and lie about it (Lying)

sticky board Storyboard some adventure associated with your Disappearing Point

build a signpost or house to mark your Disappearing Point (Celebrations that Stay)

Turn to Stone

Time: 10 minutes
Materials: none
Organisation: work as individuals within the whole company

A variation on the Disappearing idea that evolved around work with stones and younger people. We are turning ourselves to stone to see what it is like to lie in the grass and not move very much (this is more fun to do than to explain!)

Step 1: standing in a circle, maybe facing outwards. Swing our arms, shake our legs: nimble and active

Step 2: take one big step and move more slowly. Our arms are getting stiff. They don't move so much: maybe we can still move elbows or wrists or shoulders but not all three

Step 3: take another big step and find that our arms don't move at all and our legs are hard to move.

Step 4: stumble down to our knees and feel that our fingers, our ears, our feet are all turning to stone, getting heavier and heavier

Step 5: one more stagger on our knees perhaps as we slowly crumple into the grass. Become a lump of stone: feel how hard it is to move different bits of yourself. There may be a few last twitches. Close your eyes for a moment

Step 6: now work with this. You may keep the group still and stone-like for a moment. They may open their eyes for a stone's eye view of the world. They may open their eyes and look for a little stone near them, one who has been waiting for a friend to fossilise just next door. Have a conversation with this new friend: how did you get here? what happens here? what animals do you see? do they do anything to you? do you like it here? what is the weather like? Starting points for some good Stone Stories.

Leaf People and Twig Life

You may like to combine that sense of your Disappearing point being a place where things happen with the experience of leafstrings and some simple animation to make some of the peoples who might frequent the site when our backs are turned.

Time: 15 - 20 minutes
Materials: scissors, thin string, small bits of card with a tab of double-sided tape on them, gaffer tape. For Leaf People add thin A5 or A4 card and some Copydex
Organisation: everyone can make their own people, working around a central store of materials while nipping back to their Disappearing Points to forage

Look at the illustration. Essentially for Twig Life simply tie twigs together to give bodies with arms and legs, heads might be leaves glued or taped onto card (stronger that way) and then taped onto a twiggy neck. Clothes could be leaves pinned together as in Leafstrings. For animals simply change the orientation of body and limbs. With Leaf People: stick leaves onto card and allow to dry a little before cutting out. Use twigs for arms and legs, fasten together using tape or string joints so you end with articulated puppets.

This is a very popular activity that can easily take up more time with people making more and more "twiggies' as they grow in confidence. The appearance of "Twig City" and "Leaf United" football teams in a small clearing among bushes stands out as an especially noteworthy experience. There were even goal posts and a football made of leaves.

These small puppets can be taken away or left on site to amaze other visitors. In a bigger celebration they can be set in place more securely by taping a short stake of withy to a leg or to the back of a leaf body and using this stake to fix the puppets in the ground. On one occasion they could be seen in a long winding procession approaching the path carrying placards about woodland life. "Be kind to Slugs". "Stoop and smell the bluebells". "Don't step on me".

In conclusion

Exploring activities here could go on indefinitely. I am aware of working in two ways here:

> having a basic set of activities that modify quickly to suit different sites or different themes

> making up activities that belong almost entirely to that situation

Get to know your site first and think about what will take people deeper into their understanding of that site, its occupants, its resources and any secrets it might be hiding.

There are lots of other sources of this kind of activity. The work of Joseph Cornell stands out here for relaxed and simple activities. The Institute for Earth Education's structured "earthwalk" ideas could bring a lot to these sessions and with some of their more sophisticated activities coming in as ways of exploring ecological concepts. Working with these activities might give our celebrants the information they need to move on to turning information into celebration.

Stillness

A lot of these activities come over as loud and lively. I like to cheerfully give groups the chance to be loud and lively, the freedom to run around and rummage, grubby nosed, in the undergrowth. But behind all this is a movement towards stillness. I plan activities in sequences to give people confidence in themselves and their surroundings, to have them feel safe in this place so that when we move into Disappearing or Tree Passports or A Spell, they are ready to be quiet. For me, the most potent outcome of a session like this is comes with a group that has fallen into silence through their own actions, that is embracing stillness and enjoying a quiet moment.

6

Investigating

Sometimes we need to take explorations further. People want to "find things out" and a school may want to add a stronger sense of scientific investigation and understanding to their work on a site. *Celebrating Nature* is not really the place to look at length at the details of field work and there are many other useful books you could pond-dip into for activities and information (try some of those listed in the Bibliography).

Here, however, we might look at some underlying principles that would help tie such apparently formal work to our more celebratory approach:

> **enjoy what happens!** plants and animals are interesting and exciting and fun in their own right! Field work should be fascinating. If it isn't, think about what you are doing and see if there is another way of approachng it
>
> **you do not have to be an expert!** as with so many of the creative activities described in this book, you do not need to know all the answers, you just have to be prepared to enter the activity with a sense of adventure and a confidence in the group's abilities to find things out.

why do it? work is often at its most inspired when the group itself has decided that they need more information and choose to go on a bug-hunt, pond-dip or whatever. You might suggest the activity but they need to agree that this is worth doing

approach the work creatively: give some time before the activity to plan with the group (see Shopping Lists below)

working with animals and plants: as with Shopping Lists spend a few minutes with the group establishing how we are going to work with the living things that we are examining: talk about respecting them, protecting them and see if the group can come up with some guidelines like the ones below

naming things: do not get trapped by the need to name everything or to know the names of everything. You might argue that names do not really matter and it makes no difference to a mosquito if it is named "mosquito" or "Fred", but children in particular often like to know names. So arm yourself with relevant guides or a local countryside or park ranger and hope they can help. Respect that need to have things named but then work with this information and try some kennings

recording things: make sure are taking information back, that it is in a form that will inform other activities. Shopping Lists, Worksheets and Interviews might give you much of what you need, but also take drawings: big drawings of small things are fun but can be tricky to do (big sheets of paper in a field?). I use a lot of postcard-sized bits of white card and sharp pencils and felt pens for detailed drawings

With these thoughts behind us, we can start planning our investigations. Here follow notes of some more general things to bear in mind and possibly useful activities.

Equipment

Do not worry about not having fancy equipment to do your investigating with. You do not really need it. With time you could make your own field-work kit: a good project for a summer playscheme perhaps would be to make your own equipment in one session and then go and use it in another.

Improvise:

> use small white or clear plastic tubs for holding animals in

"it is easy to take too much..."

use bigger plastic bowls (again white or a pale colour) to hold water and pond life

make nets from bent coat-hangers, the feet of tights and bamboo canes

plastic spoons and clean, soft paint brushes make good tools for picking up small animals

scrounge shamelessly: that local ranger service may well have equipment as well as people you could borrow!

if you do have any money, magnifying glasses or hand-lenses are perhaps the single most helpful tool you can have. Get enough for everyone in a group, put them on long bits of string to wear round necks, switch on your "Sherlock Holmes Detective" programme and go investigating.....

Respect the animals you work with

Think about this and think about your own possible horrors of spiders, or worms, or mice or whatever and try not to let that affect your group. You do not have to touch anything they find (although you may be called on to execute an emergency rescue of a slug in a tub at some point: be prepared).

Reassure yourself and your group:

> most small animals will probably not even register you as another living thing at all - to a spider you are a mountain
>
> most animals that are aware of you will be much more frightened of you than you are of them
>
> you can do much more damage to them than they will to you - a spider may just horrify you - you might squash it!
>
> but do be sensible - bees and wasps do sting - and this book is written in Britain where we do not have scorpions, numerous poisonous snakes and centipedes. In fact, we live among a remarkably benign fauna. If you live somewhere else, you might not.

Practical points

Regardless of whether you are looking for bugs under logs, swimmers in a pond or beetles in a meadow, you might talk about the following. These points come out as a bit of a list of negative rules, but the underlying principle is of respecting and looking after the animals we are meeting and these points are simply ways of implementing that much more positive guidelines.

always look after the animal

handle animals as little as possible - a beetle running across your hand is unlikely to hurt you but in trying to get it into a tub to examine it more closely you are quite likely to injure it. Let animals move around on you - but remember that for most of them, our skins are uncomfortably hot. For damp skinned creatures, like frogs, toads and newts our skin is both hot and dangerously dry

if you do want to look at someone more closely, most land animals can be encourage to scamper, slither or march into a plastic tub - you rarely need to actually grab and lift

don't catch butterflies, moths or other delicate winged insects in tubs or hands - the risk to their wings are just too great

keep the slimy company of slugs, snails and earthworms in containers of their own, or their slime will glue up the legs and tangle the antennae of everyone else

don't catch ants - they attack other animals and you would need to return them to exactly where you found them or they may not find their colony again

ration the numbers of animals in any tub - don't go for a "let's see who can fit the most beetles in a yogurt pot"!

Practical Plants

The above points and most of this chapter is talking about finding and examining animals but you might encourage your group to see the plants the animals live in, on and around as just as deserving of care and respect. Discuss the fact that plants are living things, too, and they can be hurt just as much as ourselves or the animals we examine.

Finding things

Too much talking can really kill an activity. Practical points can come from a quick group activity. Shopping Lists might then grow from the ensuing discussions. Then issue whatever equipment you've got and go adventuring.

Look: under stones and logs (lift gently and return gently)
- in the leaf litter under trees
- in grassy tussocks: if gently tapped with a foot, wolf spiders often run out and up to the top of a tussock
- on the undersides of leaves
- in the cracks on rough tree bark
- in moss - get noses right in there for a good sniff!

In ponds:
- be safe
- have one net to a group of 4 or 5 children and work on sharing
- encourage lots of looking - see Pond Gazing and Pond Viewers
- keep pond animals in water! and not in your net - clean pond water in washing-up bowl is a good way of looking at exciting finds. Use plastic spoons to transfer things to smaller tubs for closer examination but return them to the main bowl fairly quickly

Shopping Lists

Time: 20 minutes
Materials: big sheets of sugar paper, chunky felt pens
Organisation: groups of 4 - 6, followed by whole company

Use this activitiy to give your group a chance to set the parameters of your investigation. You may already have talked about what animals or plants they think they might find, so here invite them to think about what they might want to find out about a parti-cular animal. Tie this back into their storyline, but usually the same basic information comes up every time: what does it really look like, up close and personal; how does it move, eat, breathe; what does it eat, what eats it and so on.

Pond Animal Shopping List
slide
swim
> movement
walk
crawl
where in the pond?
snorkel
nostrils
> breathe
gills
aqualung
skin
food - any clues
colour
home
age
baby?
life-cycle
how old?
adult?
enemies
can it fly?
can it move on land?

After a few minutes in small groups, gather the whole company and pool ideas to create a group List. Take this with you and have it available at pondside or while imm-ersed in wildflower meadow. Often we don't actually refer back to the list as much as we might have done but going through the process helps structure the investigation with the group and gives them a greater sense of ownership of the activity than if you had just issued a set of worksheets telling them what to look for.

Worksheets

Time: 5 minutes to explain, then ongoing through a session
Materials: enough copies of A5 sheet (on colourful paper?) for 2 or 3 for each child, pencils, clipboards?
Organisation: working as individuals or with a partner

Following on from Shopping Lists, above, we might give people blank worksheets. Here we offer a boxes of different sizes and invite people to use their information from Shopping

Lists (or where time is more pressing, from a quick discussion) to decide what particular bits of information they will try to discover about some of their finds. They decide what goes in each box. Usually, we get things like: name, a drawing, size (measured), movement, breathing, diet. Sometimes, it is worth deciding as a group on several things we all think we should find out: so everyone has several definite questions to answer while still having blank spaces for their own choices. Sometimes, we'll print a couple of questions in boxes in advance while still leaving most boxes blank.

When to issue these? It could be at the start of a session, but often I find it better to do Shopping Lists, out of which come a chat about our sfatey and animal safety, then Pond Gazing perhaps, and then get dipping, or bug-hunting or whatever. After 20 minutes or so of that, we invite people to sit down,

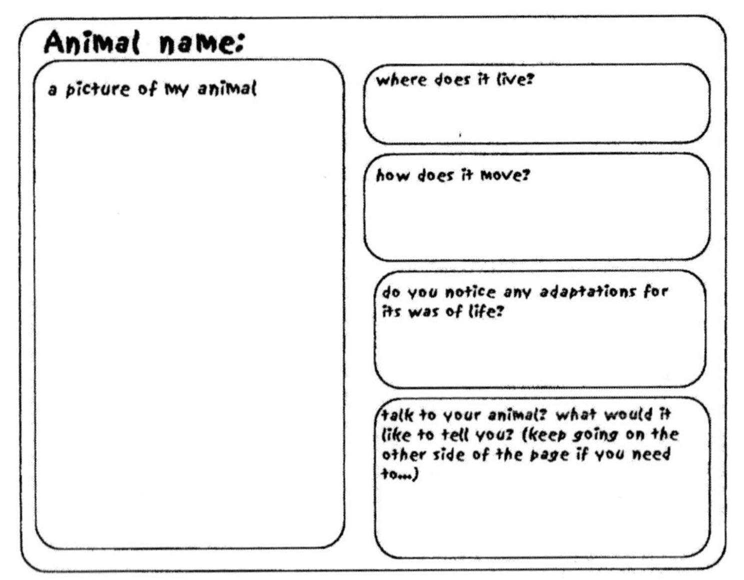

Example of a **worksheet**: questions in boxes could be included on printing, or boxes left blank for group to fill with their own ideas

have a look at their finds and at that point bring out the worksheets.

This usually complements a more general information sheet: a guide to pond animals or something similar. Worksheets is a very simple activity but very valuable. Sheets can be used later to inform other work and perhaps incorporated into a Wild Book.

Interviews

Time: 10 - 15 minutes
Materials: enough copies of A5 sheet for 2 or 3 for each child, pencils, clipboards? - the same blank sheet as used in Worksheets could be used here
Organisation: individuals or pairs? up to the group to decide

A more freeform variation on Worksheets. Tying in with ideas like Tree Passports and Disappearing, we might go on to interview the Tree we have just met or the Stone we disappeared beside. Talk this through briefly with the group, maybe agreeing some basic common questions and then send people off to talk to their trees.

Look at Storyboards in the Story chapter for ideas about approaching trees, but we are essentially asking people to let their imaginations run away with themselves. After sometimes slow beginnings, this usually warms up. People can take it anyway they like: formal interview with clipboard,

snuggling up close to a friend and sharing secrets....record the answers to your questions as words, or drawings, or in strange tree languages...

Pond Gazing

Time: 10 minutes
Materials: none
Organisation: spread out around the safe edges of a pond or other body of water

Sit down and watch. That's it. Better still, lie down and look into the pond: no nets, no sticks, no disturbance, just look. How many animals can you see? What are they doing? What does it look like? The contrast that comes from looking at pond from a short distance away (often looks quiet and unexciting) and what you see below the surface can generate interesting comments for poems.

Try the same activity with flowerbeds.

Pond Viewers

Time: 15 minutes maybe
Materials: clear plastic bags (freezer bags are about the right weight), a margarine tub each, scissors, rubber bands
Organisation: everyone can make their own Viewer but younger children might need help with the cutting

Cut around the inner ring of the base of your margarine tub (there is often a small step about 1cm in from the edge). Cut open your freezer bag and cut a section of it big enough to cover the top of the tub with a good 5 - 8cm plastic clear on each side. Fold the plastic over the top of the tub and hold in place with a rubber band or two.

Lie down on the bank of a pond, place the Viewer, plastic side down, in the water and peer in through the window cut in the base of it. You might need to push it a little under the water. This should give you a lovely view into the underwater world without ripples and reflections to get in the way.

By now

By now, in the development of our celebration, we will have talked and played and dreamed and come up with our first ideas. We will have gone exploring, found things out, got to know our place, our theme and our storyline a bit better. Out of that experience we may already have started shaping up stories of "adventures that happen here". We might have written some poems, shaped some stories, done some drawings and leaf sculptures of what might come next.

So now we move on and into playing with our inspiration, our knowledge and our understanding. Now it becomes time to make.....

7

Puppets: eyes to see and hands to hold

Puppets come in many shapes and sizes and styles. In Creeping Toad projects we tend to work with small rod, occasional glove and simple giant puppets and these are the styles that we will explore here. Similar principles and techniques can be applied to other sorts of puppets, but as with everything else here, you need to experiment and find the best ways of working into the techniques that animate any particular style.

Waking the world up

"Animation" is about bringing things to life: giving movement and maybe a voice to things that may not usually have these. Think of animation as a way of encouraging communication, giving a "voice" to the voiceless: a chance for the silent to speak.

While masks are agents of transformation, puppets often feel safer. Put on a mask and to some degree you become the the character the mask represents, but pick up a puppet and the character involved remains independent of you: a new friend on the end of your arm. That sounds like a very safe way of describing a process that is much more subtle than that.

Work with puppets and you will find soon enough that any puppet will have its own character which emerges as you work with it. Puppets are not necessarily passive little objects for us to project our personal interpretations of the world upon. Make a puppet and you may soon find that it seems you are simply the agent by which the some aspect of the natural world is being given eyes, hands and a character. At other times, puppets can become a wonderful medium for individuals to speak through, perhaps without recognising how much of what comes out is their own inner feelings and thoughts. In puppets and in their interactions with each other, we can play out our fears and anxieties and reveal some of our unguessed joys or let that habitat, those plants, these animals act out their own stories. Puppets may be quick to make, or slow and involved in their creation but do not ever think of them as insignificant or pointless.

Enough of solemnity. Puppets are fun. People love puppets and techniques that allow a degree of freedom in character, size and manipulation will result in a spectacular array of characters for your group to celebrate with.

If you have time to experiment, try leading your group into animation gently, slipping around a lot of standard preconceptions about what a puppet should be ("on strings") and release the group into a wilder animated world.

Where has my puppet come from?

Often starting points for puppets will have come from earlier work. Devising a story might have revealed characters that you would like to meet and work with. Or Disappearing might have led you to a place where some animals or woodland person might also sit and you feel this would be a good person for visitors to your celebration to meet. Or you might just be sitting with your group in the middle of a field wondering what friend from this field would like to walk home with you.

When do puppets become masks or costumes?

At first this may seem very obvious: puppet on hand, mask on head. But as you work with larger puppets, the boundaries begin to blur. Tall Tree People often seem close to complete costume masks in the way they envelope the puppeteer: are you still a puppeteer or are you now wearing the puppet and assuming an identity? Animal Heads do likewise, especially when costumes spread over the rest of the body while some Boggart Masks have grown out of Animal Head puppets.

Generally, I would let a group go where it would in this sort of border territory and use the description that suited themselves rather than feeling it necessary to insist that these were masks and those were puppets. You could say that you manipulate puppets by hand while you look out of and through masks. But the exceptions are instant and leap right out and bite you.

Activities to introduce animation

Opening discussion

It might be helpful to talk to people about puppets first. Other times, just let everything grow out of some simple starting ideas. Certainly for more involved and longer puppet-centred projects it can be useful to sort out a few starting points first.

What sorts of puppets have people seen or met in the past?
Try to establish:

- string (marionettes)
- glove
- shadow
- and rod puppets
- any others?

How are these puppets worked?

- on strings

a hand inside them
a light shining behind them with puppets on sticks?
strings?
by hands and rods
what else could we do?

Now might be a good time to talk about some key points: the importance of eyes and that there are lots of different ways of joining things together to make puppets. Maybe bring out some examples from the activities below to demonstrate Joints and manipulation. Often people think first of intricate marionette which can take more time and skill than we have available. Look at puppets that are combinations of "hand inside" and "rod" for dramatic and effective results.

"Find an eye!"

Time: 10 -15 minutes
Materials: carrier bags (1 each), string, tape perhaps, scissors, maybe
Organisation: working as individuals or in pairs

A useful starting principle is that if we can find an eye we can bring almost anything to life. This will be undermined by the child who ends up with a blind, mouthing and mumbling carrier-bag worm that is full of character. But it gives us a starting point and a first quest. Send your group looking for things that could be eyes: acorns, pine cones, pebbles, knots and knot holes, snail shells. Try making faces using your hands (see Hand Faces) with these found eyeballs as eyes. Take it further by issuing green gardening twine and maybe carrier bags for a bit of body and let people experiment with faces made out of found things. The eyes are important. Eyes on their own can reveal as much character as you might need.

Eyes

Time: 20 minutes
Materials: cardboard, scissors, pens, double sided tape, carrier bags maybe
Organisation: working as individuals or in pairs
Preparation: cut card into 3 cm squares, add small piece of double-sided tape to the back of each

Eyes will start it all. As an alternative to Find an Eye, issue some ready made eye-cards and ask people to build a face around them. I usually use small squares of cardboard with double-sided tape on the back. Table-tennis balls and permanent pens are an even more exciting alternative (cut a hole in the back to stick a finger in). People can draw eyes onto their cards or balls then stick them onto things. Or stick the card on fingertips and build faces around them, holding grass and twigs between fingers while the eyes are mobile and as active as your fingers can make them. Practice blinking: duck fingers down to "close" eyes then snap them up and forward so eyes suddenly "open" and "stare".

Experimental worms

Time: 30 - 40 minutes, or more (how much time for decoration?)
Materials: long socks or stockinette: 1 sock per child, eye-cards as above, felt pens, cardboard, paint, brushes, etc, glue, ribbons
Preparation: eyes as above
Organisation: working as individuals or in pairs

Eyecards as in Eyes with socks or surgical stockinette (tie a knot in the end, and that can give a very expressive tongue!) give wonderfully animated hands and arms. These instant puppets give lovely snakes and worms (colour with felt pens but remember to take them off your arm first!) They can, however, go much further. Draw snail shells, butterfly wings, flower heads: just about anything, onto tough cardboard, paint, cut out and glue ribbons onto the back (to tie shell onto arm around puppet body) and you can have a whole field ecosystem in an hour.

Eyes and one thing to move

Eyes look at and respond to the world. If we add a separate moving part to a puppet we give it the chance to interact with the world around it. Go back to Eyes above and try adding a puppet hand (or equivalent) to a corner or torn streamer of carrier bag and moved by a thin piece of willow.

Leggy bugs and boatmen

Time: up to 60 minutes

Materials: tough card (cereal packet thickness is good), scissors, glue, paper fasteners, decorative bits (look for nice things for eyes), streamers

Organisation: working as individuals or pairs. These are really one-person puppets so maybe people could work in pairs to help each other but aim to produce a puppet for themself as well

See the illustration in the Bestiary below. It helps to have a couple of examples to show people. Moving slightly sideways from the flexibility of the above, we might work with drawing of animals we have seen and make realistic if sometimes slightly strange puppets. This works particularly well with insects and arachnids with round or oval shapes but it can accommodate all sorts of things. After perhaps, a bug hunt, work on tough card and:

draw round your hand in pencil to give a working size

now draw an animal bigger than your hand outline

cut out and decorate vigourously

while paint or glue are drying, make some legs. These might be like the tape joints described below, attached to the underside of your creature with a cardboard loop also fitted to the underside to slip your hand through and hold the puppet. Or you might try a swivel joint to give you more control over another pair of legs or wings, or fins. Slide your hand into the loop and hold the cane between thumb and forefinger. Twiddle it so the cane-mounted legs will move

try to persuade people to add lots of streamers to hide hand

perform enthusiastically

Joints

Rather than a specific activity, this is more a set of demonstrations you could show your group. Different ways of quickly joining things together to give different degrees and styles of movement.

Try making a few examples beforehand. Introduce your group to any of the following suggestions for joints that allow movement in your puppet.

mouths: folded card with finger straps stapled onto the outsides of upper and lower jaws so fingers can slide in from the back of the puppet. Build the rest of the head around this. For bigger puppets, try folding paper plates in half

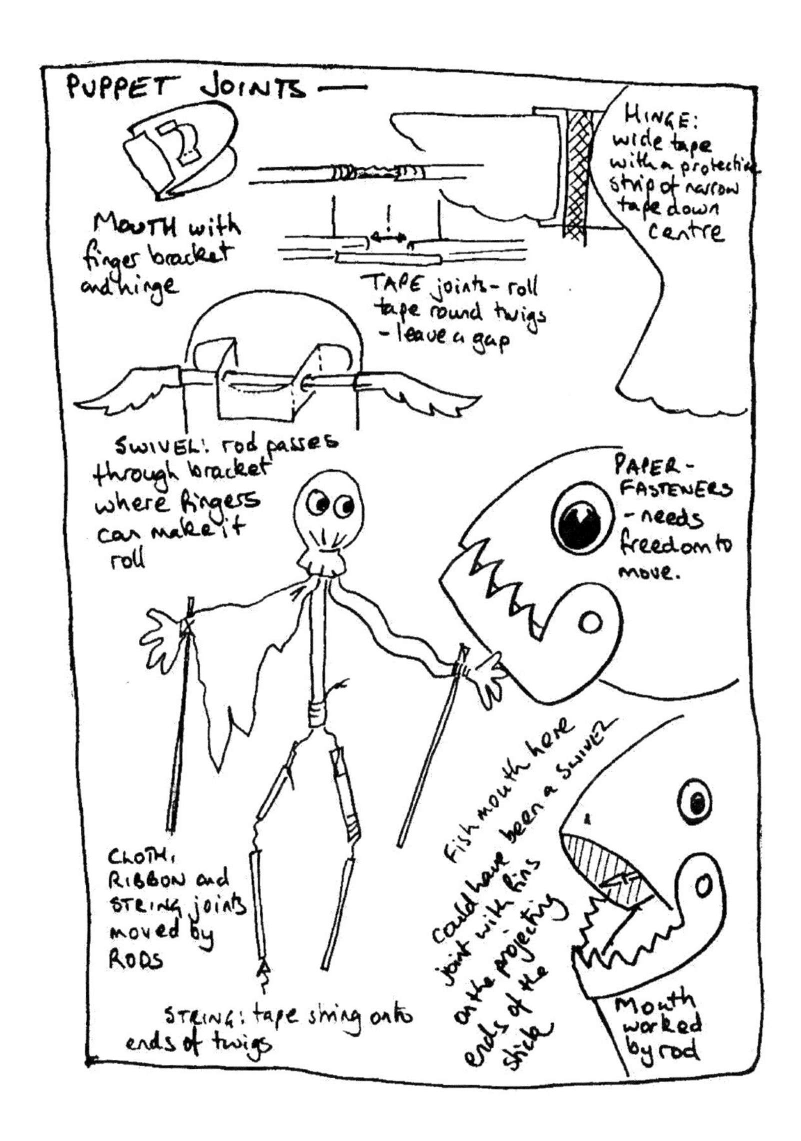
PUPPET JOINTS —
MOUTH with finger bracket and hinge
TAPE joints - roll tape round twigs - leave a gap
HINGE: wide tape with a protective strip of narrow tape down centre
SWIVEL: rod passes through bracket where fingers can make it roll
PAPER-FASTENERS - needs freedom to move.
CLOTH, RIBBON and STRING joints moved by RODS
STRING: tape string onto ends of twigs
Fish mouth here could have been a SWIVEL joint with pins on the projecting ends of the stick
Mouth worked by rod

tape: lay withy lengths, or twigs, on masking or gaffer tape with about a centimetre between the ends of the sections. Roll tape around the twigs, a bit like a roll-up cigarette, and you have a strong, flexible joint

hinge: a piece of gaffer tape with a short strip laid across the centre to made a "dead" space. Then attach other ends to the two sides needing movement

swivel: make a loop of cardboard that will fit round a hand. Pierce this with a piece of withy so that fingers in the loop can take hold of the stick and roll it back and forward. Attach legs, wings or fins to the projecting ends of the stick. An animal's body can be stuck onto the upper side of the loop. Use the same idea to pierce a 2-sided duck or fish so that the cane sticks out on either side. Add fins or webbed feet for a swimming animal

string and cloth joints: replace tape joints with string taped onto each limb piece

ribbon: try to get away from needing rigid limbs with joints and use ribbon, long bits of cloth or foam rubber instead (see Ribbon and Sock puppets below)

paper-fasteners: an old favourite: good for close-action joints: jaws, limbs on cardboard cut outs, any joints on bigger shadow-puppets

rods: (no, not a joint but a good point to turn to a basic manipulation tool) look for something slender and strong that is easy to attach and work with. With large groups, I tend to use bits of withy: plentiful, cheap and easy to use. With bigger puppets, we use bamboo of different sizes and with smaller groups and more delicate puppets we might use rigid florist's wire

Preparation: you need to experiment and to have some maybe "not quite finished" examples to show people, going for examples that people can look at, see how it is made and decide they could do better themselves. Core materials are hopefully obvious from the notes, while you can pull in any amount of natural or recycled material for body and decoration. A lot of these ideas I would use shamelessly with just about any age group, simplifying things down a bit with younger groups or giving more freedom with interpretation (rather than trying to make things more complicated) to older or more able groups.

Bodies

There are a variety of suggestions in the examples below. When people are planning their puppets; there is often a tendency to make heavy, solid bodies because they seems more "real" while flimsy rag or floaty-cloth bodies seem insubstantial. The latter are much easier to work with, however. Solid bodies add weight and need support or extra hands to move them and they slow you down. Apparently flimsy bodies give you much more freedom.

Exaggerate

Make things bigger than proportions: limbs need to be a bit longer than they "should" be to allow for more dramatic gestures. Eyes are vital: make them big and obvious. Heads can be too big for bodies, hands too large for arms.

Think about the animators

How many people will a puppet need to become active? Try to ensure that everyone in a group has a role: add foot rods or ear flappers if need be, or try to rein back the person obsessively developing a life-weighted elephant that they reckon will be a brilliant marionette for one person to operate.

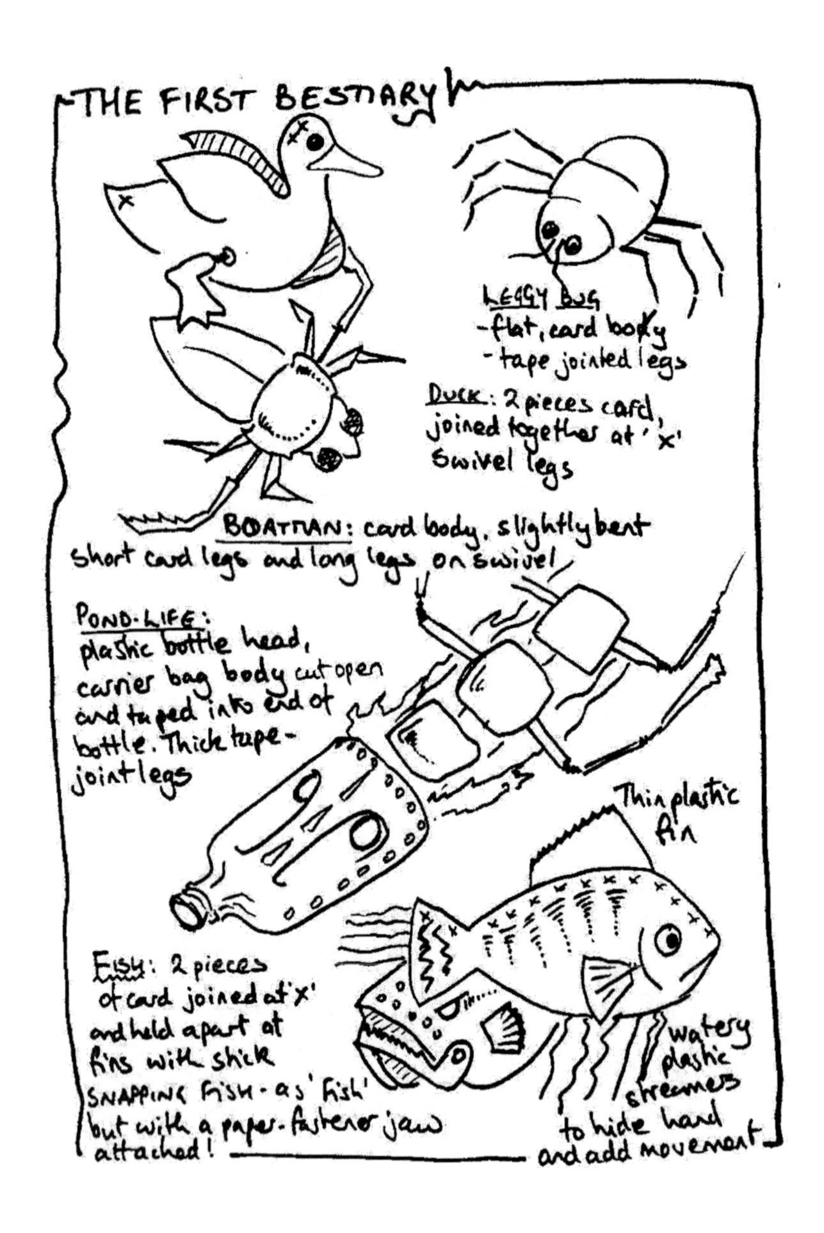
THE FIRST BESTIARY
LEGGY BUG
-flat, card body
-tape jointed legs
DUCK: 2 pieces card, joined together at 'x'
Swivel legs
BOATMAN: card body, slightly bent
short card legs and long legs on swivel
POND-LIFE:
plastic bottle head,
carrier bag body cut open
and taped into end of
bottle. Thick tape-
joint legs
Thin plastic fin
FISH: 2 pieces
of card joined at 'x'
and held apart at
fins with stick
SNAPPING FISH - as 'fish'
but with a paper-fastener jaw
attached!
watery
plastic
streamers
to hide hand
and add movement

The Bestiary

Here are some notes to accompany the illustrations: a collection of strange creatures and unpredictable people

fish and snapping fish: often used in the same workshops as Leggy bugs and boatmen: simple two-piece puppets, with identical shapes fastened together along the upper edge and braced open with a rod supporting fins. A "V-shaped" jaw, with open ends folded up and paper-fastenered into place can give a moving jaw, manipulated by the other hand , maybe at the end of a thin rod. Works well with fish, rabbits, tortoises, the heads of foxes with biting teeth and so on

pondlife: plastic bottles with built-in handles offer so many possibilities! Held vertically they give very dignified human faces: all nose and eyebrows. Horizontally they are wonderful animal faces. Bodies can be made from a cut open carrier bag, taped to the inside of the bottle with its end cut off, then with the open side of bag taped up. Cardboard segments and rod legs add structure to the body

twig life and stick people: see entry in Exploring chapter

mantis: work out from twig people and build more complex characters with fuller articulation. Sticks work well for insects and praying mantids with four legs to walk on and long grasping forelimbs might unfold from the debris

Boggarts 1: build onto a small cross of cane: maybe 10 x 5 cm. Wrap one end with foam or scraps and cover with cloth or plastic for a head. Add arms (move with rods at hands) dress with scraps or pinned together leaves. Simple, absorbing and very effective, but fiddly

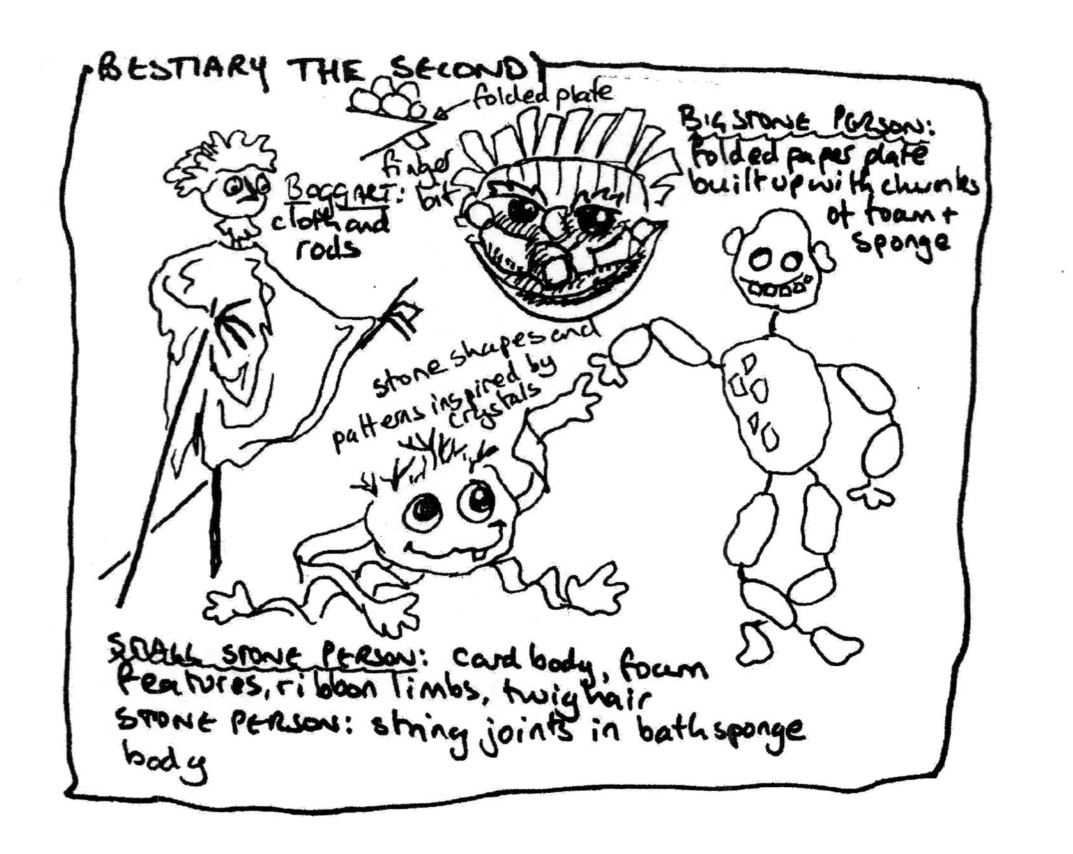
BESTIARY THE SECOND!
folded plate
finger bit
BOGGART: cloth and rods
BIG STONE PERSON: folded paper plate built up with chunks of foam + sponge
stone shapes and patterns inspired by crystals
SMALL STONE PERSON: card body, foam features, ribbon limbs, twig hair
STONE PERSON: string joints in bath sponge body

to prepare as you really need the cross made first (fasten with gaffer tape)

Stone People: the following two groups arose out of art and geology projects. Participants worked with either individual rocks and minerals or simply pebbles and rockforms and turned these into "people", developing characters and features from their understanding of the original rock. There were pale-skinned Talc people who crumbled if you even shouted at them, glittering Mica magicians, elegant Calcite princesses with crowns made of crystal towers, a Boulder King and a villainous lump of sulphur who was going to take over the world and find an effective deodorant. These ideas gave us the following puppet types:

small pebble people: working with bath sponge bodies with limbs of string or ribbon poked into holes punched into sponges and glued in place with latex glue. Features are built up on flat sponge faces with more sponge and found materials using latex and held in place with pins until glue has set (sometimes needs overnight). Slower with the glue than one might like but results are good. Faster bonding can be achieved with hot glue-guns but you might need to think about using them.

big stone people: bigger version of the above. Here bodies were large pieces of foam, limbs were hacked up water-pipe insulation and heads were chunks of foam built up on folded paper plates for opening mouths. The finished puppets generally needed two or three people to operate them.

snapping mouth animals: a small version of the Pole Mask heads with a lower jaw added (hinged with strips of tape) and the whole manipulated by fingers slid

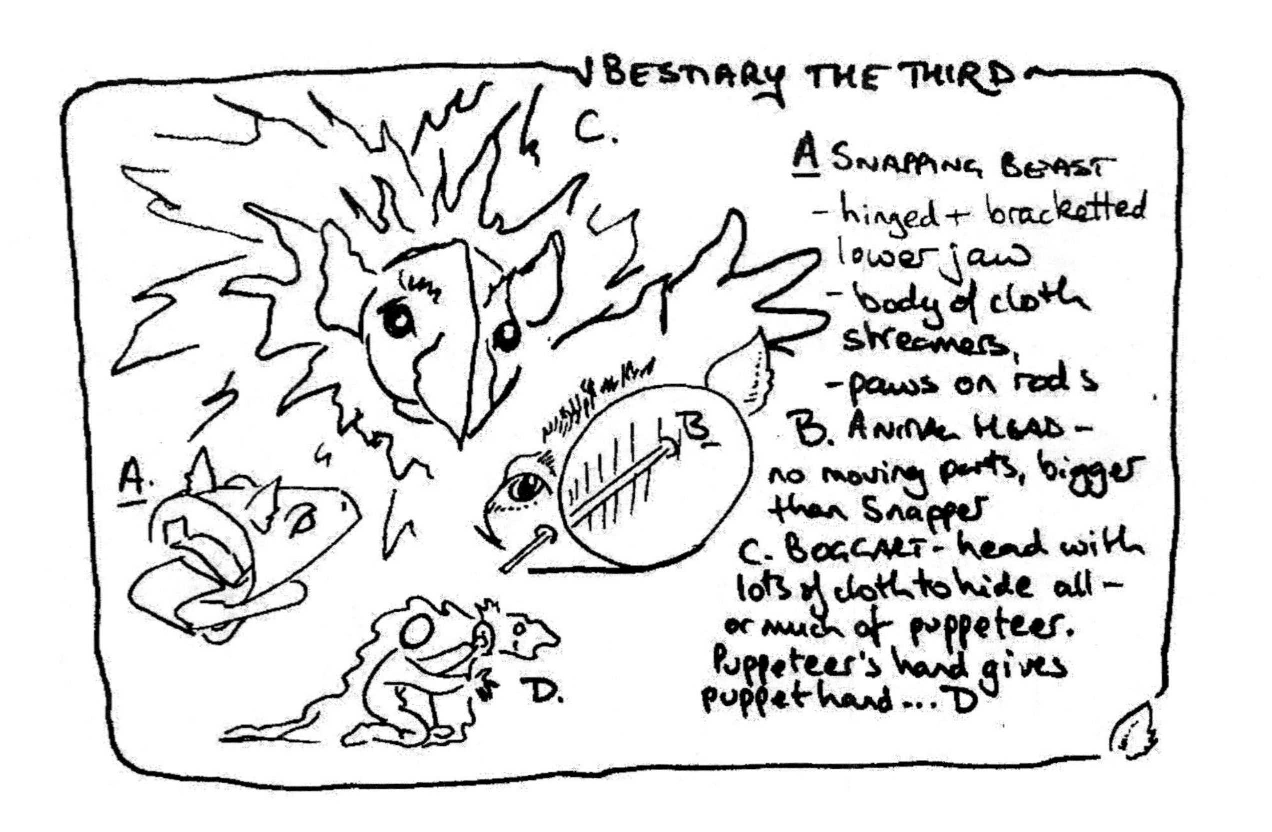
BESTIARY THE THIRD
C.
A SNAPPING BEAST
- hinged + bracketted lower jaw
- body of cloth streamers,
- paws on rods
B. ANIMAL HEAD -
no moving parts, bigger than Snapper
C. BOGGART - head with lots of cloth to hide all - or much of puppeteer.
Puppeteer's hand gives puppet hand ... D
A.
B.
D.

under card strips fastened inside main head and under the jaw. Paws on cloth streamer limbs and moved with rods added a finishing touch.

animal heads: again working Pole Mask constructions but now without the carrying pole and a shorter stick slid sideways through the head. Ends may be concealed behind ears. Puppet manipulated by holding this stick, arm hidden and movement added with lots of streamers

Boggarts 2: as with animal heads but now with cascades of cloth that cloak the whole puppeteer giving a lumpy, hump-backed body, a long neck and a very mobile head

small tree people: simple rod puppets with faces that were smaller version of the tall tree people, mounted on short bamboo with bodies of cloth streamers and rod-managed hands attached to one or two of those streamers

paradise bird: a simple but effective combination of plastic bottles, hinges and cloth joints that took 2 people to work effectively and looked quite distinctive

big snake: a good collective project for a group working fast. Simply stuff plastic bottles with materials of your choice, join them together with carrier bags (cut open, and trim off handles, then wrap around and tape to each segment, leaving a gap maybe as long as a bottle between sections). Mount with numerous bamboos and experiment. Go dancing

Waking your puppet

Time: minimum of 10 - 15 minutes
Materials: maybe paper and pens, music
Organisation: for short times try working with the whole company, or split in two to have an audience and performers, then swap. In longer periods work in pairs or groups of 4 - 6.
Preparation: make sure you have a basic set of scenario ideas in your head or to hand
Working with puppets might call for something as simple as a short procession and a chance to wave them and feel excited about them and the achievement of making them. You might have time to do a quick puppet performance as a dance or try the hasty adventure described below. Or try working through some of the notes below and see what comes out

Try this first:

first activities: sleep, wake, walk around, encounters: friends, greetings, basic behaviour, response to frightening things (think of unusual or non-human responses: freeze/invisibility, stalking). Take your puppet slowly through a sequence like this. Encourage it to repeat actions. Stylise encounters, repeat effective movements. Greetings, hunting, waking up: anything can become almost a dance. If you have time to do little else, this can give you an elegant set of movements and laughter to present.

Other things to think about:

interview your puppet: name?, home (go and find it), favourite places to do things, what does it do in these places? ambitions, secret desires, friends

combine puppets with storymaking activities, perhaps building a story gradually around the adventures of a small group of puppets, weaving in more and more characters as the story unfolds. From the notes in Stories, try repeating ideas about attempted solutions, failures and helpful friends or new enemies until everyone is involved

you don't need a puppet theatre! Encourage your group to perform in the open. Watch each other and realise that we all watch the puppets rather than the people. So make sure we can see the puppets, unless they are "off stage" (behind your back) getting ready to perform: slow action down, repeat things, give the audience time to see and appreciate what is happening

Clapping Puppets

Time: 15 - 20 minutes
Materials: maybe a supply of percussion instruments or a range of junk and natural resources: or just hands and bodies
Organisation: groups or 5 or 6 people
Preparation: the group really needs to have done Clapping Symphony in the Bumblebees chapter for this to work easily.

In their groups, ask people to take it in turn to be musicians or puppeteers. Choose a phrase that describes a particular puppet or puppets, collect, find or make instruments and when musicians are playing the rhythm of that phrase puppets can move, in time to the music.....and when groups meet, the different phrases start telling stories as foxes go hunting and rabbits freeze as their music stops when the fox comes round the corner....

Hasty adventures

Time: 20 minutes
Materials: none
Organisation: whole company working together, maybe sitting in a circle grouped according to puppet friendships or other alliances.

That idea of gradually drawing everyone in can be done very quickly, if rather hysterically, in a sort of demented version of "The Gingerbread Man" by hurriedly selecting one or two puppets (maybe start with small or apparently vulnerable ones: the ant and his mother) who need to find something (check out rest of puppets: strands of golden hair from a magical horse?). And then set off, grabbing new puppets in as you meet them rather than trying to assemble any sensible order (the Bug Boys who try to boil the young ant, his mother who rescues him him from the Lazy Lizard). This adds a huge degree of unpredictability as our heroes fall over villains, friends and the downright peculiar with no logic at all. Add people to the journey, so that while we might leave some characters behind, other will join the heroes, or track them, so that we build a mad procession of friends and foes. Finally reaching the goal is no guarantee of success as by that time the Golden Horse has got bored and is watching the telly. Or doesn't notice the Ants and stands on them, or sneezes and blows them back to the start. Or welcomes them as old friends and invites them in for tea.

Chaotic, full of laughter and a good way of ending a workshop collectively, You need to be ready to think on your feet and improvise. Try building up a mental (or scribbled on paper) list of puppets as the workshop progresses.

Dancing

Time: 10 minutes or more
Materials: music and player
Organisation: for short times try working with the whole company, or split in two to have an audience and performers, then swap. In longer periods work in pairs or groups of 4 to 6.

When time is short, use music. Forget words, other than to start with a narrated sequence and wake, walk, explore, befriend, be scared, be brave, have a party, go back to sleep.

Work with very simple outlines: "if you could see the school garden at midnight". Or the Pond before, during and after our pond-dipping.

Run through a couple of times. Be at the front and lead some group sequences and at other times let the puppets fly free. Slow it all down. Quick storyline. Casual. And often remarkably beautiful.

And to finish this chapter, a set of more defined puppet styles to work with.

Ribbon Puppets

Time: 45 - 60 minutes; shorter with small groups, longer with bigger ones
Materials: 1 sheet A4 (or A3) card for everyone, but allow for mistakes, scissors, pens, double-sided and masking tapes, ribbons (allow about 60 - 100cm per person), lots of staplers, pipecleaners: 1 per person and 2 x 30cm lengths of willow or cane per person
Organisation: working as a company but with everyone making their own character

The nicest way of doing this is to work without a starting example: the stages of the process have their own shock value then!

Stage 1: draw a character: out of a story you have heard? who might live in your wood? - animal or humanoid, both will work. Keep shapes big and bold and have limbs spread out (don't fold arms, or have seated cats and the like)

Stage 2: cut out your drawing (we can colour them in later)

Stage 3: cut off their heads! And limbs, and hands and feet. If they have a waist, cut them in half as well - don't worry! don't worry! we will put them back together again!

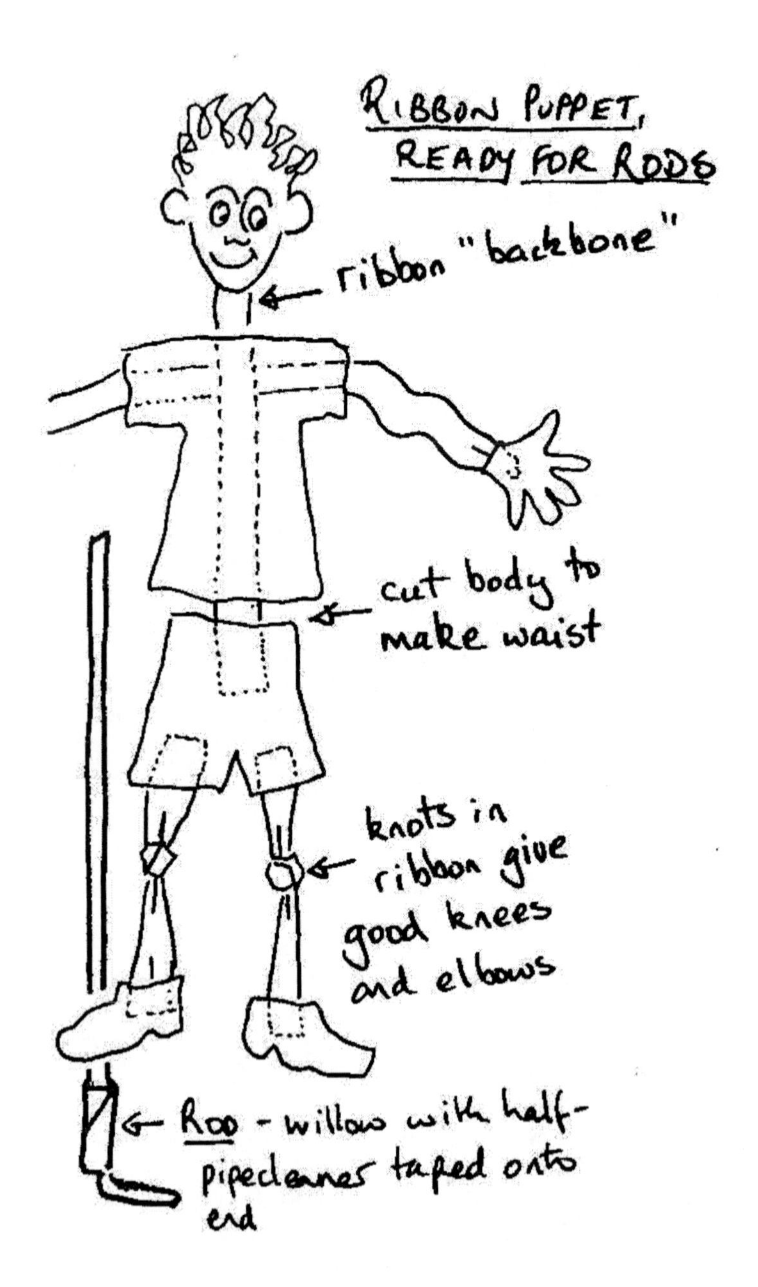
RIBBON PUPPET, READY FOR RODS
ribbon "backbone"
cut body to make waist
knots in ribbon give good knees and elbows
ROD - willow with half-pipecleaner taped onto end

Stage 4: now give them a backbone by stapling a ribbon along the reverse of the drawing, connecting torso pieces and a small scrap of card instead the head (keep the head free of staples for later).

Stage 5: limbs can be separate pieces of ribbon (a bit longer than they "should" be works well), either with drawings of arms and legs stapled onto them, or discard limb drawings and just attach hands and feet. Knots in ribbons work well as knees and elbows

Stage 6: by now we should have a headless puppet with a bendy waist and bouncy limbs. Make 2 rods by taping half a pipecleaner onto the end of cane. Staple these onto one hand and the back of the head card (people), body and head (animals). These will be the bits of the puppet we manipulate. Everything else follows these two rods so you might want to experiment a bit

Stage 7: now add the head, using a bit of double-sided tape

Stage 8: decorate

This activity produces lovely puppets. Make sure you draw to fill an A4 card: too small and drawings are easily damaged by the making process. Much bigger and the card wobbles about too much. We have even done this with photocopies of medieval courtiers stuck onto card and the cut out to make a very quick King Arthur and his Court as the opening of a production using bigger Sock and Face people.

Building bigger puppets

Time: a day and a half?
Materials: gaffer tape, heavy card, cloth, junk, paint....think it through for yourself
Organisation: usually working groups of 5 or 6. Tall Trees usually work in groups of 6 - 8

Preparation: maybe have a tree face to show people or small versions of other things. Or maybe start by making small individual puppets to introduce techniques.

While most of the puppets described in this chapter are relatively small, you might want to make bigger characters. A few suggestions to start us off:

explore strength and lightness: we need puppets that are tough but light. Willow and bamboo frames covered with paper or calico soaked in PVA or Latex glue are good or covered with shredded plastic woven in and out of the frame. Large amounts of cloth get heavy very quickly. Turn to the Willow chapter for techniques.

> papier mache can be moulded over clay forms to give light and strong heads that can be fitted over willow armatures.
>
> simplify designs so that your puppet is very straightforward.
>
> look at books like "Engineers of the Imagination" for more ideas!
>
> carrying: you can carry puppets like the Tall Tree People simply in your hands but they grow heavy quickly and you might be better to prepare shoulder straps that hold the pole in a holster at your hip. Old rucsack frames can support an even stronger structure and carrying the structure supported on your back and hips is quite the most effective way of doing so and still being reasonably manoeuvrable.

Big ideas:
Pond Animals: start working flat on large pieces of card to draw a giant pond animal: a water scorpion maybe. Cut this

out and shape it: cut, fold and glue, tape and paper fasten corners curve the whole thing round plastic hoops (helpful for extra decoration and as handles too). Break it into sections and joint these with cloth or tough but flexible plastic (give yourself enough of a joint for strong exaggerated movement. Manipulate this beastie with a crew underneath it, so hang lots of watery streamers off the hoops and body to hide puppeteers if you want to.

Birds: a head might be made of a big plastic bottle, beak attached, or with a Pole Mask design. Body: another bottle. Neck and wings are cloth or plastic. Tail likewise: or maybe a bouncy curve of decorated plastic tubing. Everything mounted on bamboo poles and worked by a group of 3 or 4 people.

Tall Tree People: combining a range of techniques, these 3 - 4 metre tall folk, have faces made from folded card, foam and anything else that will stick; leaf crowns made from willow and tissue, bodies of cloth streamers and painted Flags, hands of card, branches or more willow leaves, all assembled around a large plastic hoop and a heavy bamboo pole, using gaffer tape and cable ties. They are carried with shoulder harnesses and manipulated by two or three people. Making a Tall Tree Person is a useful group exercise: see the workshop outline at the end of this chapter.

Working with big puppets...

takes time and practice! Do not expect great delicacy and subtlety but do expect expansive movements! To make an impact they often do not need to do very much. Just sailing majestically past can be impressive enough!

Organise your company into teams, taking it in turns to manipulate puppets. With the Tall Trees where groups of up to 8 children may have contributed to its construction there might be two teams of puppeteers to a puppet with one team working the puppet while the others are the Tree's attendants: masked supporters running around their friend until it is their turn to act.

Music helps here, even just a strong drum beat, and work with puppeteers to choreograph simple dances within which they can move and interact with each other and maybe the participants of your celebration. Their size and slowness gives big puppets a certain lumbering grace.

Sock and Face People

No, not sock-faced glove puppets but one of our most effective designs for smaller puppets. The characters who come out of the following have detailed faces and a lot of effective movement in their bodies. I would aim to let everyone make their own puppet and small versions can be manipulated by individuals, but as they get bigger, maybe standing up to 1 metre tall, they are best worked by teams of two people

Time: faces: 1 hour initially then another half day at least to finish off, paint and make bodies (usually at least a day later)

Materials: faces: clay, cling film, plaster cloth, scissors, bowls, boards to work on (stiff card covered with cling film), beads for eyes maybe. Bodies: socks, (or thick tights) soft stuffing (eg foam pillow filling or foam chips), strips of foam about 4 - 6 cm wide, (length depends on size of puppet), string, rubber bands, latex glue, paint, scrap cloth....

Organisation: each person can make their own puppet but often it is helpful to work in groups for resources and moral support

Session 1: Faces. Often working out of doors, after time to explore, write poems, invent character, in clay we make the faces of...the trees? Animals that might live here? Strange people from under the tree roots? Ourselves? You could go for faces standing up from a board that reach as far back as the ears, or you could work in the round and make whole heads. Carefully cover the clay with cling film (means the

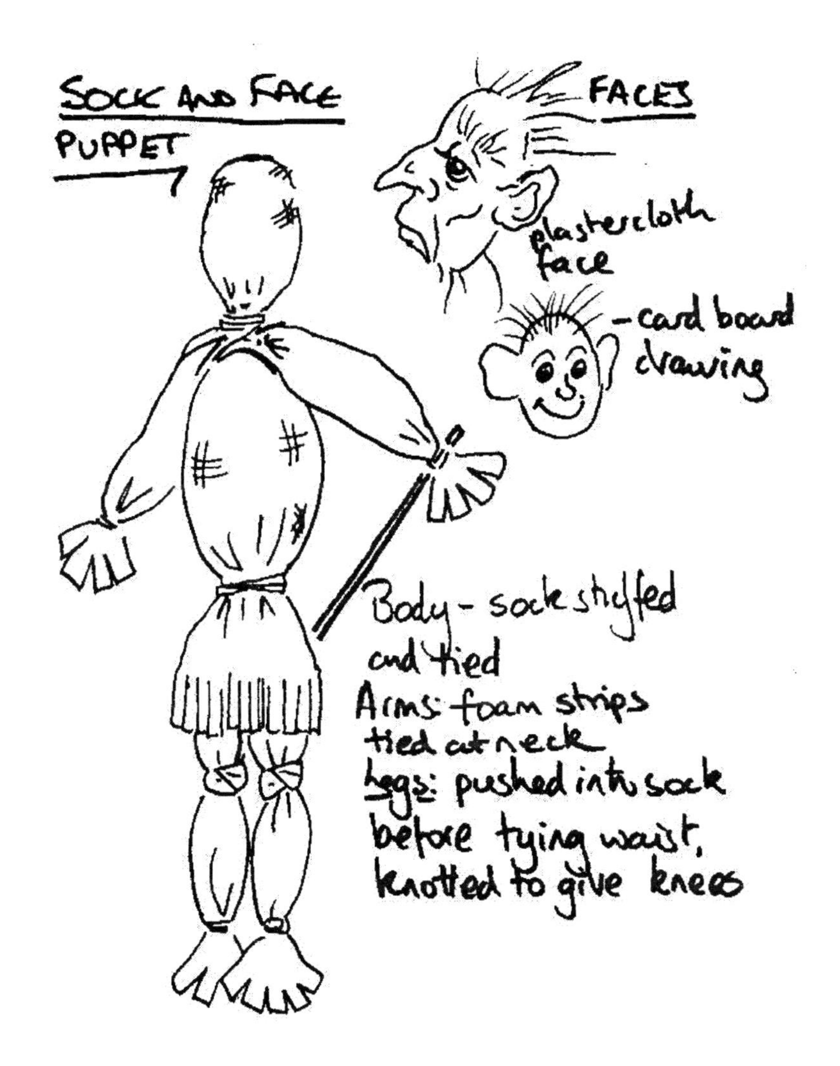
SOCK AND FACE PUPPET
FACES
plastercloth face
-card board drawing
Body - sock stuffed and tied
Arms: foam strips tied at neck
Legs: pushed into sock before tying waist, knotted to give knees

plastercloth dries quickly without the wet clay getting in the way, and that the plaster comes off easily). It sometimes helps to reinforce areas like the edges of ears and the fine tips of beaks with pipecleaners, running round the edge and onto the main head. Beads are useful for making round eyes and these are sometimes best left out at this stage, simply leaving rather gruesome eyesockets just now.

Cut plastercloth into pieces about 10 x 5 cm. Dip them in water for a count of 10, until they are wet and soft. Wring them out a little, spread out the crumpled plaster cloth and smooth it onto the clingfilm-covered clay. Build the plastercloth up like papier-mâché, going for 3 layers of cloth, pressing it gently but firmly into the folds of your clay. As it starts to dry, the surface of the cloth can be smoothed with fingers. Eye-beads can be added with a spot of glue and some rolls of plaster cloth pressed around the beads to give eyelids. Beads can be swivelled around so that their holes give pupils.

Leave the plaster to dry. After about an hour (or less maybe) the plaster can be lifted off the clay and then left overnight somewhere warm and dry to dry out fully. If you have made whole head moulds, you might need to leave the plaster longer, until it is dry enough to cut. Then carefully cut through the head behind the ears, with a craft knife, remove clay and use latex glue and small bits of plaster cloth top glue the halves back together (hold together with rubber bands while everything dries)...or separate the halves but don't glue them together until you have a stuffed head to fit them around.

Overall: this is a familiar papier mache technique, used here to give quick and dramatic results. The plaster is heavier and coarser than paper and glue and fine features get lost in the process. You could always use the plastercloth as a mould, now and take a papier-mâché cast from the finely featured inside of the plaster but this all takes much more time than we usually have with groups, as does simply doing the whole process with paper in the first place.

Session 2: Bodies. Back indoors, in our next meeting, we paint our faces (may need some patchwork repairs first when we see where plastercloth wasn't thick enough: pad thin areas from inside with plastercloth or glue and tissue). A coat of white acrylic gives a strengthening undercoat, then off you go.

While paint is drying, stuff a long sock or one leg of a pair of tights. Stuff vigourously into the toe, making a ball big enough to fit firmly inside your head. Tie off with string. Now stuff the next bit of sock for a body - how rotund is your puppet going to be?. Before you tie this off, slide two foam strips into the end of the body for legs, then tie tightly, making sure the foam is firmly fixed in. Foam arms can be tied with more string round the neck knot. Knees and elbows can be made with more string tied round the foam at appropriate places. Now dress. Anyway you like: glue leaves, twigs and bark all over your puppet, use scraps of cloth, make "proper" clothes, cover with scraps of fur fabric. A coloured sock often needs no more work, the open end of it becoming a skirt or shorts against the legs. Colour foam with slightly watery acrylic paint.

Hands: card or thin foam shapes can be fitted (glue and staples) onto arms, twig fingers might be tied in place, but the simplest hands are made by snipping 2 or 3 cuts into the end of the foam then tying a thread 3 cm or so back from the end of the arm, splaying the fingers to give simple but effective hands.

Feet: likewise, or for larger and more substantial puppets, try fitting them with baby shoes (raid charity shops).

Animals: clay heads can be made longer, try starting with a cone and building animal features onto that so that we have a longer head. Bodies can be made as above but think of your puppet more horizontally, so legs tied on at the neck and tail ends of the sock can be tied round and underneath the knot so they hang down.

Fixing heads: apply generous helpings of glue to the inside of the face, then stuff in the front of the sock-head and hold in place with rubber bands. Hair can be added to plaster and sock (work around the rubber bands). For whole heads, glue both sides of the head then fit them together around the sock, sealing the join with tape and small bits of plaster cloth and holding ti all together with rubber bands

Manipulation: with one puppeteer: hold at back of head and one hand (you might want to put thin rods on hands)

with two puppeteers: Person 1: back of head and hand as above, Person 2: puppet's body and other hand

Experiment and enjoy.

Carrier Bag Puppets

Time: 20 minutes or lots more
Materials: carrier bags (at least 1 each), newspaper, string, eye cards, maybe willow or cane sticks, scrap thin card
Organisation: everyone can make their own puppet but often helps to work with a friend to help with knots

Here is a very simple, recycled material puppet that is quick, versatile and lots of fun.

Start by rolling a sheet of newspaper into into a ball. This will be the puppet's head, so make the ball quite tight and an appropriate sort of shape. Stuff this into a corner of the bag and tie a piece of string (or use rubber bands instead of string to make these joints) round the bag to hold paper in place: keep everything tight and as firm a knot as you can manage. Long neck? Measure out 5 cm or so of bag and tie another string in place. Body: maybe 2 sheets of paper rolled into a reasonable shape. Fit in the bag against the next knot and draw the bag around this ball. Tie. Now the remaining bag might be split up the middle and divided for legs, shredded into streamer-feathers, or rolled and taped for a tail. Arms or front legs might be half of another bag rolled up and tied round the neck knot. Bird legs might be twigs with taped joints. Feet might be scrap card or foam or pipecleaners. Beaks and ears can be card, cut and taped in place. Antlers and horns: pipecleaners. Wings: carrier bag opened out and cut into shape, gathered and taped along back. Eyes: eye cards. More decoration: double-sided tape is best. Paint is very

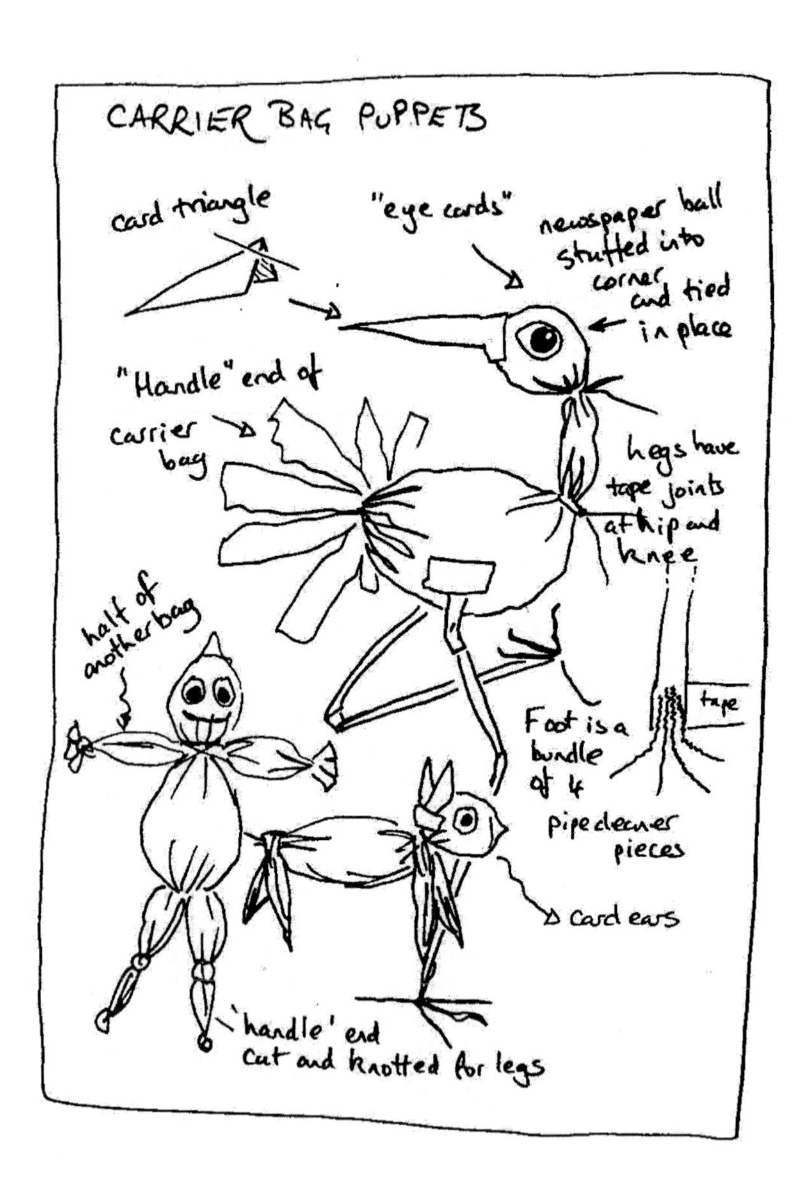
CARRIER BAG PUPPETS
card triangle
"eye cards"
newspaper ball stuffed into corner and tied in place
"Handle" end of carrier bag
Legs have tape joints at hip and knee
half of another bag
tape
Foot is a bundle of 4 pipecleaner pieces
card ears
'handle' end cut and knotted for legs

BIRD OF PARADISE: plastic bottles
with cloth and carrier bag decorration
wings: card, hinged with tape and edged
with streamers, moved with rods
2or 3 people to move: body + head (1)
wing + foot (x2) - or (body + wing) &
(head + wing)

messy and doesn't take well to the plastic. So, use tape - stick it to the body rather than the decoration - usually easier to lift off the protective layer then

Manipulate: with hands: one to support body and wiggle limbs, one to move head.

Variation: try using rubber bands instead of string and knots

So we reach the end of the Puppet chapter. This one feels like a bit of a marathon and, I hope, not too overwhelming. But I make no apology for the weight of this section. Puppets are wonderful and invaluable tools in celebrations and offer so many different avenues to explore, it is worth giving them, and us, time and space to explore possibilities.

Tall Tree People

Here are the outlines of a set of workshops that took us through to the creation and performance of some wonderful, 3 metre tall Tree People. Each session was 4 hours of workshop time, with breaks for lunch and the like. In a more whirlwind version, we have worked with several artists and whole classes to do all Sessions 1 to 3 in one day; the artists have then assembled the puppets and the company has gathered again just before a final celebration to meet and rehearse with their puppets.

Session 1: talking about trees, swapping personal tree stories, playing "animals by numbers" and adding in trees and hand faces for trees. Exploring to meet local trees: 4-shout, leaf-pinning, tree passports,sticky picture scoreboards, stillness and writing a Tree Spell.

Final activities: A2 sheets of paper to design their tree people and write collective "These Roots of Mine" poems (groups of about 8)

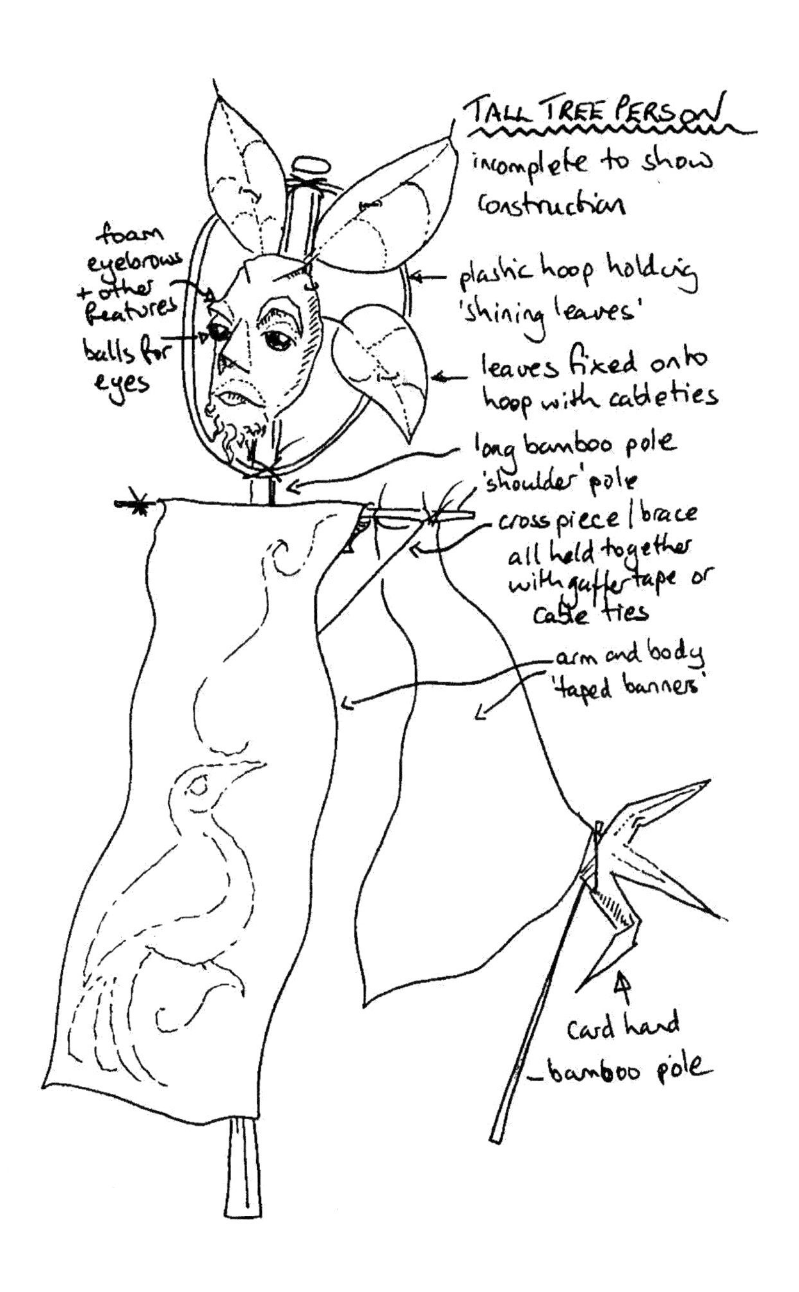
TALL TREE PERSON
incomplete to show construction
foam eyebrows + other features
balls for eyes
plastic hoop holding 'shining leaves'
leaves fixed onto hoop with cableties
long bamboo pole
'shoulder' pole
cross piece / brace
all held together with gaffer tape or cable ties
arm and body 'taped banners'
card hand
bamboo pole

Session 2: everyone makes willow and tissue leaves. Extra time? invite people to make Animal Head masks so that they can become their tree's animal attendants

Session 3: split into teams of about 8 people. Group 1 (3 people) big Tree Faces. Group 2 (5 people) Flags (2m x 1m) as main body parts - images inspired by tree: animals, bark, leaves, associated flowers. Extra time or people? Make long but thinner flags as arms

Session 4: assemble puppets: tie head so that it hangs in the middle of a large plastic hoop. Arrange a crown of willow leaves around the head (keep back 2 as hands). Fix in place with gaffer tape and cable ties. Hang flags from lower edge of hoop as body and arms, add more cloth streamers for a bit of bulk (and as arms if need be). Netting gives a bit of body too, and with less weight. Strap whole thing onto a 3 metre long bamboo. Fix willow leaves and bamboo rods at end of arms. Stand whole thing up and find it won't fit in the room. Stagger outdoors and have a celebratory parade: 1 person on each arm and 1 or 2 carrying body pole.

The Dance of The Tall Trees

Stillness. A soft drum beat.Attendants of each tree recite the Waking Chant that brings their tree to life while they leap out, masked and impressive. Trees dance: a slow circle first, then right hands meet in centre and as a star the trees wheel round their circle. Then slowly swap, swinging right arms out and left hands in, wheel in other direction. Open out. Each tree does its own thing in turn with loud storytellers reciting These Roots poems. Then all dance, circle facing inwards. Turn and circle facing outwards. Process, inviting "audience" to join the waltzing forest...

8

Personal moments

A lot of our celebratory work revolves around groups exploring places and ideas and growing activities and stories out of these. Often this is very individual work: we might work in small groups or as a whole company but we draw upon and grow from individual ideas. We are also usually working towards a finale that is rooted in the company as a whole: people contribute towards a communal experience. In this context, it can be easy to lose those moments that belong to us as individuals.

To find ways of coming back to the personal within the group experience can complete a cycle of growth and creativity for the individuals within the company. We need to look for activities that are effectively personal projects even though everyone in the company is engaged upon them. Look for activities that could be done by one person on their own just as effectively as by a whole company.

Personal moments can encourage personal reflection. In a bigger project they can offer time to slow down, step back and listen to what we are feeling, to appreciate our achievements. As one-of activities they can offer a chance to reflect: to distill the essence of what a place, an animal, a season, whatever, holds for us as individuals. "Reflection" does not here need to imply some deep soul-searching or potentially awkward emotional examination. Effective creative activities allow people to relax and in the development of the activity quietly incorporate their feelings into their work.

When planning for the activities that follow:

> give activities as much time as you can
>
> draw on other activities - poetry and the shorter story ones can be very useful here
>
> return to activities - particularly on a long project - half an hour at the end of a day can become a valuable and anticipated "wind-down" period, allowing ideas rooted on one day to grow into the next

These reflective activities also work well as small individual celebrations. Private indulgences and delights perhaps. Or you might offer your quiet, personal celebration as a present to someone else. Make of it something more: "A Recipe for a Garden Walk" (mapstick?), "Design for a Woodland Chapel" (triptych?). Make a ceremony of the whole thing: a box of the necessaries, an invitation written on nice parchment - or just roughly cut crinkly brown paper, rolled into a scroll.

Use your imagination and give the chance of a celebration quietly to someone else.

Postcard

Time: 10 - 15 minutes
Materials: postcard sized cards (A6), pens, pencils
Organisation: work alone or beside a friend. Usually we would set this up altogether and then spread out a bit to find a quiet corner to work in

Simplicity itself: invite people to send themselves a postcard. Ask what people like to find out when they get a postcard.

Encourage thoughts about how the writer was feeling. What they had been doing that day? What were they hoping to do? Any little dreams or secrets that might be shared?

Work within your storyline and see who, or what, people have met they would like to receive a postcard from....tadpoles can send some very excited postcards with pictures of mud and pond-weed and much anticipation of turning into frogs. Anglo-Saxon peasants sent some rather weary and equally muddy messages to their friends in the the future. Their Norman neighbours, meanwhile, had pictures of their new castle with its flags flying and talk of freedom, adventure and riding through the dales.

Don't talk too much, just let people get on with it. Share a few together at the end if people want to.

Leaflet review

Time: 25 minutes
Materials: sheets of sugar paper, 1 each (usually A4 sized), pens, pencils
Organisation: stage 1 sitting in a circle working as a whole company, stage 2: individuals anywhere appropriate

A two stage process that allows us both to share experiences as a company and to reflect as individuals. You might do both stages or simply the second one

Stage 1: circle of people sitting on the floor. Working on only one side of the paper, draw a small logo in one corner that will allow you to identify your own sheet, then pass your sheet to the person sitting to your left. On the new sheet of paper that should have appeared in front of you (slid there by the person on your right) now write or draw....Decide upon the question here. It might be "something I learned today". Or it might be what people enjoyed doing. Some brilliant idea from some other situation.

Set one question and don't change it because now, after everyone has drawn a single image or written a word or two on that new sheet of paper, they slide that one on to the left and meet another new one approaching from the right. Same question: different response? same response? Up to the individual but keep those sheets moving! It is up to you whether you tell people to move sheets on or ring a bell or just let them get on with it. There will be log-jams where sheets get held up. There will be people shouting for sheets to hurry up. There will be laughter and chaos. But eventually everyone should get their own sheet back (look for the logo) and have a chance to see what experiences everyone else has shared with them

Stage 2: now turn over the paper and fold it into three. Three spaces. Three questions. Perhaps: what have you enjoyed - not enjoyed - would like to do again? What have you learned? - could do again right away? - need to go away and experiment with? What made you happy - sad - what did you find out about yourself?

On completion these answers could be shared with the company, or with a friend or two or folded away and kept private and concealed. Often the process of answering the questions is enough and public revelations are not needed.

Mapsticks

Time: 30 minutes
Equipment: lengths of wool, scissors, maybe thread or thin twine, found twigs
Organisation: usually working with friends but making individual mapsticks

This activity is described in much more detail in *Talking to the Earth*: Mapsticks and Storylines where it was used as a way of recording landscapes without pencils and paper. Here we use it as a way of mapping experiences: encouraging people to think back over a workshop and chart activities and their personal responses to them as colours wrapped, found materials tied, or little models bound onto the sticks. And that's it: rummage, collect, thinking all the while, bind wool onto a twig adding features as you go.

Hints:

scrape bark off sticks where possible

you could always just use natural sources of colour and stain scraped wood with mud and juice, bind with wool and plant fibre

for younger groups we sometime run glue, or double-sided tape, along sticks to help the process

encourage people to make their own minds up about colours to use for 'exciting moments" and achievements. They do not need to conform to stereotypes about the language of colour (red = anger, grey = dull ?).

Wild Books

A lovely activity for recording personal thoughts and changes during a project. Described in full in Chapter 18, Holding onto words.

Triptych

Time: 60 - 90 minutes
Materials: basic kit, strong card (approx A4 is a good size), materials for decorating: tissue, paint, leaf rubbings, etc
Organisation: work on individual triptychs
Preparation: cut some sheets of card into 3 pieces of different proportions: 3 equal pieces, 1 large - 2 small, wide, thin, thinnest. They need a straight base allows to stand and straight edges for hinging but free sides and top can be cut into interesting shapes

A Bog Book
WILD BOOK AND MAPSTICK
BOOK: pages of sugar & brown papers and acetate. Cover decorated with pipecleaner animal and beads.
MAPSTICK: wood, grass, feathers, berries, flowers and twig people

Inspired by the Icons of Russian Orthodox Christianity, this is a simple but very engrossing activity. Essentially, we are making folded card displays but the resulting triptych can be as simple or as intricate as the maker desires and the layers of decoration displayed is limited really only by the imaginations of those involved.

A triptych can be a record of personal moments: "my favourite bits of the garden", "my favourite season", "a special place". It becomes a small, portable celebration all of its own. Encourage imagination and working with a variety of ideas. Mix elements from the list below and encourage people to draw upon previous activities. This can be an ideal opportunity to fix some of the fleeting experiences of a walk in more permanent forms.

Basic process: cut card into three pieces. Show your samples. It is important to cut and hinge the card with gaffer tape rather than simply folding it. Cutting and hinging gives a much crisper finish. That is it. Then decorate.

Consider:

shape: play with the silhouette of the card (tree shapes, the domes and arches of a building)

internal cuts give windows or the spaces between tree branches

light: back internal cuts with tissue or acetate and set the finished triptych up where it will catch the light

colour: lovely opportunity to have thin paintbrushes and acrylic paint to work with miniature paintings

words: incorporate poems or stories from other work. Stillness poems and other similar activities fit beautifully

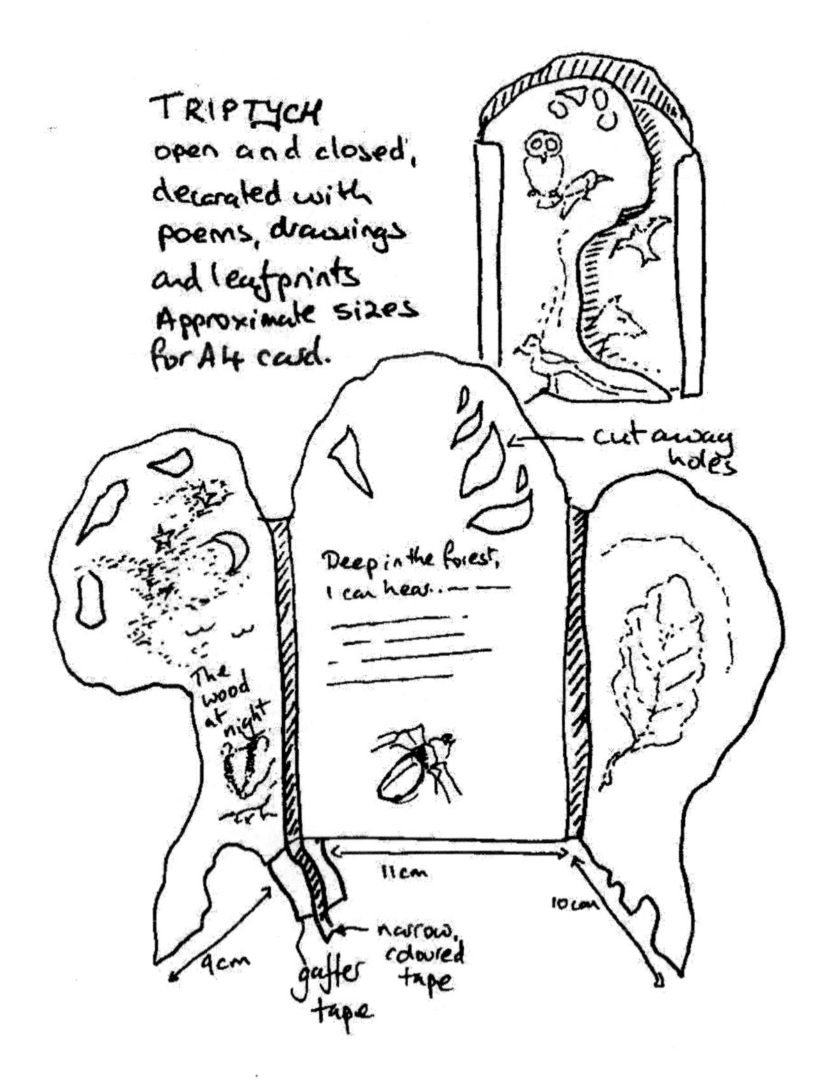
TRIPTYCH
open and closed,
decorated with
poems, drawings
and leafprints
Approximate sizes
for A4 card.
cut away holes
Deep in the forest,
I can hear...
The wood at night
11cm
10cm
9cm
narrow, coloured tape
gaffer tape

special places: use material from sticky boards, leaf or bark rubbings texture: create appropriate textures on different faces of the triptych

think in story terms: a triptych is like a book with 5 pages (or maybe 6 if you count the very "back" section), each page offering a different stage in a story

add body: a fourth leaf might be added, folding down to give a floor between the three "standing" pages - or folding up to give a roof. To this could be added thin streamers and twists of ribbon or shredded plastic as plants in a pond or the leaves of an unfolding flower

stand back: and see what ideas your group come up with all of their own

Variation: let people experiment. We are not creating Icons in a set classical style. You might find someone wants to make a four-folded tower to hold a secret. Why object?

Blocks: a finished triptych can fold flat (and perhaps be tied shut with a ribbon) to become a sort of portable celebration, ready to be opened up and shared wherever you like. More permanent displays could incorporate a plaster slab that sits between the uprights and braces them open. Cast your block from clay pressed into a margarine tub of a size to sit between the open wings of your triptych and impressed with leaves, stones, seeds or shells found on site to give another expression of the special place, moment or season that the triptych represents. See Coffins below for more notes on plaster.

Coffins

Time: 60 - 90 minutes

Materials: basic kit, strong card, clay, cardboard strips (50 cm long, 4 com wide), paper clips, plaster, jugs, plastic spoons, rulers, range of things to make moulds with: plastic animals,

shells, seeds, nuts, leaves, etc. Possibly a set of templates for coffin boxes. Pieces of stiff card or hardboard to work on.
Organisation: working alone or in pairs

Possibly a rather curious activity but a very popular one nonetheless. Here we can design in miniature the coffin that we would like to be buried in - or perhaps we design a coffin for friend or a loved pet (hamsters, goldfish and stick insects have all featured in the past). Inspired by a Ghanaian tradition of carving spectacular coffins for people that reflect the life of the deceased, here we can approach the ceremonies of death as a celebration of the life that had been lived. In one workshop, a Granny accompanying her grand-daughter made a jewellery box as she felt that would be the most exciting thing for her to be buried in!

Start with talk about life and how we are living our lives, what our priorities are, our favourite pastimes, our prize possessions. We might list the most memorable and most delightful qualities of our friends and share these around the group. It is up to you how you manage such a process - keep to positive statements about each others habits and features!

There are 4 main stages to building a miniature coffin:

1. Design: think and maybe draw your coffin design. In this version, we will make a strong cardboard box - which can be painted - with a lid sporting a plaster slab displaying the features we have chosen to celebrate

2. Lid: settle upon a shape (if you are using templates for the coffin body, this will give a limited range of lid shapes). Roll out a slab of clay to about 1cm thick, measure and cut to shape. Compose your lid design by pressing or cutting shapes into the clay: bold and simple stands out best. Remember that this will be cast so you are making negative images: ie everything will be reversed when it comes out as plaster so

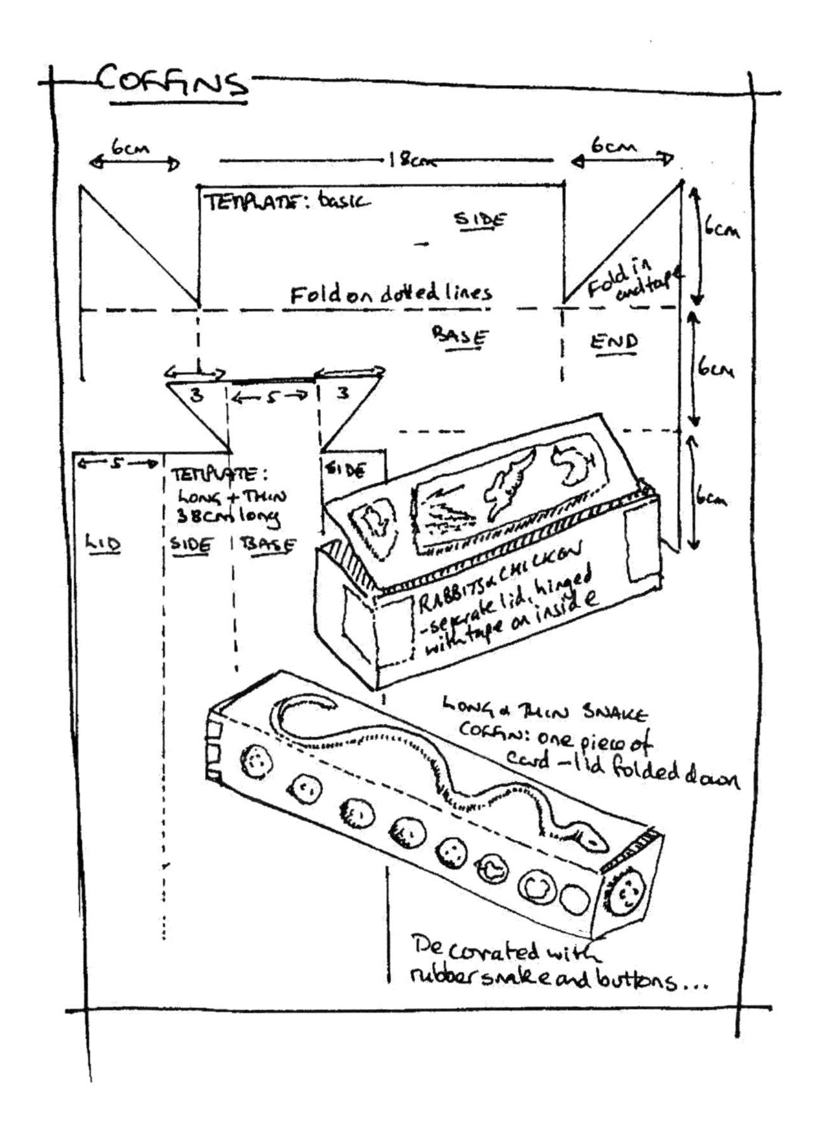
COFFINS
6cm
18cm
6cm
TEMPLATE: basic
SIDE
6cm
Fold in and tape
Fold on dotted lines
BASE
END
6cm
3
5
3
5
TEMPLATE: LONG + THIN 38cm long
SIDE
LID
SIDE
BASE
6cm
RABBITS & CHICKEN - separate lid, hinged with tape on inside
LONG & THIN SNAKE COFFIN: one piece of card - lid folded down
Decorated with rubber snake and buttons...

letters need to go in backwards. You might be able to find a an old printing kit to use. Letters designed to go on cakes might work.

3. Casting the lid: use a cardboard strip to make a wall round the slab: overlap the ends of the card and hold them together with a paperclip. Roll out a sausage of clay and press this to the base of the wall to make a watertight seal with the board. A good test is to look round the inside of the wall, where it meets the coffin lid and look for light peeking through.

Mix plaster: add water slowly to plaster, stirring gently until a thick creamy consistency is reached. Try spooning some plaster into a jug then adding just enough water to cover the powder. Let it stand for a few seconds then pour slowly into the mould. Do not stir vigourously or shake up the mixture or you will end up with plaster full of bubbles which mars the face of your casting.

Leave to set. The time this takes depends upon the consistency of the plaster. Some may be ready in 30 minutes, others will take an hour. If they are taking longer than that and there is water standing on the surface of the plaster, cheat and gently sift a bit of extra plaster dust into the mould. This can make for rather friable plaster so try to get the initial consistency right.

4. Coffin box: while the plaster is setting, make the box itself by measuring, cutting out, scoring and folding card. Glue tabs in place (rubber bands can hold the whole thing together while glue dries. Tape along edges can add extra strength and provide interesting decoration. Make a card lid as well and hinge that in place with strong tape.

Decorate the coffin with paint, tissue, beads, sequins.....

5. Finishing the lid: when the plaster has set, gently open up the mould and peel the clay away from the cast. Ideally, it should dry out still further before painting, but usually people want to plunge straight in. So, decorate. Glue onto the cardboard lid.

6. Process off homewards bearing coffins!

Variations

You could avoid the whole plaster component by working with cardboard sculpture and building bigger coffins with a stronger 3-D element......incorporate relevant shapes into sides or ends of coffin box by extending these outwards when working on the flat. Fold up sides and fasten together above the "box" bit to give animals or other forms standing above the box where the "body" would go.

Hints:

prepare a number of lids for casting so you can line them up and do a run. Plaster does not keep once mixed!

have some extra clay sausages handy to press quickly onto the inevitable gaps where plaster leaks out from under the card wall

try mixing a little plaster beforehand: judging quantities and consistency always feels far more an exercise of instinct than measurement. You can read what should be needed but in the end, the plaster always seems to need something different!

if plaster lids crack coming out of the mould, this might give you a very ancient coffin (prepare a sample one perhaps, suitably "aged"

we have never yet got around to making little dolls to go in the coffins. That might be striking a little too close to home!

Treasure Chests

Time: 30 - 60 minutes
Materials: basic kit, tissue paper, paper picnic bowls, lustre or iridescent paint, "special" things: metallic threads, big sequins, acrylic "gems", permanent pens
Organisation: working as individuals but sharing ideas and helping friends

A round, dark box sits on a table-top, brown as earth and camouflaged with dead leaves, twigs and curls of bark. Lying on a woodland floor or in a flowerbed you might walk past it without ever noticing that anything was there, but for a sudden glimmer, a gleam of sunlight catching a reflecting facet. There, half hidden under a twist of bark, a gem twinkles to lure you in. Opening the strange box, you find colour, a haven lined with bright tissue paper and painted in gleaming colours, and treasures! Small, unexpected things: an oak leaf gleaming golden, a feather stained lapis blue, a bundle of twigs (a rope ladder for pixies? firewood for a fairy? a do-it-yourself broomstick kit for a very small witch?). There are silver pine cones and spells written on the narrow pages of willow or eucalyptus leaves....

Treasure chests are lovely and they encourage a close and excited investigation of wherever you are working.

1. Make the box itself: hinge together two paper picnic bowls (the deeper, the better usually) with gaffer tape. Maybe staple the tape onto the bowl as well as just sticking it to the bowl

2. Paint the outside of the bowl: probably with earthy and leafy colours (some folk will still go for "spectacular" both inside and out!)

3. Line the inside of the bowl with tissue paper glued in place, or paint it. (If the waxen surface of the bowls resists your water-based paint, try mixing in a little PVA with the paint - or just use acrylic paint). Set it aside to dry, leaving box open, with the lid propped up (so it doesn't stick to the table-top)

4. Now go hunting for treasures! A good forage will turn up all sorts of things and it might be up to you and your group to set any necessary parameters: prickly, or stinging plants, live animals! appropriate bits of dead animals....

5. Encourage people to think into **stories** about their treasures as they go: what have they found? why is it special?

6. Back at base, use lustre or iridescent paints and fingers to gently **stain found treasures**. I try to avoid giving things heavy coats of paint and look for a veneer of paint giving a sort of gleaming varnish that allows the natural colours and qualities of the treasure material to shine through. Write messages, with permanent pens, on leaves and bark, tie bundles together or string snail shell and knopper gall beads onto silver thread

7. Guard, protect and **show your treasures**, telling the stories that accompany them.

Treasure maps

Time: 10 - 30 minutes
Materials: selection of drawing materials, paintbrushes, thin paints for colour wash?, a selection of different sizes of paper: cartridge paper has a good solid parchment feel, brown paper looks aged and crackles nicely, tracing paper is delicate and frail to the touch....ribbons
Organisation: working as individuals but sharing ideas and helping friends

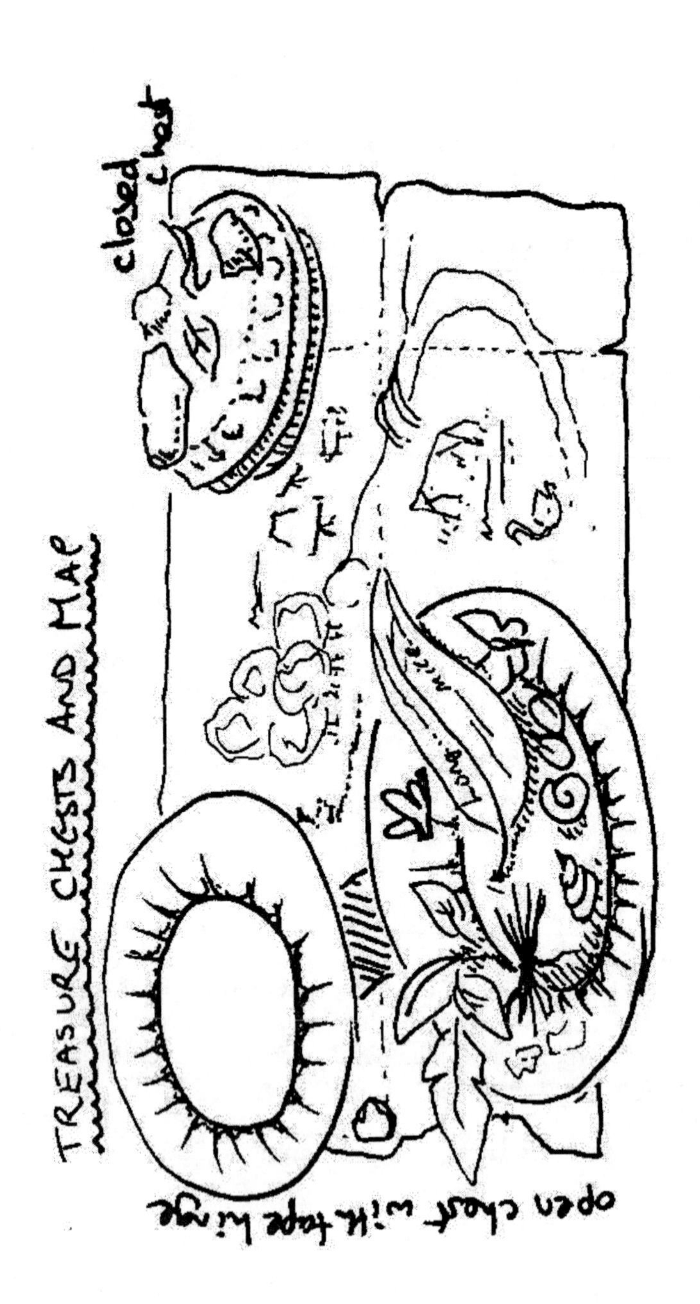
TREASURE CHESTS AND MAP
closed chest
open chest with tape hinge

An almost inevitable development on from Treasure Chests: simply drawing a map to show where your treasure is hidden, or more probably where it was when you found it. Treasure Maps often work best where you map the area you are working in (some people will make completely fantastic maps, while others might map their home street or back garden).

Now, encourage people to look at the area around themselves as people with a secret to hide. Invent new names for places, discover terrible perils that treasure hunters will have to overcome. Our local park produced: the Wild Woods, the Old Woman Bench, the Red Dragon Caves (where the model train was stored), deep waterfalls, crocodiles, and fearsome rapids on the small stream, instructions to "feed the Snow Birds first" (swans), "watch for the guards/ogres/cannibals" (Gardeners!).

Draw maps with as much detail as you can muster. Add colour in small ways or as exciting stains running across the maps.

Fold it, crease it, age it with earth rubbed into the folds. Tear off a corner. Nibble the edges with fingers.

At the end, fold it small and tuck it away, or roll it tight and tie with ribbon and either take it home or leave it for some other traveller to find and adventure with: only to discover that someone else got to the treasure first!

At the end of your quiet personal moment, like a treasure map, fold it small and tuck the experience of it away in your heart: something that is yours and is just for you. Share it if you will, but these are intended as personal moments within all the hustle and bustle or bigger, louder and more public processes.

Gently revolting

For myself, I feel one of the main goals of any education should be to give people the confidence to think for themselves. As educators, we might bring in information, teach the skills to find and to use that information but the heart of the process lies in empowering the people we educate.

In environmental education, we are encouraging people to explore the world for themselves and to develop their own sense of the world around them. This can be a risky process. I know that I hope people will grow into a rich appreciation of this world but I need to recognise that they may not. If I believe in what I am doing educationally, I have to be prepared to accept that, for me, unhappy, conclusion. If I create workshops where people are given a defined emotional outcome ("you will accept this, you will believe that, you will do the next thing) then this is indoctrination, not education. Education is a risky business!

But effective education is not just risky for us. I hope that environmental education promotes, or provokes, change. Environmental work should encourage people to reflect and review, to change as individuals and through them, change will ripple, or reverberate, through social, political and technological approaches to the world.

Environmental education promotes revolution - or maybe renaissance is a better term? - or maybe a butterfly metamorphosis.

Through *Celebrating Nature*, we might hope that some of those metamorphoses can happen through creativity, wonder and delight.

9

Small spaces and smaller celebrations

As we said at the start of Personal Moments, a lot of the examples and activities in Celebrating Nature tend to assume that you are working towards an outdoor finale, and often with a fair number of people: 30 or more maybe. We have been planning processions and performances. dances, stories and masked extravaganzas. You might, however, want to work indoors or with a smaller group of people (or large numbers of people in a hall...the variations are endless!).

This might call for some new ideas, new ways to create special places where that final celebration might take place. This chapter pulls together some ideas for ways of decorating smaller spaces, and looking at and thinking about settings generally. Most of these notes are designed for indoor spaces, some will transfer happily to outdoor events while others would be in grave danger of sagging damply and looking very forlorn.

Creating celebrations for smaller groups of people will draw upon the same principles we are using for other groups and some further ideas to experiment with are presented in a section at the end of the activities.

Look at the space

Be it living room, bedroom or village hall, give yourself time to simply look at the space you will work in. Whatever else you do, your activities could also become a celebration of the space you are working in. Acknowledge the space as well as other themes you may be exploring. So, look at:

light: windows, light sockets, other power points

shadows: mysterious dark corners?

hidden spaces: cupboards that things could swing out of (experiment with string on door handles and puppets hung on the back of the door), fireplaces where other things could slither down the chimney

people in the room: doorways, where do people usually stand or sit? would it be interesting to change this?

features: anything else to note? amazing carpet, picture rails to hang things from, wonderful ceiling roses... just about anything might spark an idea?

stories: hopefully you will be bringing a new celebration into this space but is there anything about the room itself you feel it would be good to recognise? Anything that might add to celebrants' appreciation of the space as well as the whole celebration? This might just lead to an opening sentence or two introducing the space or it might inspire your decorations. Is this the room where your family has birthday parties? A Victorian school room now seeing livelier forms of education, a place where someone died and you hope their memory would appreciate the warmth you bring to an old space? A new room in a new building and may your celebration's sense of wonder will set the scene for future uses?

Bring the outside in

You might simply draw upon activities described in the Flags, Lanterns and Celebrations that stay for ideas to use in creating your enchanted place, but there are other, smaller, ideas you could add.

Lights

Ideas for small scale and cosy illuminations

i) cheat: use "Christmas tree" lights anywhere and everywhere

ii) flowerpots or other bowls: sit a night-light (or "tea-light") in the bottom for a warm golden uplit glow

iii) sea-shells: intriguing variation on the 'night-light' idea. Take the wick out of a night-light (usually these are attached to a small metal plate and will just slide out). Then grate, crush or otherwise reduce the wax to small chunks. Stand the wick in a seashell and pack the wax pieces around it. If the shell will not stand upright on its own, stand its point in a bowl of sand. Alternatively, you might get fine wax granules from a craft shop but I like the recycling nature of wax bits (you could use the remains of other candles as well) and groups enjoy the violence of scrunching them up. The results are lovely and help create a special, marine atmosphere

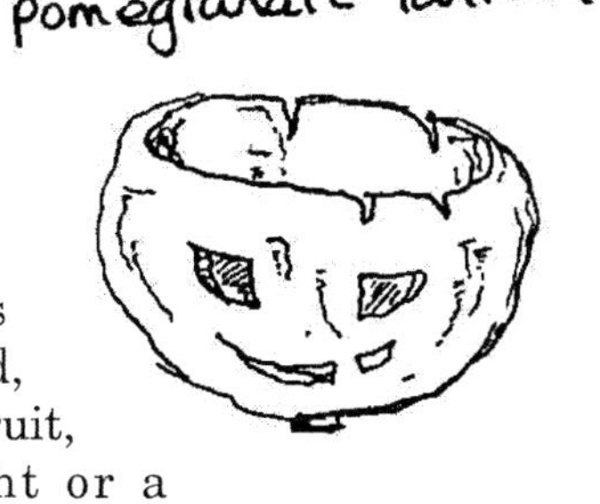

iv) pomegranate lanterns: a miniature version of pumpkin lanterns. Cut off the top and scoop the flesh out of a pomegranate. Eat the flesh. Cut features in the skin with a scalpel (or hole-punch pliers might reach in to give eyes) and, depending upon the size of the fruit, illuminate with a night-light or a birthday cake candle set in a small lump of clay. Over time, the pomegranate will dry out to a tough, almost wooden, finish. I have one that has been leering at me for eight years now and still sports a candle on special occasions. Experiment with other fruit. On this small scale, look for things that have a tough, thin skin and may dry to that husky finish

v) papier-mâché balloons: as messy as it sounds, papier-mâché a balloon and when dry, cut patterns and features through the layers. Illuminate with a night-light in a jar: Make sure there is a vent at the top and you may need to cut the bottom off for an edge to sit on flat surfaces. You could use wet-strength (or other) tissue paper, which dries to give a tough and translucent finish. Rather than cutting shapes out, decorate the still wet-surface with leaves or dribbled food colouring and illuminate with a night-light or small torch

vi) cut out lanterns: see below

vii) mirrors: and add mirrors to all the above: small ones set beside or behind other lights add depth and extra light to the proceedings

viii) Pumpkins: what do I need to say here? I'm sure you know what to do! Have you tried only cutting part way through the flesh for a softer light? Or using lino-cut tools for smoother lines and easier curves?

Cut outs

Time: 30 mins or more
Materials: tough paper or thin card, pencils, scalpels, tissue paper, glue (PVA or glue sticks), cutting boards, night light and jam jar maybe, masking tape
Organisation: work in ones or twos

CUT-OUT LANTERN & FREIZES

3 Freize designs shown
- details could be coloured in on finished work
Owls meet a wing & tail,
Cat and mouse at borders and tails (noses usually touch)
wizard - borders, beard and hat brim

Draw pictures to cut out, like shadow screen pictures. Perhaps trees in winter, leaves, flowers, birds: scenes that tie into the celebration that will follow or that reflect upon people and the place where the celebration happens......

When designing a panel to cut out, make sure shapes reach right to the edge of the paper where you need a border a couple of centimetres wide.

Cut carefully (supervision of scalpels or craft knives may be needed)

Tape onto windows

Or fold a strip of card into four sections and cut out four panels (different or all the same) and stand as an open-ended box, taping the open sides together, to make a lantern that can sit with a candle in a jam jar inside it

Variation: you could work in black card rather than white for a very different "feel" to the finished piece. With both lanterns and cutouts, you might also like to glue tissue paper across the cutout spaces to add colour to the image. Cut-outs also work remarkably well when cut from brown paper, decorated with glitter and stuck to trees.

Friezes

Time: 10 mins or more
Materials: strips of paper up to 1 metre long and maybe 10 - 20 cm wide (thin brown paper gives good results) , pencils, scalpels, scissors, masking tape
Organisation: work in ones or twos

In a similar technique to the cut-outs, revive that familiar childhood activity of making cutout "concertina" strips of people. See illustration for some examples.

Mobiles

Time: 30 minutes
Materials: animals etc already made (eg small fish), hoops: either made from willow or scavenged plastic play hoops, plastic fishing line, string, streamers and ribbons
Organisation: group of 4 or 5

A simple space filler to draw lots of small creations together. Just hang your small fish (try Bottle Fish), folded card beetles and the like at different heights from a hoop (or from several hoops). Using fishing line will make the hanging less obvious.

Add further decoration by wrapping the hoops with ribbons, streamers, real leaves and so on, and also hang these from the hoop so that fish swim through water and weeds, birds fly among floaty cloudy bits and so on.

Such mobiles might then just be hung in place or might be paraded in on long bamboos like some emperor's palanquin canopy. In one project we made mobiles using two or three hoops representing different layers of life in a rainforest river. The final celebration began with the raising of these on long ribbons (slung over a halls' climbing frame) so that they rose slowly, revealing the different layers of life as they unfolded creating the performance space in which everything else then happened.

Rocking birds

Time: 20 minutes
Materials: scrap tough card, pens, pencils, scissors, tape, glue, decorative scraps,streamers, damp willow
Organisation: working as individuals or maybe pairs

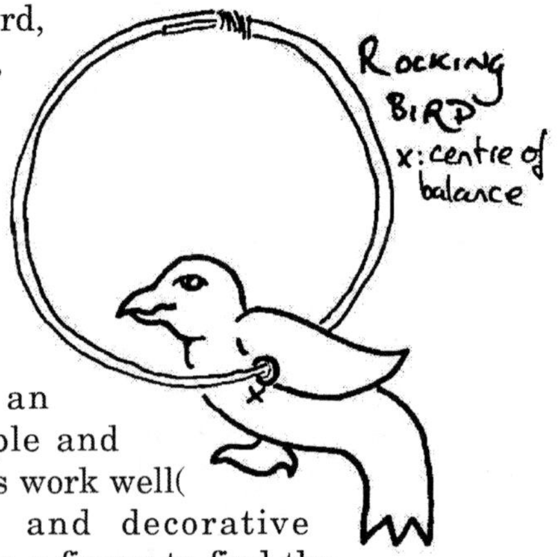

Simplicity itself: draw an animal: keep shape simple and fairly stylised...fish or birds work well(so do mice). Cut out and decorative vigourously. Balance flat on a finger to find the shape's centre of gravity and make a small hole there through which you can push a length of willow. Bend this into a large hoop so that the animal sits poised at the bottom of the hoop. Add streamers to the willow.

Make sure the animal can rock freely back and forward. Hang from the ceiling or on a pole. If the balance doesn't work, try adding paperclips or small bits of clay for weight. Try this with harvest mouse shapes to get tumbling, acrobatic mice.

Thrones

Time: as long or as little as you need
Materials: a chair, things to decorate it with: rugs, blankets, banners.....
Organisation: anything between 1 person and everyone?

I know the above directions are not very helpful. For stories and poems, for the celebration of a person, some sort of central "throne" gives focus and attention to the person in question. For storytelling performances by a group, it is invaluable: a good storytelling chair commands respect and focusses attention on the teller, giving them authority and hopefully a feeling that they are special. For some people it might also feel a bit intimidating, but if we want a story to be heard or a poem to be spoken we need that moment when everyone looks at you!

A throne does not need to start as a very distinctive chair. Drape rich blankets over a chair from the kitchen and it will be as potent as some queen's golden milking stool, spread rugs before the chair's feet, clear a space around it and there you go.

Work outwards from this: you might drape the chair with banners made by the group or hang banners behind it (see Flags). You might attach figures on tall poles to its back to give it height. Pennants may flutter red and gold above the storyteller's head. Lanterns may stand on either side.

Be careful: don't add so much material that the person in the chair disappears under a flood of streamers or surround the throne with so many things that the person cannot move without knocking things over.

Giving gifts

Giving gifts away is a lovely thing to do and helps visitors carry a celebration away with them, giving them a physical, definite connection to the activities they have been part of. Think through what you might give away. Look for something that reflects the celebration and that will give people a thought or an intention to carry away with them. Pressed and painted leaves with small messages in golden ink, golden acorns to grow a new story from, bundles of dry earth and lavender tied up in small bright bundles to hang on a tree at home, delicate scrolls of brown paper carrying fragments of poetry, painted feathers....Again, we look for gifts that encourage reflection, invite wonder and hope that people will be inspired to act. We usually avoid gifts with a stern command, unless that ties in with a "wonder moment" ("switch off light bulbs", while a worthy action is not necessarily a moment of wonder). "Listen to the moths in the darkness, so switch off lights" was a more intriguing, if rather curious, command. On another, celebrants left with leaves bearing small requests from tree saplings: "talk to me when you are passing", "will you be my friend?", "please don't let the grass grow too long around me"....

Smaller celebrations

As we have already observed, most of the work in this book assumes that we are working with tens of people but the same principles that we would use with 30 excitable 8 year olds can also apply to a small family gathering celebrating the birth of a new child.

With small groups, especially those who know each other, the strong skeletons of bigger events may not be as obviously relevant but if you are planning your celebration carefully you may well find yourself working with those same stages, albeit less obviously.

It is still worth giving your preparations that slightly formal tone. This does not mean that an event will become stuffy and freedom and laughter suppressed, but it does give the event weight and draws people attentions and intentions together.

Think it through:

wait for people to arrive: a sense of anticipation both in yourselves and in arriving guests. The preparations have begun, special clothes are worn (have you asked for something special: dress as your favourite garden flower perhaps?)

gather the company and welcome them. Thank them for their attendance. remind everyone why you have gathered

Set the proceedings:

time to make decorations? think about what they might like to do, learn a dance, (no, wait, keep the food for later)

invite contributions: give this space and attention, make sure that everyone who wants to contribute publicly has done so

(quiet spaces: a time and a space for private moments?)
do things altogether: sing? dance? laugh

share food: always a good strategy (think about gift giving mentioned above)

end by thanking everyone, again. Hugs and more laughter

As ever, do not get trapped in the structure, but do use it to hold ideas together and make sure people know what it is happening, why it is happening and what they can do to participate (except for those moments of surprise)

Watch timing as well. It helps to start when you say you will: I always think giving a start time is like a pledge. Some people will be late, but maybe they always are. There are, however, those others who noted your stated intention and respected it and made the effort to be there for the time you gave. Why should their effort be ignored because some folk have not done so?

An event for a small group of people may not need to draw upon the activities we would use for a larger company, but then why should you not spend time before - or during? - the event making masks, animating puppets, painting banners and faces?

Working alone, or with a small group (your family perhaps) can actually be harder than with an organised group. It becomes ever so easy not to bother and to hurry away to the next job or slide quietly into a TV programme. Give yourselves time. Grant yourselves a spell of freedom from other things Start with a walk in a wind-blowing, leaf-flying autumn, or a picnic in a summer, swallow-blown, pigeon-cooed park and grow your activity out of that.

A few domestic group themes and thoughts:

gardens: throw a party for your garden, inviting people to come as their favourite piece of garden: masks? costumes, puppets?

planning your garden: invite the garden to a planning meeting with human guests taking on the cause and role of different parts of the garden , facilitate a debate about new developments and next year's planting plans

new life: greet a baby with naming celebration, and painting a banners before inviting the company to make and hang small tokens of love, affection and good wishes round the edge of the hanging to make a "dream blanket"

fairy godparents: again for new children - or a new stage in anyone's life, you might invite people to come as the fairy godmothers from story.....think about the gift you would give and the implications of same. Reflect that "wicked fairies" may just have been those who brought the truths no-one wanted to hear.....

old year/new year: decorate a room with tokens from high points of the last year and look at hopes, plans and fears for the year that comes

funerals: sad but celebratory, too. Perhaps for that cherished pet: look at Coffins for an activity or maybe Cut-outs showing moments from the life that has passed or giving us a chance to describe cherished moments shared with the passing one

Overall, small celebrations are just as valuable as big ones. They can wake just as much of imagination and creativity as anything bigger. Relax. Enjoy. Cherish the delight of a small group of people having a small occasion of wonder and delight

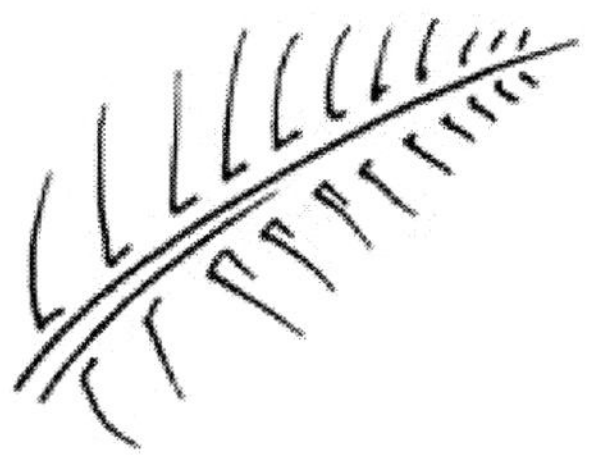

10

Stories

One way or another, stories are how we explain our world. Through stories we make sense of the world around us, using tales to shape the landscapes we walk through, to describe the features and behaviours of the animals and plants around us. We use stories to guide our own actions and decisions and emotional responses and to justify our relationships with each other and the world.

All our explanations can be seen as stories. Whether we call them myths, legends, fables or hard fact, they are all stories. Our most precious scientific processes are still stories: patterns spun to explain observations, rhythms of words that change and grow as our understanding changes, patterns that might help to explain what is going on around us and that might help predict more accurately what may happen next than some of our myths or fairy tales. But they are still stories and what we might accept as firm scientific fact now may in another hundred years be laughed out of the laboratory as a piece of rampant folly.

People can be very quick to dismiss stories, discarding the richness of imagination and wonder tales as "just fairytales" and "only for children" but we all hunger for stories. Think of the stories we follow and hold onto. In films, on radio, on TV soap operas with ridiculous plots and outrageous characters. We might laugh at fairy tales but we devour these stories, talk about them, wonder what we would have done in that situation, even use them as reference points in our own interactions.

We may not consciously compare ourselves to the heroes, villains and victims from our favourite TV programmes or consciously decide to act as he or she did but such stories do give us a gauge to measure ourselves and our actions against. Story-behaviours give us a starting point for discussion or for personal reflection.

Older stories work just as well. Slipping away from our modern communications media and simply sitting and listening can seem both very simple and very hard. Children will readily give themselves to a story, letting it fill them and inspire them while adults may not be used to just sitting and listening. The hunger is there in grown-ups, too. It is sometimes maybe harder for us to admit to ourselves that it is wonderful to do this, not for the sake of the children or the group but just for ourselves.

We can turn to those older stories and there listen to voices from hundreds of years or thousands of miles away and from environments and cultures far removed from our own but where human situations still echo in our experience of ourselves, each other and of how we live in the world.

Stories in celebrations

In our work as celebrants, stories are there right at the beginning of it all and persist throughout the process, like the breath of our celebratory creature, waking it to wild and laughing life. No matter what scale we are working on, reaching out for stories provides fuel for imagination and inspiration and shape the celebration that grows.

As we begin to shape a celebration, we might separate the idea of "a story" into three main forms:

> story itself in the sense of a narrative with defined characters and actions. This might be a story we are "given" as something delivered by a storyteller or taken from a book or it might be a story or stories we create during the course of our other activities
>
> storyline: a less defined situation - a pattern to work with, a loose sequence of events rather than the tight structure of a story itself
>
> scenario: even looser format, the opening paragraph that sets the scene, an idea we are exploring

These three forms are dynamic, changing from one to another as we work. The situation you are in will probably suggest what you work with. Storywork here in *Celebrating Nature* will revolve around spinning new stories and poems out of our experiences and imaginations. Learning and telling established stories is another skill and that one you will have to pursue in other ways: look in the bibliography for reading ideas or track down a local story-telling club to listen and try for yourself.

Where we are working with a group over several sessions we might use a traditional story or two to set a scenario in motion that over the course of a number of workshops evolves its own storyline that may then coalesce into a definite story that holds the whole of a final celebration together. Where time is short, we might work within an established story, using its characters and experiences to help us explore an issue or a place.

Stories in workshops

In workshop terms, we can look for activities that encourage people to look at the world "as a place where stories might happen". This allows us to use anything and everything to fuel our imaginations. Recognising that adventures are happening all around us, all the time is a wonderful way of engaging with a place and the with the life and processes of that environment. Seeing adventures everywhere promotes a sense of value in all those places. Finding adventures in our own housing estate, playground or the park at the end of the street is a great way of recognising that everywhere and anywhere can be special and that even the most discouraging of landscapes has its own secret wonders for us to discover. Finding adventures everywhere can lead to anything from quick poems to epic sagas and helps people find for themselves some of the connections between the living and non-living components of the world around us.

Stories and science

It might be argued that using the world as a source of stories might exclude scientific observation and understanding from our work and give a totally anthropomorphic worldview. This is a risk, although there is no reason why our experience and understanding of the world should be limited to a scientific rationale. If we are working to explore a group's sense of connection to a place and to each other, we are as likely to be looking for emotional responses to places as scientific records of species and processes. If we also approach "science" as "adventure", we can enliven the whole process of investigation and discovery. Children often have large amounts of knowledge that does not get heard : things learnt from TV or internet, processes met in the classroom or as notes and diagrams can now feed into an adventurous view of the world (see Lifecycles below for a good example). Again, we might be concerned about anthropomorphising objective processes but encouraging people to 'feel" their way through a process can provide a strong sense of understanding and appreciation of that process. It is up to us as facilitators to find the balance within that relationship between "scientific fact" and "artistic impression" (or "flagrant fantasy") that is appropriate for our groups and ourselves.

I aim to create stories with a group that will describe the landscape we are working in and the animals and plants that live there and the adventures that are, or have happened there, but also encourage people to try to see things from an animal's perspective, say, or a tree's. Then instead of simply dressing every fox in trousers and a hat and turning it into a hairy human, we will have tried to think "fox" and put that with its needs and priorities into a story-form.

Activities

The activities here range from some that simply play with words, going for increasing confidence in both use of language and setting imaginations free to those designed to build full scale stories out of our experience of a place. In building a bigger celebration with a group, we might find we have 20 or 30 individual stories by the end of some of these processes which will be just too unwieldy to work with later on. These stories might go on to feed puppet or mask work or provide individual characters for just one or two collective stories woven from elements drawn from the range we create here. This process will be looked at in "Pulling it all together".

Instant Adventures

Activities from other chapters you might use include Past, Present and Future, Stillness Poems , Getting ready for adventures, Storybundles and "Listen to me, I have seen...." from Exploring.

Kennings

"Kenning" means "knowing" so a Kenning is a phrase that describes "knowing" about something. It is a pattern, usually a pair, of words that holds the essence of the object described. An Anglo-Saxon term, some traditional kennings include the names of swords: Widow-maker and Foe-hammer; or the descriptive names of people. "Hairy Breeks" for example, is a particularly evocative kenning. For us, introducing children to kennings sets word-play in motion and out of that more can grow...

Time: 5 - 10 minutes, extending to 20 minutes if you get into simple riddles
Materials: maybe some scrap paper or small A6 pieces if card and pencils
Organisation: start with a couple of examples as a whole company then split into individuals or pairs

Take an animal, plant or other feature of the place where you are working and start looking at ways of describing it that tell us more about the subject without quite naming it. Look for 2 word pairs or adjectives.

So we might have:

owl: silent flier, mouse frightener

deer: wind runner

This can feel quite limiting very quickly, so let the kennings run together and we start creating riddles:

Owl
silent flying,
night piercing,
loneliness calling,
mouse frightener.

Wolf (no, not familiar creatures in most British landscapes)

wood runner,
deer killer,
mountain climber,
moon singer.

Riddles

Time: 20 minutes
Materials: scrap paper or card, pencils
Organisation: do one together as a whole company then work individually or in pairs or small groups.

Riddle games are a very old entertainment and delightful in their simplicity and challenge. Good riddles have you guessing right up to the end and the answer that you have not guessed should have you saying "O, of course!" in mixed frustration and laughter.

With groups, riddles are a good way of building on kenning ideas and encouraging people to play with words and images, stepping out of descriptive clichés and giving people the confidence to find their own imagery.

To start: try a few traditional riddles on the group to whet appetites. Then...

Think about an animal: maybe brainstorm lots of kenning descriptions and see what feels good to work with. Toy with

appearance
behaviour
friends or foes
how you, or other people, react to it

Then work with phrases rather than word-pairs (but not necessarily). The results do not need to rhyme but a sense of rhythm helps the delivery.

When a group feels their riddle is ready, let them try it quietly on another group until the company can reassemble. Then play a riddle game: a riddle can be said three times and there are three guesses at an answer. Invite people to nominate someone else's riddle for speaking, rather than promoting their own.

So we might end up with

> Hedgehog
> An army of spears,
> marching on four legs,
> a rolling ball of teeth,
> prowling through the flowerbeds.

Riddles in the Dark

Old riddles to work with often turn up in poetry collections, so try combing through those. J R R Tolkien's novel "*The Hobbit*" has a wonderful riddle match with lots of excellent examples in the chapter "RIddles in the Dark".

Life Cycles

Time: 20 minutes (allow 30 mins for performance bit as well)
Materials: large sheets of sugar paper (A2) and pens
Organisation: small groups of 4 or 5 people

This is good as a round-up after an investigation session outdoors or perhaps as a first composition and drama activity before moving onto more determined performance work. In small groups, choose and talk through a life cycle (butterflies, dragonflies and frogs are all popular) or natural process (water cycle, food chain with some decomposition, perhaps) that they know, or have just been investigating. Then:

> draw the cycle as a set of stages
>
> describe the main activity of each stage (may not be necessary?)
>
> add a "feeling" for each stage: excitement, frustration, waiting...
>
> write the words, thoughts or feelings of the animal at that stage of its cycle in the first person
>
> perform the whole thing!

Easiest performances are just to speak the words and experiment with that delivery. Try it as a single small voice, a whispered chorus, a loud chorus, separate lines delivered by different individuals, a chanted round (everyone reads same lines but with a staggered start). Often groups add drama as well, so try some body sculpture with the group shaping themselves into forms that capture process and feeling and out of which they can then grow into the next stage of the cycle. Using Animals by numbers as a warm-up at the start of such a session can establish some useful skills.

So we might meet:

> butterfly egg, contained excitement, one egg hanging under a leaf
>
> small caterpillar, (1 finger = caterpillar, lots of people as a single leaf)wriggly excitement, leaves so big there are huge amounts to eat

bigger caterpillar (= more caterpillar, less leaf), slow stuffing of stomach, non-stop eating, slowing down

chrysalis: stillness, a little movement hidden inside

butterfly: escape, space, room to stretch wings, ready to fly

Or perhaps:

water in a pond, lazy under a hot sun

water evaporating, lots of little movement, escaping, flying up into the clouds

clouds travelling, drifting, sailing, freedom

raining on a hilltop: lots of uncertainty, falling

a stream runs down the hillside: roller-coaster squeals and laughter

to rush back into the pond again and wake the lazy pond water with the fresh, bright stream

Beginnings and endings: encourage people to think about how their life cycle performance should begin: walking onto an empty "stage"?, small shapes curled on the ground, flat on the floor, already moving, standing upright but still? And at the end, are we looking for a dramatic closing: "freedom!", or a quiet "death"?

Remember that cycles do move on, the butterfly might be in its "freedom!" shape or might have died but one of the group could form a new egg to start the story again.

Bigger Cycles

Time: 1 hour or more
Materials: big sheets of sugar paper, pens, smaller sheets of scrap paper or card, chunky pens, writing pens
Organisation: initially whole class, then smaller groups as seems fitting

This is a longer and wider version of the above. Working with the water cycle as an example, as a whole company, we take time to

> brainstorm their ideas about rivers, seas, water life
>
> play Animals by numbers using some of those first thoughts
>
> compose a water cycle on a big piece of paper collectively: going initially for physical stages, then adding thoughts about active bits, still bits, delights and dangers facing a drop of water
>
> break this whole cycle down into maybe 10 stages, naming each stage and writing that name on a card
>
> divide the company into that number of groups, and let each group choose a card
>
> work as with Lifecycles above: compose the thoughts of our adventurous water-droplet at that stage of the cycle: what does it see, or experience, how does it feel? Find a way of conveying that experience to others
>
> then perform the whole thing in sequence

This generally creates lots of short poems, often full of unexpected imagery and a range of movement drama. Try offering groups different cloths to play with and we might find sandstorms that whirl across the stage, hills that can grow and fall and a creator Rainbow Serpent who ripples in a long ribbon of fabric from one group to another.

Lying

Time: 10 - 15 minutes
Equipment: none
Organisation: whole company together, mingling

If a group scatters through an area, ask them to bring some token back with them when they gather together again, perhaps something found at the foot of their special tree or at the place where they Disappeared.

We have already noted that everywhere we go we are surrounded by adventures. Many of these will be happening when we are not here but this thing that you have just picked up is actually evidence of something that happened here.....

Then take that thing and simply make up a story about it to someone else. Lie. Tell the wildest lies you can while still using the thing you have found. You do not have to say very much: maybe just a sentence or two to get started. Help each other. Woodland, wilderness journalists interviewing. Ask people about this thing they have got. Aren't they worried about holding it? Isn't it dangerous? O! How sad!

Look for where one story feeds into another, where one odd item actually seems to also be part of someone else's story.

Feedback as a company: listen while one or two people tell a story that they have heard (i.e. not their own tale). While this is happening, the original teller should not speak and the new teller needs to describe the thing she is telling the story about. While good for building skills as listeners and in description and development of stories, Lying can be tricky.

Sometimes a group are just not ready for that open-endedness and having done some of the earlier activities helps a lot in priming people, giving them confidence to simply let their imaginations out of the door and off adventuring.

Two Tree Tales

I usually use the following activities when working with trees but the principles can easily be applied to other situations. Change the contexts to suit your group.

"These roots of mine"

Time: 15 minutes
Materials: outside: A5 card and pencils, inside: A3 paper and felt pens
Organisation: solo, pairs or groups depending upon the situation

Get to know a tree (try Disappearing and Tree Passports). Let your tree talk, describing itself and what it does. Work your way up, or down, your tree discussing each feature of it in turn. The key phrase helps hold all these observations together and gives the finished product its own rhythm.

These lines might offer physical insights:

> "These roots of mine hold me firm against storms"

or qualities or delights:

> "These leaves of mine enjoy fluttering in the breeze"
> "These leaves of mine shelter my friends from the sun"

Or extend to other species associated with the tree:

"This ivy of mine is my blanket in the winter"
"This ivy of mine is a beard full of birds"
"These brambles of mine keep me safe from burglars"

If you are working on an activity like the Tall Tree People, poems like these can be combined from several groups to make composite statements spoken now by the collective presence of a forest represented by the Tree People taking shape on the work-room floor.

Sticky Storyboards

Time: 20 - 30 minutes
Materials: long sticky boards c 20 cm x 8 cm, pencils
Organisation: individuals or pairs are best

Visit a tree, Look at it carefully and remember that a lot of its history will be written in the patterns of its trunk, the form of its branches, its scars and wounds. Check out the immediate surroundings for other clues. Sit down and talk to the tree itself.

Tell us something that has happened to your tree, working from an observed feature. The Storyboards are simply there to help hold an idea together. Sometimes you don't need them and people will happily work "freehand" straight from the tree to the rest of the company. But storyboards help most of us gather our thoughts.

In building up this story (think of it less as fiction and more as an account of something, the final evidence of which we can still see). Try working backwards:

"and from that day to this, this tree has...."

Then start thinking around:

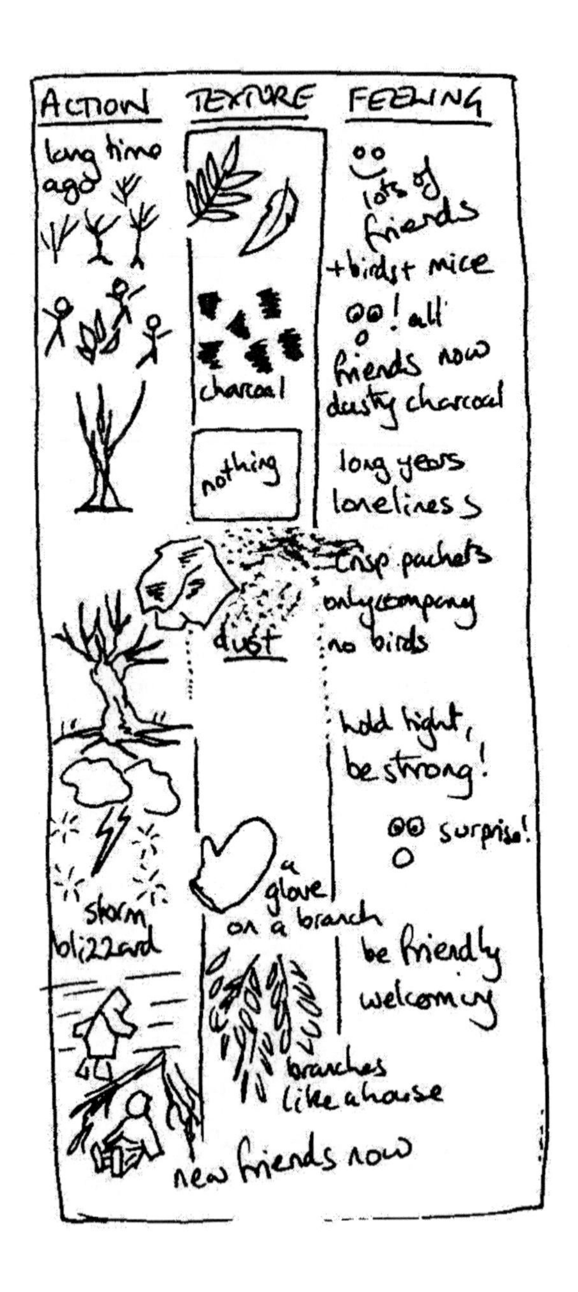
ACTION
TEXTURE
FEELING
long time ago
lots of friends
+ birds + mice
charcoal
all friends now
dusty charcoal
nothing
long years loneliness
crisp packets only company
dust
no birds
hold tight, be strong!
surprise!
a glove on a branch
storm blizzard
be friendly welcoming
branches like a house
new friends now

what was your tree like once (before the Incident)

how old was it? what did it look like then?

how did it feel? was it always sad? cheerfully growing in a forest?

what sparked this incident?

what actually happened?

and from that day to this.......

The storyboard effectively comes in three columns so try using one for writing or drawing notes on action - what was happening, the other plain card column for feelings, how did the tree feel at any particular time and the central sticky column for texture, collecting materials to give description to the story: bark as rough as dinosaur skin, leaves as green an moss and bright as new grass......Or use the found objects to move the story on: a falling twig did this, a bird (feather on board) did that.

Sagas

Time: 20+ minutes
Equipment: pencils, card, masking tape
Organisation: initially pairs then groups of 6 or so

A frivolous story-building process that is useful when moving around.

We are going to build a saga, a story-poem, which will probably not be nearly as heroic as most of those original northern sagas are. Our sagas are usually successions of transformations growing from an agreed starting point and rambling off in all directions, eventually reaching a finale.

Settle upon a starting verse: something that sets the idea in motion. Being enchanted or bewitched is a useful beginning.

> "Once I was a boy,
> Running by the sea,
> But I stepped on a starfish
> Who put a spell on me."

With this (or something similar) in mind, the group then wander in a given direction making up new, and frequently terrible, rhymes about the adventures that befall our hero. That seaside one gave us:

> "I became a sea urchin
> And sat upon the sand.
> Then I sat upon a rock
> And stuck to someone's hand"

And

> "When I was a fish,
> I made a delicious dish"

> "I became a stone,
> And was sat on like a throne.
> I let out a tone,
> Like a trombone,
> And became famous as
> The first musical stone"

Suggesting that people think of 'what I might have been" can help, giving us opening phrases like "When I was..." or "I became...". This could, then turn around and become, "As a butterfly, I flew so high, I hit the sky". The rhymes can be awful, if they are there at all. I try to encourage rhythm more but rhymes seem inevitable.

This is a good activity for wandering and scribbling and when everyone has maybe two or three verses that sound good to them, start getting into bigger groups. Now compare verses and look for some sort of progression. Does our hero get larger or smaller through the phases of her transformations? Does he go from animal to plant to mineral? Look for a good terminal verse. Does he return to his original form (very rare!)? Does he die? Is she now the tree that we are sitting beside?

Shuffle cards around to get a good sequence and then stick them, in sequence, on a long piece of tape and practice reciting the saga before presenting it to everyone else.

Developments: works very well with simple folded card sculptures to mark the changing phases of the hero's adventure, or even simply drawing that stage, writing the words within the outline of the shape and cutting it out

Bigger stories

Most of the above activities give us scatterings of ideas: anecdotes of things that have happened in this place, moments seized from bigger stories. Sometimes this gives us enough to work with as we come out of these activities with ideas of who lives here and what they do and how we might interact with them, but we might need full fledged stories to work with.

If we think of a story as featuring a number of stages (a bit more than just "beginning, middle and end"), we can use that to give a structure and way of working that can take a group from feeling uncertain about their story-making skills to having lovely tales all of their own.

Rather than dumping the whole structure on a group all at once, we can slide them through it by simply asking them some questions with each question leading us into the next bit of the story. It is good to write, here, or draw: use something to record answers to questions and when you are asking questions encourage people to take the first thought that comes into their heads. Grab the spontaneous response rather than the considered one.

One set of questions follow for a basic adventure, with some further suggestions for variations. Different routes into big stories might come with Character sheets and Diaries, described in New Characters.

Story questions

Time: 30 - 40 minutes for first stage, another 15 or 20 for following-up with other activities
Equipment: pencils and paper for everyone (card if you are working out of doors, or maybe clipboards)
Organisation: best with people working on their own. Trying it with whole company can be a useful introduction. Then just maybe in pairs or small groups

Questions might be answered with a scribbled word or phrase (don't worry about writing sentences just now) or you might divide your paper up into 8 boxes and do a quick scribbly picture in each box and build a storyboard rather than a written piece of work

1) Starting point: agree that we are discovering the stories of this place perhaps or maybe stories of the animals of our pond .

What we exclude: you might want to agree with the group about things that should be avoided. I generally ask if we can avoid aliens, robots, zombies, machines and big bombs as these often get used a bit like "deus ex machina" and save the day (often by blowing everything up). That list changes with group and recent television. Zombies are often there for some reason as may be werewolves and vampires, although we have had some lovely atmospheric horror stories about werewolves in midnight woods. I point out that stories are often much more exciting if our heroes do things themselves and solve puzzles and escape from dangers by their own wits and with the help of "ordinary" friends, rather than gun-toting marines, laser-armed aliens and body-ripping ghosts. An "ordinary friend" could still turn our to be an adventurous hedgehog who rolls herself down the hill as a prickly bowling ball to trip up and stab the slavering hound that is chasing you. But at least she is doing a hedgehoggy thing and hasn't just whipped out a machine gun and shot everyone.

Anyway, to get back to the story bit.

Sit the group down. Relax. Get ready. Here come the questions....watch the group carefully as you ask questions...keep them coming quite quickly but not so fast that people are floundering. Be ready to move around and eavesdrop or help (good role for supporting adults providing they don't take over).

2) Questions

1. Where does our story begin and at what time of day and what is the weather doing?

2. Who is our story about? Who is our hero? Tell us one special thing about them (remember a hero can start as a very ordinary person to whom wild things happen)

3. What is our hero doing at the start of the story?

4. When suddenly, what problem or danger faces our hero?

5. How does she feel when this happens? And what is the first thing she does to try to solve the problem? (usually the first thing doesn't work)

6. How does she feel now? Does she have a friend or some object that might help her? (often an object that was Lied about earlier can suddenly come into its own here) It may be that there is no-one who can help and our hero is on her own.

7. What does our hero with, or without, her helpful friend do to solve the problem?

8. What happens at the very end ("living happily ever after" is always an option)

Now, people have answered these questions and hopefully they have the shape of a story on their paper and in their heads.

3) Give them 10 -15 minutes to write it out quickly or to go back over their pictures and add more detail

Have you written Stillness Poems at some point? Could those come into the story as descriptions of what the hero hears as

she walks through the wood?
Shut up and let the group get on with it.

4) As people finish off, get them to pair off and read their stories quietly to each other.

5) If there is time, you could play with these stories a bit and try:

> a) after reading your story, swap notes and listen as your partner reads (or tells from memory as much as she can remember) your story back to you...and do not interrupt
>
> b) have your partner read your story while you act it out (may give some movement to accompany your reading of your own story later)
>
> c) read your story while a partner (or partners) provide a soundtrack on sticks, stones or small percussion instruments. This can provide pace as the musicians advise on when to speed up and when to slow down, when to be loud and when to be soft.

6) Gathering the whole company together, find out how people got on, how comfortable they are with their stories. Are these stories finished? Do they tell us about things that have happened or people that lived, or live, here that no-one had ever heard of before? Even though we all worked with the same set of questions, have we got some very different stories?

Could we hear maybe just two or three stories?

Variations

This is a basic set of questions. You could play around with them and add or remove questions as seem appropriate. Make sure you keep a basic structure: that includes: setting, main character, supporting characters, dilemma, resolution.

a) Settings: you could add a question about a particular spot within the general habitat... "homes" are useful or specific landscape features: stepping stones, stone circles, large, lone rocks, very old trees

b) Hero: tell a bit more about the hero

c) Dilemmas and resolutions: in traditional stories a hero often builds up to a final solution through a number of variously successful stages. You could repeat questions 5, 6 and 7 almost indefinitely to give a journey looking for help (a familiar story theme) or wildly increase tension by one attempt after another piling mishap upon disaster until some sort of result is achieved

d) Origin tales: the stories of "how...." are very useful in environmental settings but they deserve their own section.

Origin Stories

You might want to look at stories that explain how they things we meet in our lives came to be: "how hedgehogs got prickles", "why swans are white", "why there is a waterfall here".

A question format still works here (but see the variation below) but now it might be worth establishing the answer to #8 at the start: "And from that day to this, hedgehogs have had prickles".

Think about:
Question 1. Who is the story about and when did it happen?
2. How were our heroes different then from how they are now?
3. How did they feel about their condition then (remember

they might have been very happy then and not so pleased now)
4. What problem or dilemma faced them (pushing them towards a change: did they jump or were they pushed?)
5. First attempt? Failure, or partial success?
6. Helpful friends?
7. Another attempt?
8. And from that day to this?

A variation on this might be to take a subject and brainstorm impressions of it: picking up ideas about what it looks like, what it could be made of (swans have started off muddy brown or been made of ice and snow or of icing sugar), the subject's feelings, who could have caused the change, how the thing in question could have brought the change itself. Even more open-ended than the question format, this can open up huge possibilities but often needs a group who are feeling confident already about their own abilities as 'tellers. Works well in pairs or small groups where different people's ideas can all be woven in together. Maybe ask that in the final story their is one major idea from each person in the group.

Once we start unfolding stories it can be hard to stop. So we'll end this chapter here. You and your group might use some of the ideas that might come out of a story activity to create full grown stories to write, record or tell (look at Mapsticks, Wild Books and Water pictures for some ideas) or they may just remain undeveloped as background information that we know about a place or a character. Before we leave this chapter, however, we should make sure we.....

Tell Our Stories

Time: 15 - 20 minutes
Materials: none needed but sometimes "special" rug or cloth or chair would be helpful
Organisation: whole company together

If a whole class has been working on individual stories then there probably won't be time to hear them all, but to give everyone a chance to listen to a few is always rewarding. If possible, create a special space for stories: somewhere where we can all sit down (do you need some tarpaulins to spread on wet grass?), a place for the 'tellers to stand or sit (dramatic log? chair draped with colourful blanket? rug to stand on?)

Then you might ask the company if they would like to recommend someone else's story that they think we all should hear? Support your storyteller, be near if not behind them, allow people to tell in groups (do they need a bit of rehearsal time?). Make sure they speak up and out so we can all hear them. Applaud everything, including the ones who fall apart a bit or whose story fizzles out in embarrassment or giggles.

So now we have stories. This is a big chapter and deserves the bulk. Telling stories and developing stories bring us into some of our most ancient and deep rooted cultural practices. Respect stories but do not be overawed by them. They may bring a magical atmosphere and serenity, stillness and deep thought, or they may - and they may - leave us all helpless with hysterical laughter.

In the development of our celebration, story work may firm up ideas around our original themes and storylines. We might well come out of this work with confirmation of those original plans or find that we've gone way off target. It would now be up to you and your group to decide which stories we use and how we use them....

Embracing Biodiversity

It feels almost redundant to say that recognising, appreciating and working to protect the richness of our world must be one of the single most important issues facing us all today. Biodiversity concepts encourage us to embrace the wholeness of our world – recognising our place as part of those intricately woven webs of life.

Exploring biodiversity and working with ideas of sustainability lie so embedded in the very essence of Celebrating Nature that it can be difficult to step back and consider them separately. Our celebrations might tend to work towards "recognition" and "appreciation" rather than "active protection" but as we have discussed before, the first two are needed for the latter to become relevant and truly engaging for a community.

Scottish Natural Heritage and the Royal Society for the Protection of Birds identified 6 key concepts to use in interpreting biodiversity. These offer a useful framework to think about our work.

> the variety of life: biodiversity means "the variety of life" – the total variation of all living species, their ways of life and the places where they live
>
> keystone species: tipping the balance, recognising that certain species play pivotal roles in their ecosystems
>
> hidden wealth: resources lying still undiscovered: perhaps even " a cure for our ills"

natural inspiration: cultural history, personal inspiration and national identity all include strong contributions from local biodiversity life support systems: all life on earth, including our own, is supported by the natural balance of living systems

it's in your hands: action for biodiversity: recognising and taking responsibility for, the impact and implications of our lifestyles and technologies

Do these need further examination to pin down their relevance to the activities here? I hope not. For me, these are principles that should inform how we approach a project, how our participants approach the world and the work and the message that is inherent in that starting phrase "we live in a world worthy of celebration"

Rather than now sitting down and trying to decide that this activity would match that biodiversity point, while that activity would fulfil this one, let these issues lie within your discussions. As group leaders, reflect upon these, let them infuse your imaginations. With your groups, let the relevance grow: encourage them as discussion points, get people to talk and think. You might widen your discussions and look at how we may apply similar ideas to our human social interactions: welcoming the richness of different ideas and different imaginations, sharing resources and existing skills, learning new skills from each other, sharing experiences, using materials carefully: recycling, re-using, replenishing. Grow new ideas and new plants side by side.

For more information on SNH's Biodiversity initiatives visit their website http://www.biodiversityscotland.gov.uk/. You could also visit http://www.biodiversitystories.co.uk/__

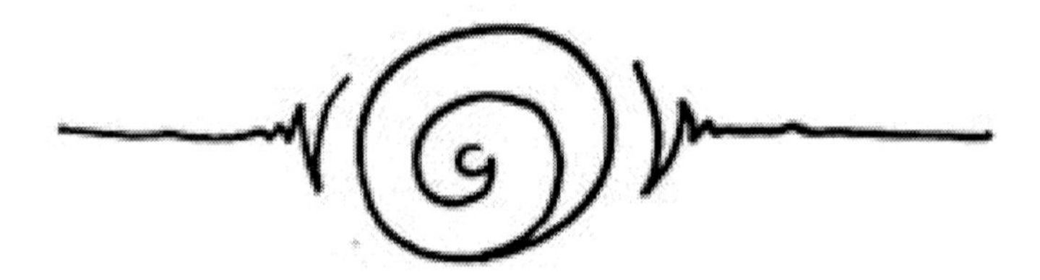

11

Lanterns and shining leaves

Throughout *Celebrating Nature*, I have tried to avoid repeating material already published in "*Talking to the Earth*". I have even tried not to refer to activities there too much on the grounds that this might irritate readers beyond measure. But now we have arrived at a set of activities covered once in "*Talking*" but so valuable in their own right as to merit their own chapter here. While many activity groups (puppets, say, and masks) are common to both books, we hope that here among the lanterns is the only place there will be a major cross-over of activities themselves.

Lanterns. Lights shining through the trees. A gentle glow in a village hall. A

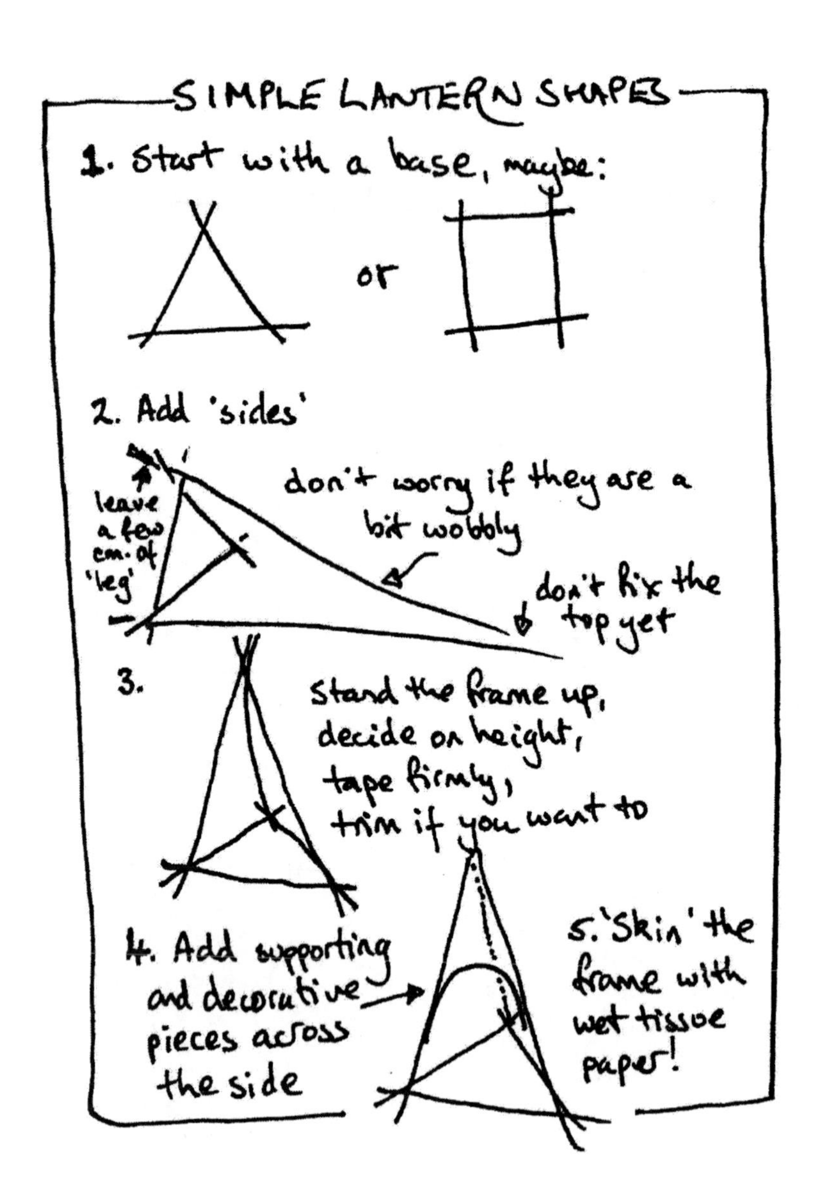
SIMPLE LANTERN SHAPES
1. Start with a base, maybe:
or
2. Add 'sides'
leave a few cm. of 'leg'
don't worry if they are a bit wobbly
don't fix the top yet
3.
Stand the frame up, decide on height, tape firmly, trim if you want to
4. Add supporting and decorative pieces across the side
5. 'Skin' the frame with wet tissue paper!

flicker reflected in a city park's pool. There is little to compare to the gentle power of a paper-covered lantern.

Making lanterns, or by the same techniques, other willow and tissue structures, is a lovely, messy, rewarding process that when handled carefully can have everyone producing exciting pieces without too much frustration or glue all over the floor. Of course, when it goes wrong, frustration and excessive glue can both result. Often, even when everything goes well, the glue is still there.

Taking it in stages.....

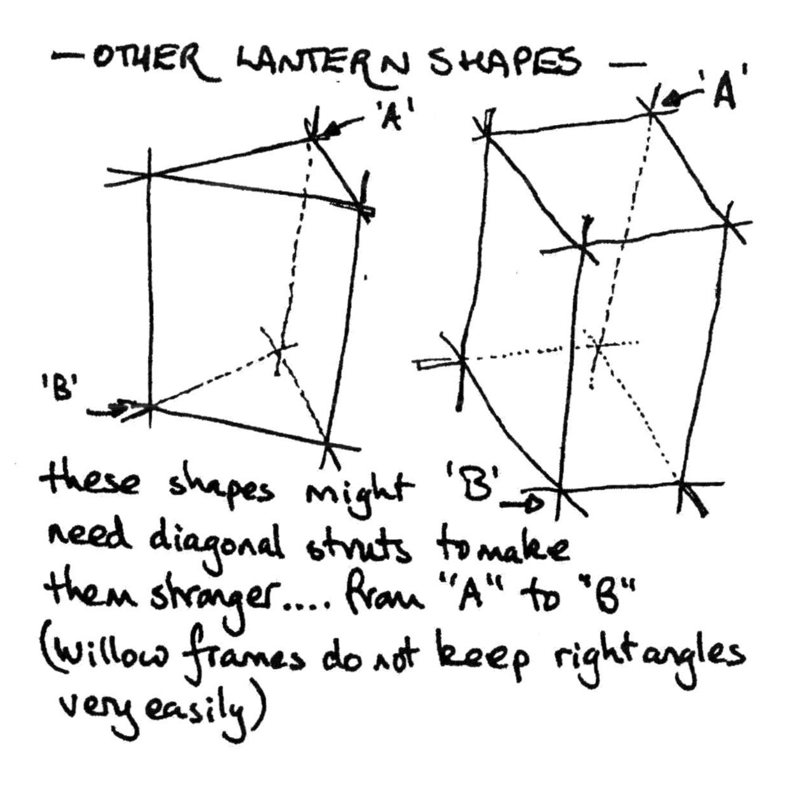

Frames

"Withy", willow stripped of its bark and dried, is the usual material to work with. There are alternatives:

green willow: cut and used when still fresh

dogwood: either fresh or dried

hazel: best used fresh

birch: best used fresh

other things: wire, plastic tubing, pipe insulation foam, almost any flexible plant material that will dry to hold the shaped form

If you do have access to a site growing thin flexible shoots, this becomes a lovely exercise in understanding resources when the group cut their own frame materials.

Dried willow needs to be soaked; either immersed in a vat overnight or sluiced down with water and rolled in a tarpaulin. We generally do the latter: this gives nicely bendy shafts, not quite flexible enough for basketry, perhaps, but good enough for the larger curves of lanterns. Immersal is good but can be hard to set up: don't drop your willow in a pond unless you are prepared to spend time the next day picking out the tadpoles (or unless you are simply very ruthless).

Joining frames together

We need something to hold the cross pieces together. Try masking tape (1cm or 2.5cm: narrower tape is often better but harder to get). Gaffer tape is good but a bit unwieldy. Plastic tapes tend not to resist the water at all and joints tend to slide apart.

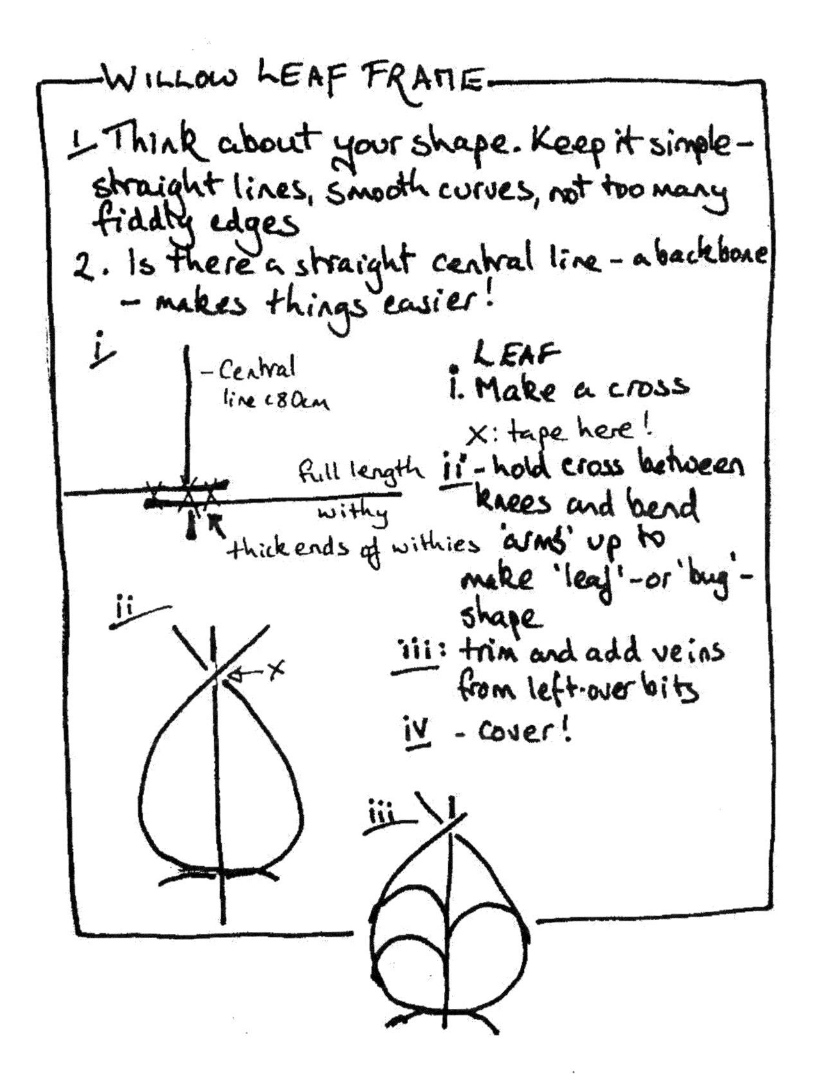
WILLOW LEAF FRAME
1. Think about your shape. Keep it simple - straight lines, smooth curves, not too many fiddly edges
2. Is there a straight central line - a backbone - makes things easier!
i
- Central line c 80cm
full length withy
thick ends of withies
LEAF
i. Make a cross
x: tape here!
ii - hold cross between knees and bend 'arms' up to make 'leaf' - or 'bug' - shape
iii: trim and add veins from left-over bits
iv - cover!
ii
x
iii

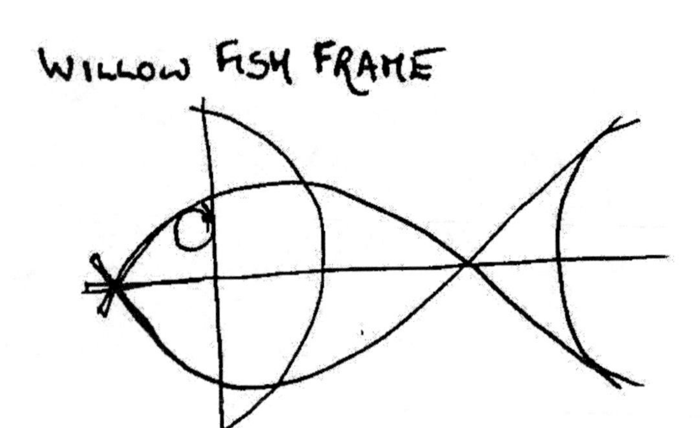

Alternatives:

wire: twisted tight with pliers or basketry tools

cable ties: good on larger constructions

rubber bands: good for simple forms and people who have trouble with tape

Coverings

Once we have made a frame (we'll come back to that below) we need to "skin" it with something:

white tissue paper: the standard skin, normal tissue is quite fragile so try working with a double thickness

coloured tissue: often even more frail than plain tissue, and colours often bleed. For some reason, yellow tissue often seems stronger than others

unbleached tissue: the colour of newsprint, falls apart at the very sight of glue!

wrapping paper: gift or other wraps can be tested: some is heavier than tissue but ideal for very colourful results

brown or greaseproof paper: traditional covering, if oiled rather than glued it becomes translucent but rather flammable

wet-strength tissue paper: elusive, expensive extra strong tissue: wonderful stuff to work with. The same material is used by hairdressers in thin strips for perms

clingfilm: sometimes used, not as a final skin but to cover the frame before using small pieces of tissue to create the skin: can make things much easier for some groups

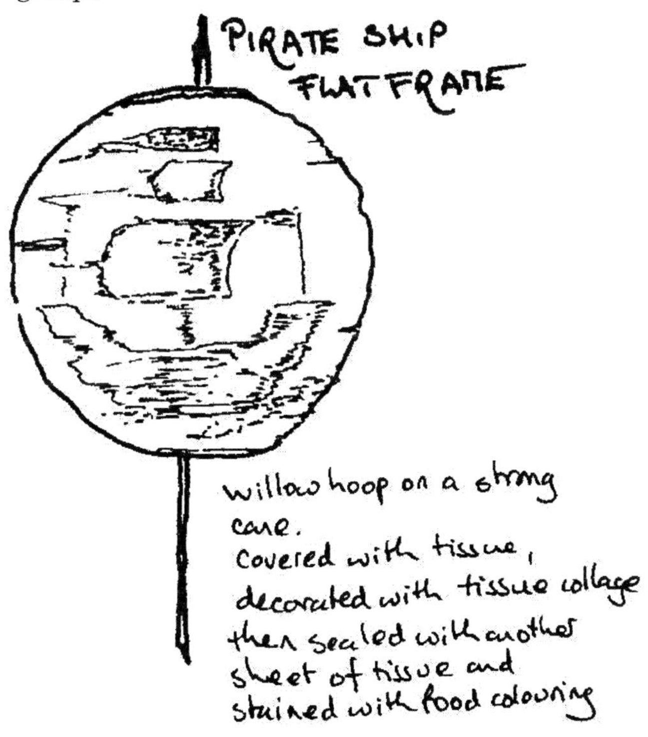

cellophane films: available in many colours and even iridescent pearls: tricky to use as "skins" but excellent in panels pasted onto tissue skins or set into holes cut out of dried tissue

Glues

The usual standard is PVA: diluted about 50:50 with water. The strength of PVA varies so you need to build up a feel for the right consistency. You are looking for something a bit like single cream, or slightly thicker. When it is dry, PVA is sort of showerproof. You could paint a layer of neat glue over the face of a dry lantern to protect it more. If lanterns do get wet, don't fiddle with them but try to let them dry off on their own and they usually tighten up again without your help.

Alternatives:

rubber-solution glue: "Copydex" or a similar latex adhesive: can be diluted and used like PVA. Better for experienced workers as you have to work fast. It is very smelly, very messy and ruins your sponges but does give very strong skins that are more waterproof than PVA ones

flour and water paste: like a thin gruel. Horrible

wallpaper paste: we know some people use this but we never have.

Experiment for yourself.

Lights

Traditionally, we might fasten a wire coil in the base of a lantern to hold a candle, or fix in a jamjar for a candle or a night-light. These do give the nicest, warmest, gentlest golden lights, but for practicality and safety, now, we often recommend small pen-light torches or similar. Candle flames are remarkably safe but can annoyingly blow out (they also need a small hole cut in the top of the lantern as a chimney) and every so often you will encounter people who will simply set every lantern they can get their hands on aflame.

Display

Lanterns might be carried on strings (not candle lanterns), or on wire loops taped onto bamboo poles. They could be hung on trees or stand on their feet on level floors.

Flat shapes, can hang from trees or poles or be taped onto poles and back-lit with a torch taped to the lower edge of the shape.

Preparing for lanterns

You can always just plunge straight into constructing lanterns, but if there is time it is good to build up to those moments of construction.

Planning: a lantern might just be an exciting light or it might hold images, ideas, poems, secrets. Discuss with your group what would be appropriate to include in a lantern that would reflect the theme you are exploring. For example, "woodland" lanterns might call for:

> real leaves, flowers and feathers: go out and collect thin, flexible leaves and leaf skeletons (nothing that will tear the tissue) - these can be placed onto wet skins and then held in place with a tissue patch
>
> leaf prints: see below
>
> woodland animals: drawings in permanent pen on small pieces of tissue paper
>
> poems: again on tissue paper

shapes: cut silhouettes out of black tissue (or heavier paper for flat sided constructions) - buildings, winter trees and pirate ships look especially good!

Leaf prints

Time: 15 - 20 minutes (longer if you go leaf hunting first)
Materials: paint palettes, plastic trays or sheets, acrylic paint, brushes, printing rollers, newspaper, mixed sizes of wet strength tissue paper
Organisation: everyone doing their own prints but sharing materials in groups

Start with small pieces of tissue, maybe 10 -15cm square. Place a leaf on a tray or sheet, lower side uppermost (veins tend to be more prominent there) and paint generously. Place a the leaf, paint side downwards, on a piece of tissue on a sheet of newspaper, cover with another sheet of newspaper and roll 2 or 3 times with a roller (inventing a little rolling song as you do so). Gently open up the newspapers and peel off the leaf. Often the first print has too much paint on it but there is also often enough paint left on for a second, clearer, print from the same leaf.

Write names on printed sheets in pencil, lift them off the newspaper and set aside to dry. You can try laying one print on top of another. Printing gold or silver onto other colours often works well. You could also print leaves onto larger sheets of tissue. Prints that do not get built into lanterns can always be mounted on card and taken home as gifts.

Shining leaves

(good practice before going onto 3-D lanterns)
Time: 30 - 45 minutes (more if this is a big group)
Materials: soaked withy (allow 3 shafts per leaf shape and a few extra), old or paper towels, tufcut scissors, or secateurs, masking tape, tissue, PVA, washing up bowls, sponges, food colouring, tarpaulins, cut open bin-bags
Organisation: work in pairs to make frames (even if everyone is going to make their own), then in groups of 4 or 6 to share resources and limit chaos when skinning

Think about shapes, about the simplest shapes that say "leaf", "fish" or "bird". For a leaf (a good practice form) we need one shaft maybe 60 cm long cut from the thickest end of the withy. (Look at the illustrations). Use two full length withies to make a cross at one end (wiping down with an old towel if the tape won't hold) of the stick, then boldly curve the long arms up and round, crossing them nearer the other end of the central shaft and taping firmly in place. Now you should have something roughly leaf- (or aphid- with those long antennae) shaped. Trim off sticky-out bits. Use left over thin pieces to add some leaf veins (act as struts to support the wet tissue).

Cover with tissue (see below)

For younger groups, try simply making withy circles with a supporting strut across the middle. When these are being covered, cut out or printed patterns or leaves or feathers can all be added

When covered, leaves can be hung from a line or stood upright on a tarpaulin (quantities of glue will run off onto the floor) and left to dry. Or lie them flat on a sheet of plastic for transport elsewhere. When the leaf is quite dry, the plastic can be peeled off. Peeling when the leaf is wet might tear the tissue: be warned. Just after covering, these shapes are still pliable enough to be shaped further to give curling leaves or leaping fish. Tie a string round the end of the mid-rib in a leaf and loop the other round the joint where sides and mid-rib meet. Gently draw on that loop until the leaf has curved into the shape you want. Tie off and hang up to dry. For other shapes, tie string round the inevitable sticking out bits of frames. Make sure you attach to strong points in the frame or you can pull the whole thing apart!

Simple Lanterns

Time: 60 minutes (more for bigger groups where support is needed and materials shared)
Materials: soaked withy(up to 8 withies per lantern), old or paper towels, tufcut scissors, masking tape, tissue, PVA, washing up bowls, sponges, food colouring, tarpaulins, cut open bin-bags
Organisation: entirely up to you: work in pairs to make frames (even if everyone is going to make their own), or in groups of 4 making shared lanterns and then in groups to share resources and limit chaos when skinning

Flat leaf shapes are fairly straightforward. So are simple geometric shapes. Encourage people to work with straight lines (or as straight as the willow will allow). Try making 3- and 4-sided pyramids (start with a base and then do the sides). 4-sided bases might need a diagonal strut to brace them. Add some curving struts on the pyramid's faces. That's it.

Towers look good but might need an extra brace diagonally from the floor to the ceiling, as it were.

Spheres and domes become interesting exercises in the maths of surface areas and become very large very quickly.

Other shapes and stranger creatures

Geometric lanterns and flat shapes are good places to experiment. When people have a bit of a feel for the materials and if you have time, let folk really go to town.....we have seen lantern versions of local buildings, giant water lilies (made a petal at a time the joined together), dragon heads, whole dragons, marvellous fish....

Willow is very good at doing its own thing. As people build frames, look for:

support for skins: make sure open spaces have struts across them (these can be decorative as well as functional)

the need for internal support: a supply of thin but strong bamboos or peasticks can save the day with wobbly willow shapes.

Ideally, experienced people will make an armature first, a simple internal skeleton that will support everything else. In practice, in public workshops, people often end up working more from the outside inwards and it may be up to us to help fit in those final stays that hold everything together.

Skinning

Time: 20 minutes for each lantern
Materials: glue, tissue paper, plastic bowls, sponges, tarpaulins, bin-bags, food colouring
Organisation: work in groups around bowls of glue, maybe 6 people (3 lanterns at a time) round 1 bowl of glue

Ready for mess?
All working surfaces covered with plastic or tarpaulin or doesn't it matter?

Trim off sticky-out bits of willow that might tear tissue.
Tie back artists' hair (pony tails can soak up a lot of glue), remove watches and maybe rings.
Work in pairs (at least) with one person having dry hands to handle tissue while the other glues (you can always swap roles).

Now...
Step 1: glue: bowl of PVA and water. Arming yourself with a sponge, spread glue on plastic in front of you. Dry Hands passes first sheet of tissue. Lay half of it down on glue, sponge another spread of glue onto flat tissue and fold rest of sheet down on top. Sponge the top piece of tissue (making a sort of tissue and glue sandwich).

Step 2: wrap: abandon sponge carefully. Lift tissue by two corners and gently wrap it round the frame (standing beside you or held by a helpful friend).
The first sheets are always hardest: look for places where tissue can be folded right round a withy and back on itself
Don't worry it it crumples a bit or sags: you can gently ease it into place and it will also tighten up as it dries.

Step 3: more tissues: full of success, try another sheet.

Step 4: decorate: when you have got a first layer on - don't cover the base of lanterns - and for flat shapes, cover one side then flip it over - add leaves, images, prints, etc.

Step 5: seal: for flat shapes, now add another layer to seal those pieces inside, sponging down quite firmly to glue top and bottom layers together

Step 6: patches: For lanterns, use small patches of tissue to seal in leaves, etc.

Step 7: staining: finally, try dribbling or flicking some food colouring onto the surface of the wet tissue (use left over bits of withy) and watch the colours spread.

Step 8: drying: Set somewhere warm to dry: a couple of hours in warm setting might do it but usually allow an overnight drying time

In all the messiness of this process, it is usually that final food colouring stage that generates most disorder. Now, we try to fix each bottle in its own plastic tub: harder to knock over or absent-mindedly tip up.

Done? All done? Wipe down your tarpaulins. Rinse through your sponges thoroughly. Sit back and celebrate with a good cup of tea and a piece of cake, while you peel the glue like lizard skin from your fingers.

Reinforcements

No, not more Sioux coming over the hills at the Little Big Horn, but you in your relationship with your group. It is easy to get very caught up in keeping the workshop process going, moving on towards what you need to accomplish in a particular session. Take time to pause. Give instruction in small doses. Release materials bit by bit (until you reach a "dive in and decorate exuberantly" phase).

Take time, too, take every opportunity, to praise people: individually as they work and collectively as a whole company. Stop, review, congratulate, ask for feedback, check up on problems. Maybe suggest changes, other techniques to experiment with.

Essentially, use your role as the workshop leader to celebrate the group, to celebrate people and what they are doing and what they have done. Build the group's confidence in themselves and their trust in you as someone who notices and appreciates their efforts. Usually, the whole atmosphere of such a group becomes lighter, more cheerful (often noisier, it has to be said), more joyous. With such a stance, also, control becomes easier: where issues need to be addressed or behaviours challenged, it can all be done much more gently and with more collective agreement than if you just come stomping in as a ferocious disciplinarian. Use anger as little as possible: your "disappointment" in a particular action is often a better expression. Separate stern-ness, firmness and anger. And make sure you do not really get angry, that you do not ever really lose your temper.

12

Celebrations that stay

The activities described in *Celebrating Nature* usually lead to some sort of performance. and most of the artforms in other chapters tend to reflect that active form.

We might, of course, wander off down other roads including, perhaps, the thought of "celebrations that stay". If we start to look at objects, at sculptures and installations, made in place or made to be set in place and to stand, accompanied or unaccompanied by their makers, we open a whole new treasure chest. With *Celebrating Nature* trending more to performance-connected activities and with many rewarding books about sculpture available, we'll give ourselves just this one chapter here to send celebrants off with some ideas to play with.

I'll call it "sculpture", using that as a general umbrella for "things made to stand alone". If you want to work on pieces like this, think of them as "celebrations that a complete stranger might stumble over and share with you, even though you are no longer there"(or "celebrations for unknown friends"). That thought of leaving something to share with (and maybe surprise?) someone at a distance, in space or time, can weave sculpture comfortably into the context of our other performance celebrations.

Rather than suggesting some very definite activities as we are doing elsewhere, in this chapter, we'll suggest some starting points for adventures and concepts to explore. Unless you are intending to work with specific tools and distinct techniques: wood carving or stone walling perhaps, most of the time with our groups the freedom to explore and experiment will be central to the development of these celebrations and with static pieces that freedom might simply need some nudges to start it moving....With this in mind, what follows here are not given the usual format of "organisation" and "materials". Treat these as suggestions and see where they take you. There are still a few activities in the usual format tucked in here and there among everything else.

Starting Points

In common with other activities, you might start by exploring a site...

Places where things might happen

We have met this before. Weave the idea into some of the Exploring and Stories activities and go looking for

> evidence of incidents: a sign, a mark, a smell....
>
> think of characters who might live, use or once lived here
>
> "sets": places that are just waiting for someone to add something: trees waiting for unlikely birds to roost in them, a tree stump like an empty throne

These ideas often generate very representational (if unlikely) work: toadstool people, willow and tissue fish to fly through a tree, giant water lilies on a pond. Useful activities to follow this up with might include some in the Puppets, New Faces, Occasionally Fish and Willow chapters.

Hidden Life

Imagine the inhabitants that we do not see. Should we see them? Or would we hear, smell, feel them as sinister eyes watching from the shadows....try making them. Again turn to Puppets and New Faces for follow-up ideas.

First contact with resources

Try Leafstrings to get people rummaging in the undergrowth.

Just go exploring

Find dens, hidden paths, secret places, special places....let your group ramble. Then perhaps leave messages without words to share those experiences with other people. (Or perhaps leave messages to make sure that no-one else will ever disturb your most special place?)

Special places

Working again with Disappearing or something similar that has established special places for individuals, we might try:

> looking out from our special place, looking beyond the edges: use cardboard "picture frames" to concentrate the eye on different views
>
> look up: lie down and appreciate the height above you
>
> look down: lie down and be drawn into the minutiae of the world beneath your feet (try looking through a cardboard tube)
> use your other senses: listen, smell, touch....how many different textures can you find in tree bark, how would you describe them?

Out of all these, start drawing some aspect of a special place that you feel other people should encounter and share.

Messages without words

Time: 20 minutes
Materials: you need a sheet of card or paper to demonstrate on, maybe a bag of sawdust, perhaps some mirror tiles
Organisation: work as individuals or in pairs

Give your group time to find interesting places (Disappearing is a good beginning!). Then gather and talk. Think about paths and trails. Think about laying a trail for someone else to follow. Think about making that trial interesting: should it be straight or curving? How should you mark it: something obvious? Something harder to see and calling for more concentration? When they get to the end, how will they approach your special place? Experiment with shapes and constructions, towers made of twigs with a mirror slipped into the foot under the twigs, a house of sticks or stones thatched with pinned leaves, a spiral of leaves and sawdust...

All this leads into thinking about visual language and how people respond to patterns. You might turn to the Patterns section below for ideas to discuss with a group but that might be to add too much at this stage. Let people experiment and play.

As a company or as little groups, go and experience each other's "messages without words"

We haven't mentioned mud yet. It is almost bound to come up as a medium to work in, is wonderfully versatile, mixes well with straw or sawdust to coat willow or other structures, gets everywhere. If you are working with a school or other group, you might need to have discussed the possibilities with a teacher beforehand. Such a shame to resist mud's temptations

and rewarding properties for the sake of some grubby clothes....

Environmental impact

It will be up to you and the group to determine what your parameters are in any given situation regarding what you can pick, collect and disturb. If I am working with a group where we are making things that we will leave behind (and not return for later), we generally aim to make sure that those will decompose fairly quickly or at least be integrated into the environment and not remain as dangerous bits of litter.

After these sorts of activities, we might start offering more complicated challenges or simply give ourselves other things to think about.

More ways of exploring

Patterns

Initially, people often come up with very representational ideas of "things we might make". They want to make animals, people, man-eating plants. If we want them to work out and beyond these forms, we need to find ways of thinking beyond those first ideas without dismissing them out of hand.

> Look for patterns. A Sticky board might record these or a sheet might hold drawings of what people find. From the suggestions below, you might ask everyone to look for all of these forms in the world around them, or maybe give people a card with one or two on. You might want to start by drawing patterns on a card as you introduce the idea...
>
> circles and spheres: easy?
>
> other geometric shapes: squares? triangles?
>
> explosions: a circle or sphere radiating outwards: a daisy and a dandelion clock can both be seen as "explosions". The dandelion flower is also one explosion pattern holding the promise of another
>
> spirals and helices: look for the spirals in seed-heads and fir cones as well as snail shells and honeysuckle tendrils

straight lines and forks: look in the bare stalks and dried seed heads of plants

meanders: wandering wavy lines, the path of a river over a plain. A snail over dewy grass

packing: fitting things in together: seeds in a sunflower head (also a spiral), kernels on corn, cells in honeycomb

cracking: the pattern when something doesn't quite fit any more: tree bark, a dried up pond

whatever else your group finds

look for patterns both flat and in three dimensions. Some groups might argue for patterns in four dimensions and talk about how a pattern will change with time

Use Patterns: go back to messages without words and try adding appropriate patterns to the design.

Expand and contract: try playing with a chosen pattern: reproduce it with other materials. Try enlarging it (how big can you go before you lose the pattern or cannot cope with the scale?) and try reducing it: there is a lot to be said for precision and miniatures.

Movement and balance

Experiment with balance:

start with the centre of gravity of different things: slide into drama and dance and create movements with balanced object: moving with the object, never losing its balance and letting it fall. Move a leaf as the wind moves it. Roll with a stone: or balance a stone into flight on your hand

try making balanced rather than solidly constructed towers: piles of stone, of twigs

add movement to the balance: something that turns or rocks perhaps: a thin twig with a leaf rocking on the top of a pebble tower

Somewhere with all this foraging about, you need to ask a group "what would you like to make?".

Individual makers might need to think about:

setting: where do they want their celebration to be sited

scale: this might influence the scale of their operation (so might time, money and materials but better to work on a scale that responds to space rather than external necessity where possible)

when will their thing be viewed: night time? An excuse for lanterns or little torches perhaps

access: how will people approach it, how close will they come, will they be able to see it at all?

joining things together: look at string, twine and rope, natural twines, using hammer and nails, when is tape effective?

You might like to add, if you haven't already, some examples of other artist's work; Andy Goldsworthy, Chris Drury and Sally Matthews among increasing numbers of other artists all produce work that can be very inspiring in these situations.

Then step back. It can be easy to offer too much at these times. We need to stop and look and listen to the group. They might have taken flight already and be leapfrogging away over your sequence of ideas moving deeply into abstract dreams. Or they might be feeling confused and need a more specific challenge.

Specific challenges

Plants and animals work well here: depending upon context, we might ask a group to:

create new flowers, fungi or animals or whatever to inhabit this space: Twig Life and Leaf People are both useful here

to have something much larger/smaller than is currently found here (will we see all of it? only a portion? all of it needing a special magnifying glass)

to use only specified materials

to have one part that moves, show one of the pattern sequence, reflects light (you decide)

Then stand back and let them get on with it.

For most of the celebrations planned in this book, the creations that might rise out of these activities, could be part of the whole development process and be lost by the time we reach a final celebration. They might become part of that final work, the sets that puppets perform around. The space where stories are told. Or they might be used as the celebration itself: a guided tour, with each sculpture calling perhaps for a different response from visitors. Or perhaps they remain simply as "celebrations that stay", small moments of pleasure offered to passing strangers, invitations to stop and share an experience with an artist who has already moved on somewhere else.

13

How are we doing then?

Taking the measure of a project should be an ongoing process. Ideally, a project evolves as it proceeds, as we respond to the inspirations of the participants and as we review activities, structures and ways of working.

Inspiration and how we deal with it are really the main body of this book, so here we will look at other areas that we might evaluate - both during the run of a project and after any final events.

What can we measure?

Look at those features of your work that can be monitored quantitatively.

You might record:

> numbers of participants: check with any external funders as to what detail they might need about age, sex,ethnicity, etc of participants
>
> return numbers: people who come to more than one session (a good sign of successful and engaging work)
>
> how the money is going: are you on target?

media coverage

spread of take up: where are people coming from, does this match your hopes or expectations?

how are people finding out what is going on? what publicity are people responding to?

how are people getting to events: is information about car parking, nearest trains, buses and footpaths working?

Most of this information comes from you watching and talking to participants. If you need a lot of information carefully recorded, you might need to assign a person to do the job. Otherwise, use these areas as good conversation points with participants. "How did you find out about the workshop?", "Didn't I see you at the workshop last week?" and so on.

Consider how you might use this information. It should give you material to think about and not just be the details you will feed back to a funding body. Within the timescale of a project there may be relatively little you can do but, hopefully, what you learn will inform future work. Points like access and publicity are definitely worth responding to immediately if you can: another telephone interview on local radio may pull in a whole new catch of people, signposting a workshop from the nearest bus-stop might help all those folk who couldn't find it last time.

Knowledge, understanding and satisfaction

Some of those key points in themes and topics (or was it aims and objectives?). Without getting into examinations, how do we measure changes in knowledge, in understanding?

Try:

personal conversation: give people openings to talk to you about different trees in the woods (or whatever), about how they are feeling today, about what is working in their activity

watch detail in activities: look for changes in how people depict animals or plants or the information they use in building stories about those things or this place

use scribble sheets: A2 sheets pinned to boards with a couple of questions (try to avoid "yes/no" answers - or make sure there is another question that calls for more of a response as well). Leave out a few chunky pens, draw people's attention to the sheets and then leave them. Do not hover, or look like you are looking too much: give people the freedom to compliment or criticise anonymously if they need to

personal activities: leaflet review and postcards can both offer us useful insights if we are allowed to read them

circle time: a few minutes at the end of a session sitting as a company and inviting people to speak if they have anything they want to share - a lot of schools have similar practices so children might well be used ot this sort of structure and respond readily to it

vox-pops: try giving one of your team a small dicta-phone and let them go and do mini-interviews with people

The Team

All the above ideas start giving us feedback from our participants about themselves and their relationship to the project, but we should not ignore ourselves in the process...

> initial briefing: before ever we begin, we need to run through practical issues with any members of such team as we might have. The list below for a de-brief, could be applied here as well. Also run through bigger concerns: Health and Safety and First Aid points. Your Child Protection Policy and Procedures if you have a one. If you don't have a formal CPP, look at how you will all be expected to work with your participants, how to clearly keep both themselves and yourselves safe. Look at your behaviour as leaders
>
> regular de-brief: try to met up regularly and give yourselves time to talk - check through practical things: materials, techniques that are or are not working, new ways of doing things. Let people talk about problems. Look at systems for responding to concerns: swapping roles within workshops, which participants to keep an eye on (and how?). If you are leading this project make sure you then respond or act upon everything you can and feed that back next time.

After the event

Now it is over, and once we have all heaved collective sighs of relief, it is very easy to turn away and leave this project behind us, particularly if it proved a bit of a struggle. Don't run away!

Gather yourselves: everyone you can: your team, some participants if possible. Not possible? Would you get responses to questionnaires? Even just letters would help?

Use some of the points above to shape a few questions to ask in either a letter or a questionnaire. Keep questions few and invite personal comments (and try not to take feedback too personally).

As a group, we might sit down after a Creeping Toad project and just talk our way through the sort of lists we have described above, listing comments and thoughts and trying to keep ourselves moving and not getting bogged down in in-depth discussions about small points.

But we tend to be creative people, so more often we end up making things: like Sunflowers below.

Sunflowers

Time: 30 minutes or more
Materials: 3 colours of sugar paper, staplers and glue, A2 paper (flipchart pad), felt pens
Organisation: working from a whole company, into individuals, into groups and then back into company again

We have three questions to ask ourselves (you might adjust this to suit)

> what worked well in this project?
>
> what didn't work quite so well?
>
> what do we need to think about for next time?

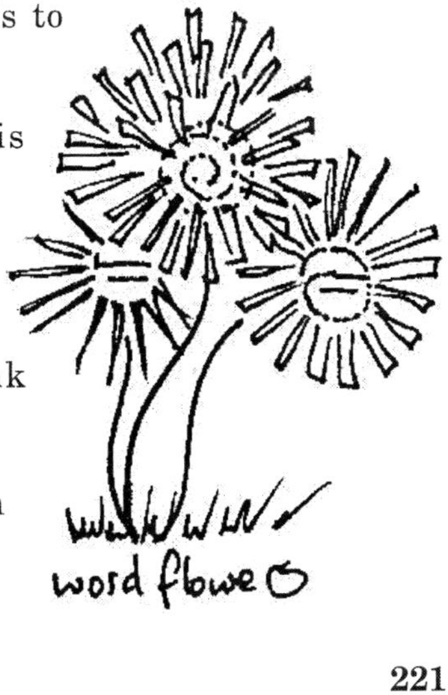

Choose a colour of paper for each question (everyone use the same colour for each question). Write

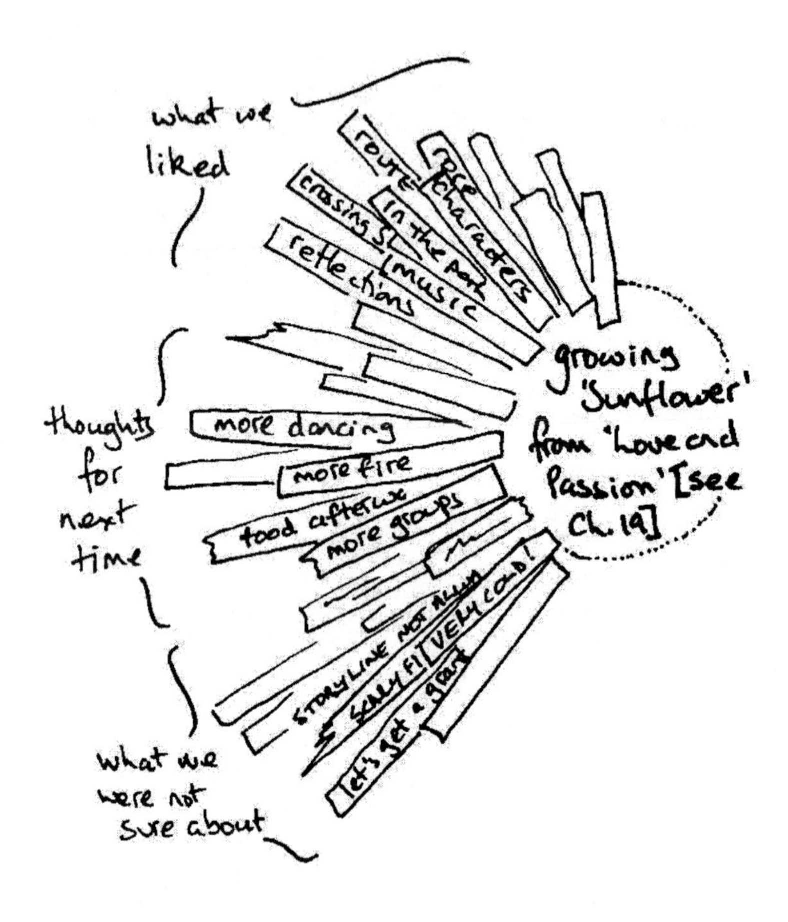

any thoughts you have in response to that question on the relevant coloured paper, leaving enough space to then tear the paper into strips with one comment on each strip. (This might take 5 or 10 minutes or more). Generally people work alone: pairs or groups tend to instantly having discussions.

Sort everyone's strips by colour and divide the company into three groups. Each group takes one pile of strips and, hence, responses to one question.

Now sort those scribbled thoughts, answers and responses into groups: some comments will be almost identical, others will be different but can be grouped by themes: money, bad behaviour, excitement, new groups and so on.

Now, use those clusters of strips to build giant flowers: each petal is a strip of paper, each section of the flower a concept cluster of related strips.

You might end up with one flower holding all responses, 3 flowers; one for each question, or sometimes there are whole flowerbeds!

Now in feedback to everyone else, each group can talk, not so much about the individual petals of their flower but about the issues that clusters of petals give us.

This helps people get away from becoming trapped in detail and pet subjects and encourages us to look at the bigger issues that underlie a number of comments.

Overall

Use evaluation as a way of monitoring progress and encouraging review and revision. Try not to let it become an opportunity for lots of nit-picking and tooth-combing through everything - and don't let it become personal. While there will be the individual points that need addressing, more useful might be that sense of an overview: looking for the bigger patterns that shape the progress of the whole event.

Evaluation should not be an excuse for pointing fingers and assigning blame, nor as a lot of self-indulgent back-slapping. Use the process to reviewing concerns, recognise success and know when the congratulations are well deserved!

14

And, occasionally, fish

I have a quiet delight in fish. Whenever I am trying out a new activity or making a sample to demonstrate possibilities, at least one of the examples will be a fish. Maybe I just like fish (as evidenced by the aquaria all over my home); maybe I am a fairly damp and swampy person, or maybe I just cannot help but hark back to all the passion of life that ever grew in and crawled out of the sea.

Whatever the reason, this chapter is a collection of odd bits and pieces that did not quite fit in anywhere else. Here there will be tiny wizards, twiggy fairies, strange flowers - and, occasionally, fish.

Plastic bottles

"Rejoice in your rubbish" could almost be a refrain running through *Celebrating Nature*. We use and re-use all sorts of things - as much of things as possible. Now it is the turn of plastic bottles.

Bottle flowers

Time: 15 - 20 minutes

Materials: empty (and rinsed) plastic bottles, 500 ml or more, tufcut scissors (secateurs or heavier cutting implements might be helpful), spray, acrylic or lustre paint, or tissue and

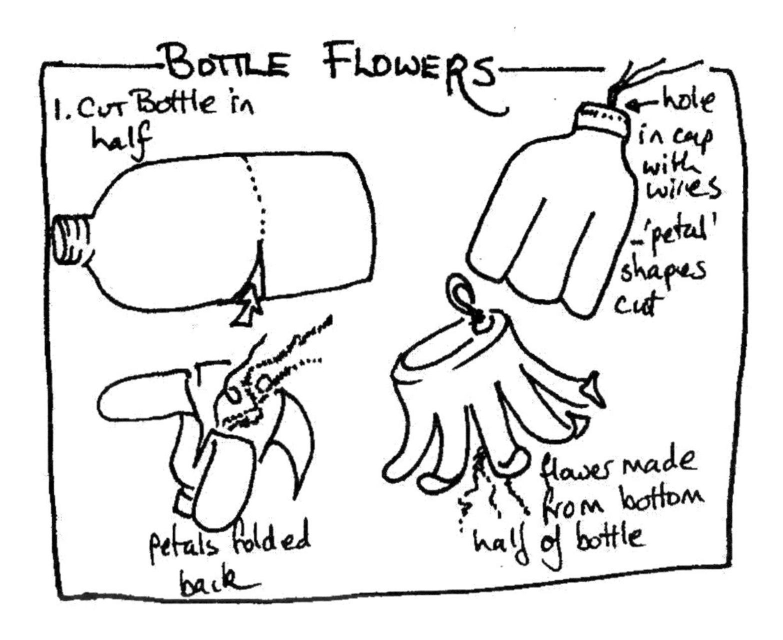

plastic films and glue, wire or pipecleaners, beads, canes, gaffer tape, awl or hand drill
Organisation: everyone should be able to make their own flower. It might be helpful to work in pairs or groups to share materials and help hold things

Cut a bottle in half. Through the base, poke or drill several small holes. In the top end, if possible, drill a hole through the cap - or poke a couple of holes as close to the top as you can. Cut the sides into long flanges: the petals of your flower. Vary width and the shapes of the ends. Splay these outwards: bend and crease or dip the bottle in very hot water for a few minutes to soften a little. You might try warming them, very gently, with a hair drier or hot air gun. Decorate the petals with paint or by sticking things on. Try to find translucent materials so they keep that sense of airiness with light shining through the colours.

Thread some lengths of wire through the holes and twist them round each other so that the flower doesn't slide up and down. Add a few beads at the ends of these stamens. Tape the wire "stalks" onto a cane.

Try grouping a few flowers together on a cane. Experiment with strips of plastic for leaves - or use some willow shining leaves . Try planing them in the undergrowth and see what you think.

You could spray your flowers with fluorescent or luminous paint for exciting nocturnal effects. Spray paint generally gives lovely effects but the environmental consequences of using aerosols might discourage you. Lustre, pearlescent or acrylic paint wiped onto petals is also effective.

Bottle fish

Time: 15 - 20 minutes
Materials: empty (and rinsed) plastic bottles (all sorts of sizes work), tufcut scissors, lustre paint or tissue, sticky plastic and plastic films and glue, staplers, string, awl, dry leaves, feathers and the like
Organisation: everyone should be able to make their own fish. It might be helpful to work in pairs or groups to share materials and help hold things

Cut off the bottom of a plastic bottle: keep as much of the "body" as you can. Dry the inside if needed. Press the cut end flat (follow the pictures), and cut a triangle out of each "corner". Still holding it flat, staple together the cut sides. When you let go, you should have a stylised fish shape with the bottle's top as the fish's mouth and those cut away triangles shaping fins and a tail.

Take off the bottle-top and fill the fish with interesting dry materials: dead leaves give lovely "leaf fish", but you are as

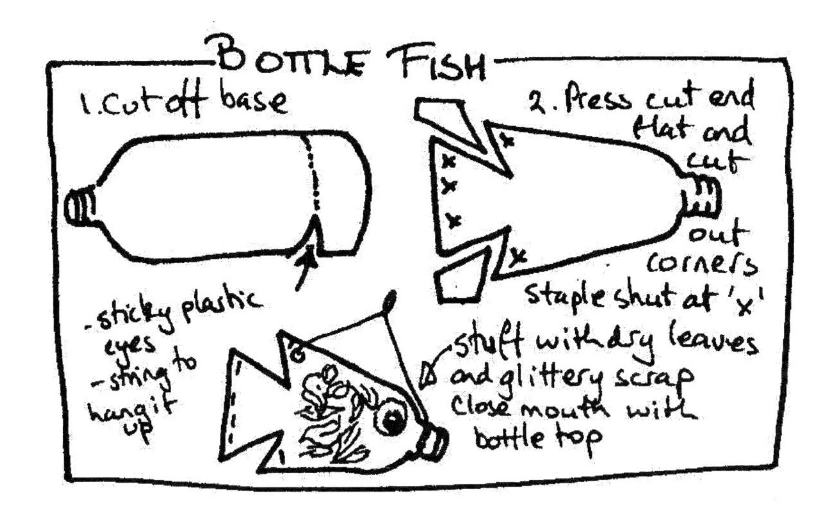

likely to find "feather fish" and "rose-petal fish" or even multicoloured "shredded carrier-bag and crisp packet fish". Stick on eyes and maybe some glittery plastic scale shapes. Use an awl to pierce a hole through the dorsal fin, threading a string through this hole and round the bottle top to give a loop by which the fish can hang from a branch, cane or classroom ceiling.

New friends: wizards and fairies

These are really "puppet" activities but they work very well as little opening sessions in their own right and the characters we make in a quick 15 minutes can then fuel the rest of a workshop with ideas

Time: 15 - 20 minutes

Materials: big beads (or compressed paper macramé balls), pipecleaners, scrap cloth, short canes or found twigs, string, net, scissors, permanent pens, glue, double sided tape

Organisation: everyone can make their own new friend

Simplicity itself. Take a bead. Give it a body from a cane, a sharpened twig, a set of pipecleaners. Add pipecleaner, or twig, arms and legs (and tail?). Do you need to tie on some netting fairy wings? black plastic bats wings? Dress with scraps of cloth or salvaged leaves. Hair might come from your scrap bag or found material and fixed on with double-sided tape. Features can be drawn on with permanent pens, or be made from sequins and scrap glued into place.

Then go adventuring with your new friend: let him, her, or it, take you into their tiny world. Add to this, ideas from other chapters and set off to make houses in the woodland, write books in grassland, have adventures, make treasure maps, find your new friend's treasure box.

Wizard hats

Anyone can make a tall pointed hat. Environmental relevance comes when we make hats for "Nature Wizards". A Nature Wizard knows secrets from the natural world, is a friend and confidante to all sorts of wonderful plants and animals and when she or he wears their hat, they will disappear into that aspect of the world that they are most in tune with. Nature Wizards usually specialise: they might be tree wizards, underwater wizards, butterfly, fish or flower-meadow or night-time wizards. So you might need to take a group out exploring and thinking and making their own connections before you actually make your hats

Time: 60 minutes for hats, longer if have a walk as well

Materials: A2 card, paint, brushes, palettes, painting sponges, glue, double-sided tape, staplers, velcro tabs, some large sequins, withy canes, paper fasteners, elastic or string

Organisation: everyone can make their own hat

Preparation: it is very time consuming but it is worth cutting a load of hat shapes first

Stage 1: after deciding what sort of wizard you are going to be, work with a friend to measure your head for a hat, wrapping the card round your head and marking where the overlap will be. Draw this as a line up to the point of the hat, on the outside(shows where to paint). For hats with brims this measure needs to be a little too big for the head

Stage 2: if you want a hat with a tip that goes up and down, staple some spare bits of card up the inside of the hat (on the back of the area marked above) to feed a cane through (don't do that yet). if you would like any doors on your hat, add these to the outside now, making a hinge with masking tape, a handle with a paper fastener and a catch with a velcro tab. Doors don't work on hats with brims (your hand won't reach!)

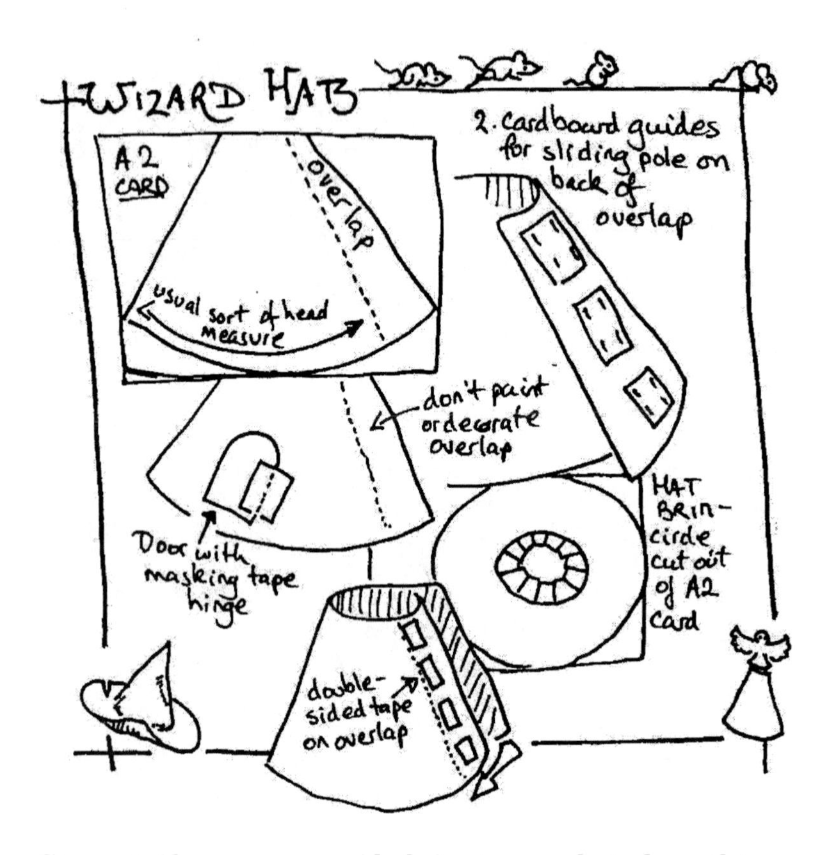

Stage 3: if you want a wide brim to your hat, draw this on another piece of card. Don't cut the middle out yet

Stage 4: decorate your hat: make it as interesting and as connected to your sort of habitat as possible. Experiment with printing, painting, smearing and streaking. Draw an animal behind your Hat Door. Make a cone to go on the end of your cane, maybe make with a small animal wearing the cone as it own hat. Add a few, special, glittery touches

Stage 5: let the paint dry for as long as you can. Then, to fit the hat together, stick 4 or 5 strips of double sided tape down the marked-off section of your hat. Gently roll your hat into a cone, aligning painted edges and pressing the overlapping edge onto your tape. Get staples reaching in along that seam as far as you can. Slide in a cane through the card tabs if needed. Cavort. Find that hats fall off. Add some elastic or string. Cavort again.

Stage 6: if you want a hat with a brim, when you have rolled your hat up, draw round the base on your brim card. Cut out this shape, cutting just inside the line. Cut a series of slits in the base of your hat cone (the "crown"): a cut every 3

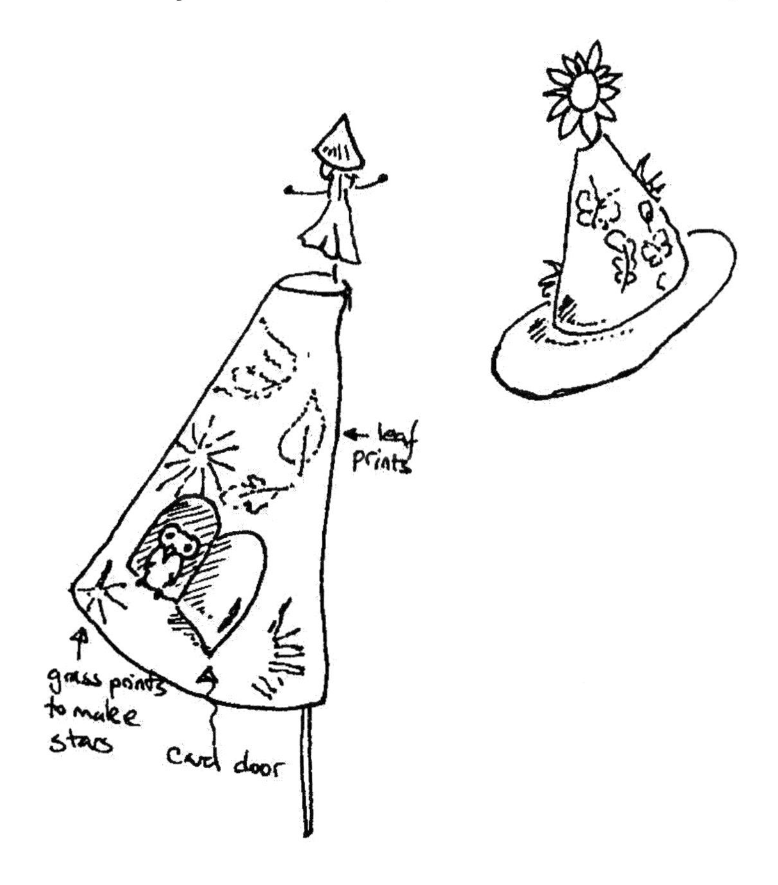

centimetres or so should do. These need to be 2 cm or so long. Fold the tabs out. Slip the brim over the crown: the tabs should hold the brim in place (it never quite works so adjust to fit). Tape and glue tabs to underside of brim. Add more decoration if needed.

Hats with moving tips (going up and down on canes) need to be held with one hand while the other makes the cane go up and down.

Now that you look like a Nature Wizard, you might want to add some writing activities and make your own wild book, collect your own treasure chest with its associated map or even just find a fallen twig to strip of its bark and decorate with lustre paint to give you a wand.

Toadstool people

Time: about 60 minutes
Materials: sheets of foam (c 1cm thick), heavy card tube, pins, rubber solution glue or hot glue gun, acrylic or spray paint, table tennis ball (1 or 2 per toadstool), double-sided tape can be helpful
Organisation: probably best working in a small groups for each toadstool

This activity produces some lovely, charming characters for setting up a in a woodland glade or corner of a playing field. The technique is very flexible, easily giving lots of different personalities to play with. The height and diameter of the cardboard tube will set the first parameters. Hold things in place with pins until the glue sets then pull the pins out

a) **Stalk**: roll the tube along the foam to measure out a piece to cover the tube. Fix on with glue, or double-sided tape and glue

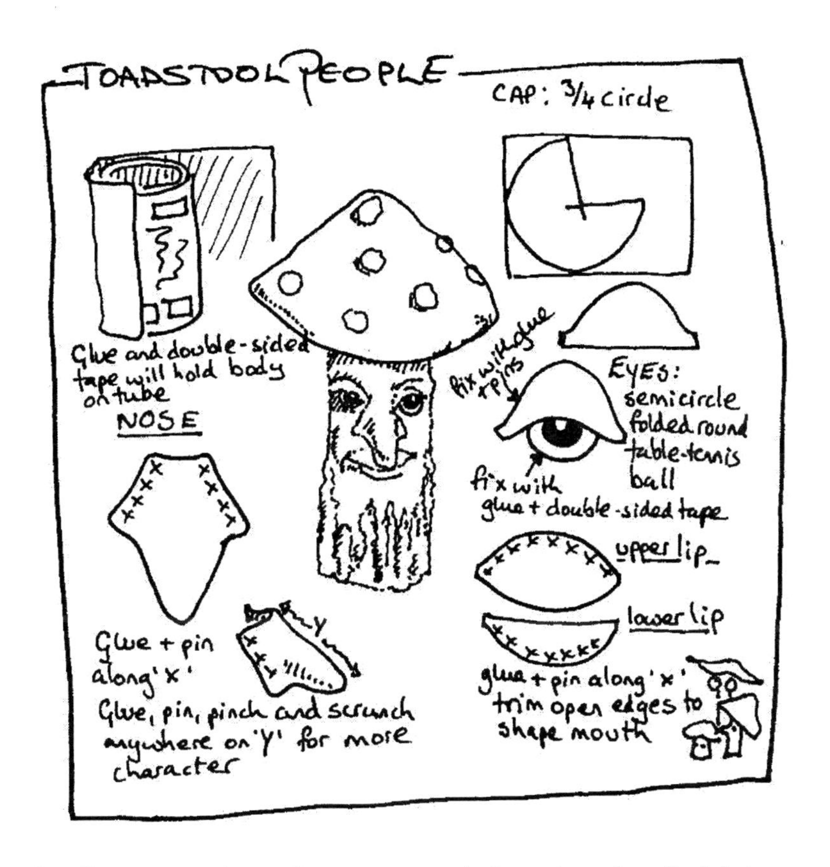

b) Cap: a semi- or threequarter-circle cut and pulled into a cone. Glue along the overlap and set aside to dry

c) Face: use scraps of foam to make eyes, lips, a nose, ears...hands? Table tennis balls cut in half make excellent eyes: hold in place with tape and then fix with glue as you attach the eyelids

d) Fit on cap with glue and pins

e) Decorate with spray paint, or acrylic paint sponged on patchily to catch that toadstool grading of colour

To install your toadstool, plant a short bamboo in the earth and stand your toadstool over this.

Usually toadstools just stand there and grimace at passers by, but if you attached thin strings to protruding arms (they need to be strong, twiggy arms for this) you can swivel your fungus from side to side and "track"" visitors as they walk past!

Variation: it can be difficult or expensive to get big sheets of foam rubber. You can improvise with cheap bath sponges, or build up surfaces with scrap card (good textures here) and use old camping mats for caps and so on.

Hobbyhorse unicorns and dragons

Time: 30 - 40 minutes
Materials: tough card (c 60cm square: old packing boxes are ideal), bamboo poles (c 90 - 120cm long), paint, gaffer tape, thin card, furry/hairy scrap, glue, craft knives
Organisation: everyone can make their own unicorn

This delightfully frivolous activity evolved during an "Enchanted Woodland" workshop for no good reason at all. And in no time at all, it seemed, we had a herd of little girls on hobbyhorse unicorns galloping under the trees (and a few zebras and a giraffe) and a lot of little boys who had become hobbydragons: gender stereotypes sneak in everywhere it seems!

Draw the head of your chosen animal on tough card.

Cut it out (maybe need an adult with a craft knife to do this).

Add ears, eyes and eyelids if desired, maybe also horns, teeth and spikes, as well. See Animal Heads and The Secret of the Ears for ideas.

Stick the pole on now: makes painting a bit unwieldy but better to paint over and decorate the tape than impose that on top of lots of delicate decorations afterwards.

Decorate excitedly, adding streamer manes, shredded carrier bag flames and whatever else.....reins perhaps?

Try to find enough time to let the paint dry.

Gallop off under the trees, whinnying as you go.

That brings us to the end of this selection of odd little moments and those final lines of Unicorns sums it up quite well: explore, make, decorate and "gallop off under the trees, whinnying as you go".

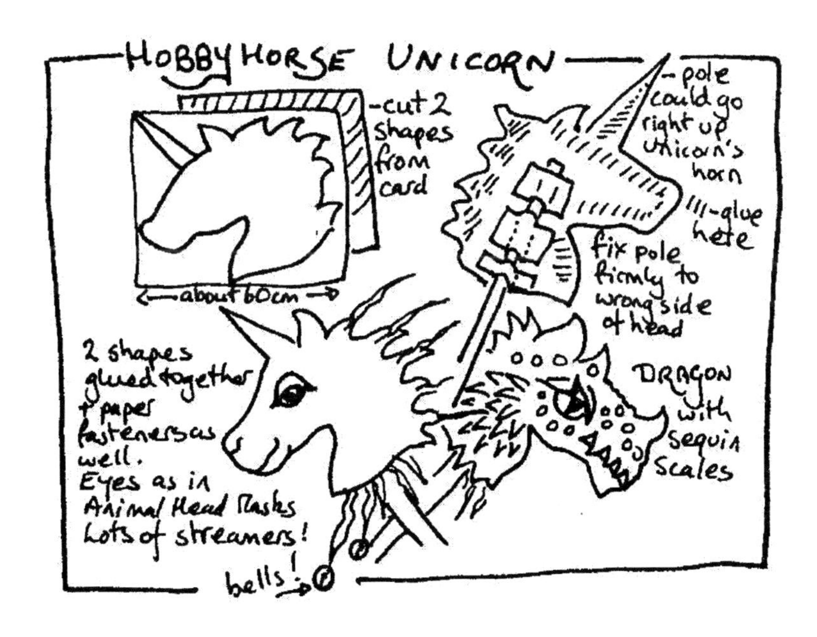

15

New faces

When we put on a mask we transform ourselves. Puppets give us someone to talk to, someone looking at us at arm's length so to speak, but the mask that covers a face turns us into something other. That can be very liberating, setting us free from our personal hang-ups and giving us strength, confidence and permission to become someone else, or it might prove very threatening.

So, enter mask work with respect. Masks are powerful. An assembly of even the friendliest and mildest-featured visages can become intimidating when encountered en masse. But for our celebrations, masks can be so useful! Through mask faces we might hear the voices of, and speak to, the places we are exploring. With masks, people might become their favourite (or chosen, or totem, or most dreaded) animal and let themselves dance, tell stories, recite poetry because now they are no longer themselves.

It need not be all escapism: the confidence that masks can bring can be part of a learning process: that tiger mask that has taught you to prowl like a big cat can leave its mark on you so that you know that you still have the tiger in your heart that lets you dance......

So, approach masks with care, aware of the profound possibilities they can bring and recognise that sometimes you'll be lucky if you have this group of excited 8 year olds concentrating for long enough to make faces on a few sticks! It is also worth noting that, dramatic development aside, some people, especially young children, do not like to have their faces covered, so masks that hover somewhere between "traditional mask" and "hat" or that move onto and away from a face at whim can all be useful. Most of the mask styles described below allow these freedoms to some extent.

Talking to the Earth has another chapter on masks with other ideas.

Starting points

My beginnings with mask work are often along the lines of "during to-day, we'd like to turn you into a woodland", or "turn you into your favourite animal to take home with you"... Opening activities might include animals by numbers and hand faces followed by one of the Quick Masks below

Quick Masks

Rubber Gloves

Time: 10 minutes or more

Materials: a pair of disposable rubber gloves for everyone - the cheap ones that go with First Aid kits are fine if you see this as a one-off activity. Have a few pairs of plastic gloves on hand for people who are allergic to rubber. Copydex or vaseline

Organisation: working so everyone makes their own mask but people might like to work in groups and experiment together

A beautifully messy activity that gives very exciting results: hence that 10 minutes can quickly stretch into something more!

Put on a pair of gloves.

Wash your gloved hands in mud. Try making hand faces now and enjoy the results.

Add leaves, bark, feathers, grass, whatever, to your gloved hands: copydex can stick things to the rubber (not if materials are very wet), but vaseline works better for immediate results.

Now experiment with masks by simply holding hands up in front of faces and peering out between fingers, through eyes made by finger and thumb, through combinations of gloves and bark.

Play with the dramatic possibilities of watching a forest wake, eyes opening in gnarled, lumpy, finger faces. Play transformation games: walking "normally", hands at sides, until the music stops, a drum beats? a twig cracks? than snap hand-masks over faces and move as your earth-masked character, until...or face paint brightly and stay hidden behind earthy hands until...

This is a nice activity to play with and gives groups lots of confidence. It could go further and might lend itself to a character activity (see New characters).

It seems so wasteful to use rubber gloves like this and then discard them. But they are rarely reusable (and that should only be by the same person anyway). So you might want to reflect upon that first. As an alternative to mud, you could wash hands in slightly diluted acrylic paint. This may offer more colour possibilities and can leave you with gloves that that person can more easily use again.

Small Folded Faces

Time: 20 minutes

Materials: thin A4 cardboard, scissors, sugar paper, staplers, glue-sticks, felt-tip pens

Organisation: working as individuals within groups or as a whole company

A quick exercise in paper-sculpture. Keep it simple and use this time to introduce the group to a few simple ideas about folding and stapling to give shape and remind them of some of the other paper sculpture ideas they might use on bigger masks.

We usually aim to make A5 sized masks: cut A4 in half and

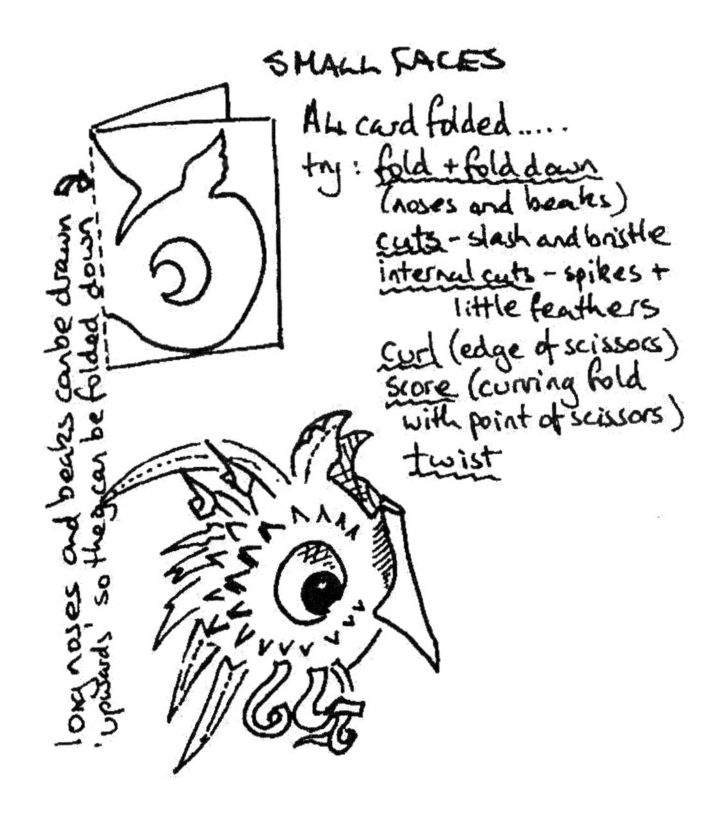

use one piece for the main "body" of the mask and keep the other for extra details (or swap with a friend for another colour). These little masks are often then set aside: we might use them later perhaps to make a community totem pole, or as faces peering out of a tree.

Netting Faces

Time: 20 minutes or more

Materials: rectangles (about A4, 30 cm x 12 cm) or ovals of tough netting, a supply of strong canes or pieces of willow (about 60 cm long), maybe a few pairs of secateurs

Organisation: working as individuals within small groups

Preparation: cut your canvas first

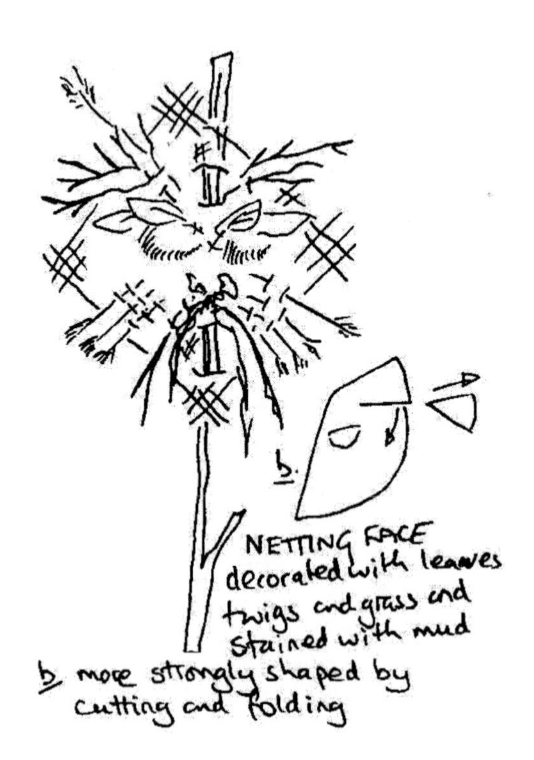

A note about materials: for netting, we usually use either strong garden shade netting or rug canvas, which can start to feel rather expensive for masks for a whole company. Shop around and scrounge. It is often easiest to cut shapes in advance which can be rather time consuming. Rectangles might also be cut and folded by their mask-makers to give more shaped heads

The process is simplicity itself.

Slide a cane in and out of the length of the canvas to give you a handle to hold. Then set-to and build a face out of natural, or found, materials on and through the netting......Leave this up to the imaginations of the group. There tends to be lots of Leafy Green People, with human eyes peering out from under twiggy brows, with rug canvas skins stained with mud. The more adventurous might have changed the orientation of their netting to make more animal-like heads, and leaf deer might now be encountered peeping from the undergrowth.

That drama game from the Rubber Glove masks works well here and these masks look wonderful when staked into the ground on their canes with the sun shining through them.

Longer activities

Animal heads

Time: anything from 40 to 90 minutes
Materials: A3 card, scissors, staplers, masking tape, pens, paint, extra decorations
Organisation: working as individuals with everyone making their own masks but possibly working with a friend to help each other
Preparation: it helps to have cut a bundle of card strips (4 cm x A3 (42 cm) long) for the caps that hold mask to head (allow 4 per person). If you are likely to make these masks a

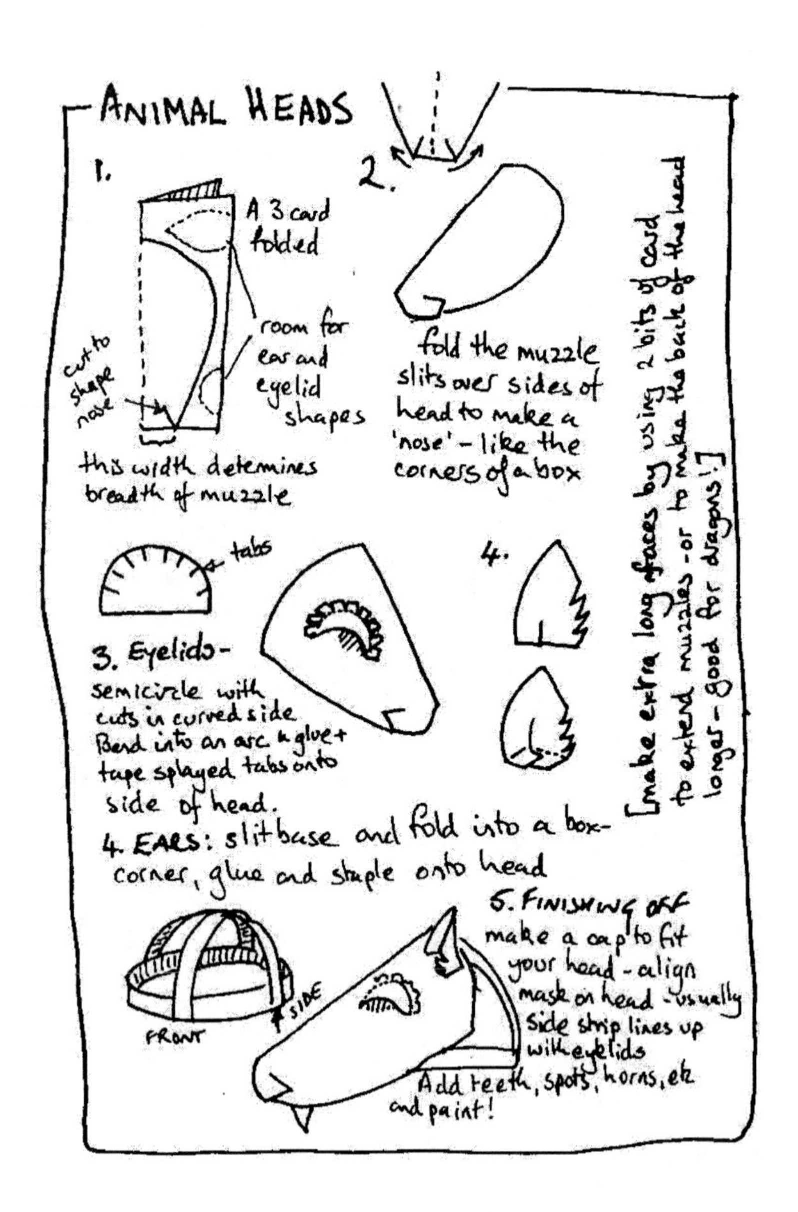
ANIMAL HEADS
1.
A 3 card folded
room for ear and eyelid shapes
cut to shape nose
this width determines breadth of muzzle
2.
fold the muzzle slits over sides of head to make a 'nose' - like the corners of a box
[make extra long faces by using 2 bits of card to extend muzzles - or to make the back of the head longer - good for dragons!]
tabs
3. Eyelids -
semicircle with cuts in curved side
Bend into an arc & glue + tape splayed tabs onto side of head.
4.
4. EARS: slit base and fold into a box-corner, glue and staple onto head
5. FINISHING OFF
make a cap to fit your head - align mask on head - usually side strip lines up with eyelids
FRONT
SIDE
Add teeth, spots, horns, etc and paint!

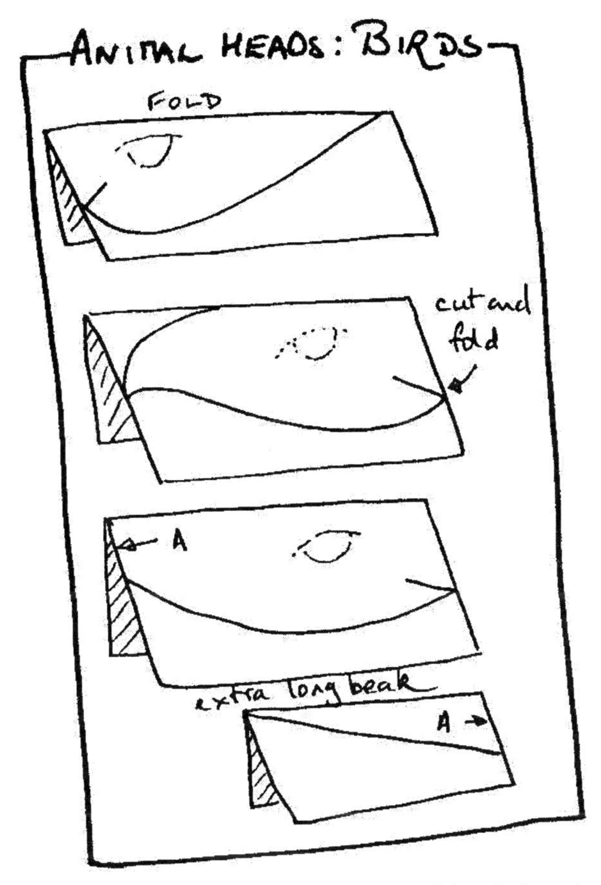

few times, it can also be worth investing a bit of time in a set of ear and eyelid templates.

These masks are a bit fiddly but very effective. This activity, can usually run side by side with human faces and catfish below. There is a slightly simpler version for younger groups in young masks.

If working with a big group (30 or so) have a few samples to show people, give folk time to decide what they would like to do, then approach construction in 5 stages. Use the illustrations to help you.

Stage 1: basic shape: fold card in half (usually lengthways, but maybe sideways for wide mouthed or wide-faced things like bats, frogs and even tigers). Using about 2/3 of its length draw a curve against the fold: note that the width of the flat end sets the width of a mammal's nose or a human forehead. Cut out, cut along the "nose-lines". Fold nose into corners, like a box, glue and staple in place. Masking tape might smooth off the joint.

Birds: fold card in half lengthways. The cuts that made a nose on a mammal (or reptile) here give us the back of a head and we use the whole length of the card to shape a beak (for owls look at human faces below), and pick up the rest of bird-making after Stage 5 for Mammals.

Stage 2: mammal ears: select a shape, cut it out. Cut ear-slits. Fold these to make a corner so that the ear stands up, then glue, staple and tape it into place. See "The Secret of the Ears" box at the end of this chapter.

Stage 3: eyes: rather than worrying about making eyes and eyeballs, we would usually make eyelids whose curve gives a strong shape to the card head. Cut out a semicircle of card, cutting short tabs in the curved side. Now bend this eyelid so that it sits like a cave with the curved side flat on the tabletop and the straight edge arching to make the front of the "cave". Glue and tape into place.

Stage 4: paint: with grace, style and lots of colour

Stage 5: make the cap that will hold the mask onto your head. Use 3 card strips to make a circlet, then arch two straps across the crown of your head. Keep these close to your scalp, not rising up like hilltops. When fixing the mask to this crown, now you make a final decision about how much you want something that covers a whole face (you might now need to cut holes to see out of) or that sits slightly tilting forward like a cap (the most effectively "animal" orientation) or that sits right back, not hiding the face at all. Usually, a mask fits onto the cap just about in line with our ears, usually where a strap coming across the head meets the circular band.

Decorate cap? add streamers? Ripples of fur-fabric falling down your back?

Bird-making: straight beaks might be cut along the fold of the card, curved beaks might need to have their tips and curves stapled together.

Then: add eyelids, and finish off as with 4 and 5 above.

Reptile-making: without external ears, for lizards, snakes and crocodiles, fold the nose as with mammals and then go straight to eyelids, perhaps orienting them strongly to the side. Crocodiles benefit from protruding nostrils made like miniature eyelids (so do hippos, incidentally).

Human faces

Time: anything from 40 to 90 minutes
Materials: A3 card, scissors, staplers, masking tape, pens, paint, extra decorations
Organisation: working as individuals with everyone making their own masks but possibly working with a friend to help each other
Preparation: again it helps to have cut that bundle of card strips for crowns.

A variation on the animal heads above, following the same basic steps but turning the original shape around......

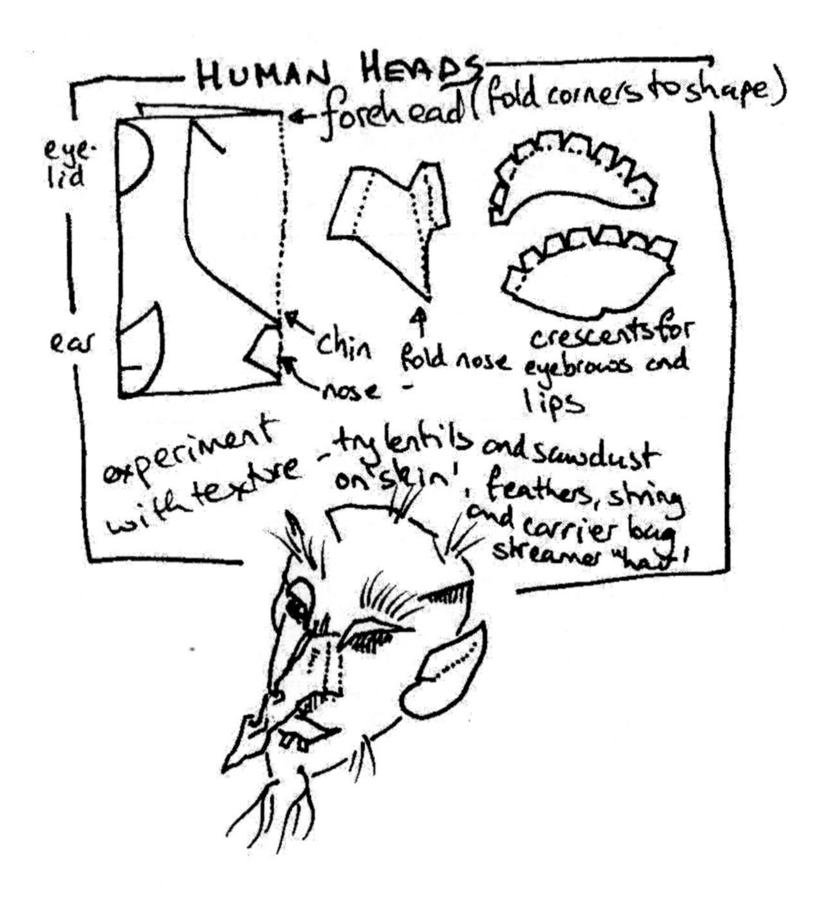

Stage 1: fold card and draw curve as above, making the straight edge wider. Cut and fold to give a forehead. The "chin" might need to be shaped: pointed perhaps?

Stage 2: ears as above, but of an appropriate shape

Stage 3: eyelids as above

Stage 4: you might want to fold and cut card to give a nose and maybe a mouth (like eyelids but made with crescents rather than semi-circles)

This orientation is also useful for owls (add a 2-piece curved beak, eyelids and maybe ear-tufts rising from forehead), monkeys, and frogs. For frogs, manoeuvre the mask so that it sits on top of head with curved edge as upper lip, add eyelids, maybe a crescent shaped lower jaw and even a flopping tongue.

Catfish

Time: anything from 40 to 90 minutes
Materials: A2 or A3 card, scissors, staplers, masking tape, pens, paint, extra decorations
Organisation: working as individuals with everyone making their own masks but possibly working with a friend to help each other
Preparation: card strips as for animal heads.

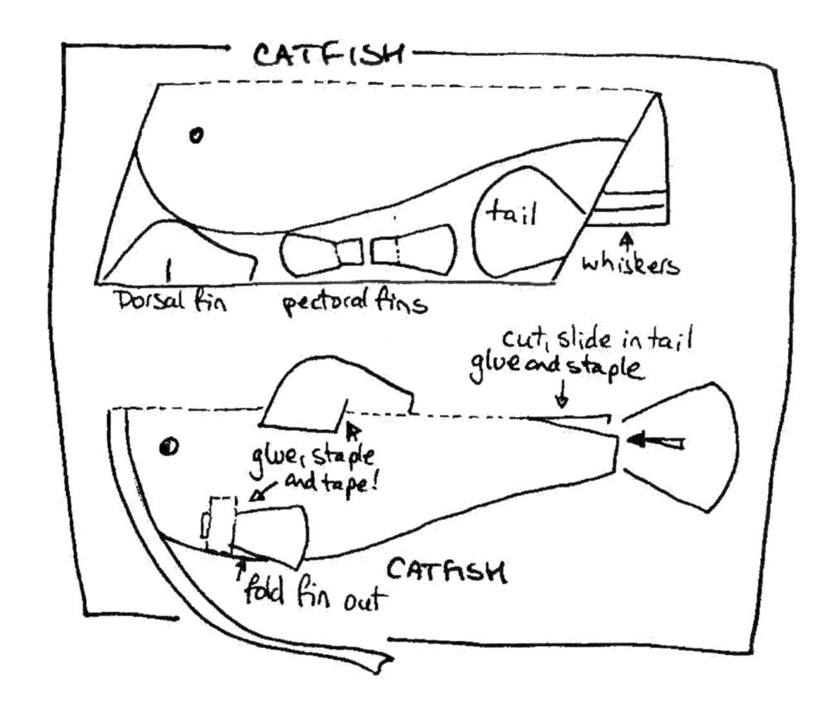

Looking at whole animal shapes that arose as a variation of that basic Animal head design above and that can work as a companion activity.

Stage 1: basic shape: work flat and draw a view of your chosen animal from above (keep it simple, big curves). Cut it out. Shape with cutting, folding and cornering where necessary. Not a lot is needed: heads on otters and crocodiles maybe. The curve of our heads will give the majority of the shaping when the animal is attached to the cap.

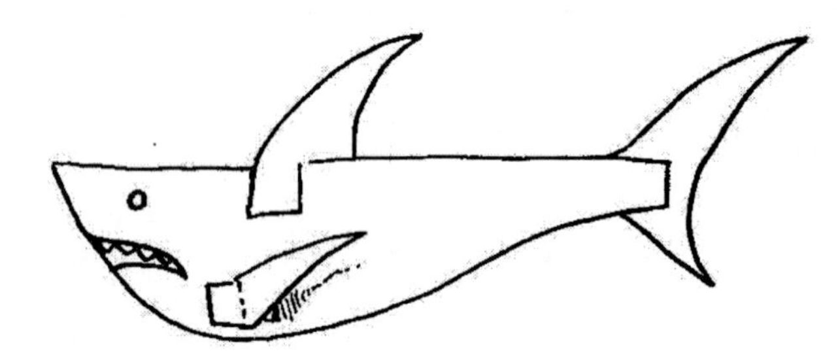

CATFISH VARIATIONS I
- shark

CATFISH VARIATIONS 2
- dolphin - 2 pieces
of card joined at
head and tail - splayed
open and horizontal at tail
to take flat dolphin tail

Stage 2: add detail: eyelids as above, if at all, fins, tails work well when slipped into a cut with a fold and a staple to lift them vertically above and below them main plane of the cardboard

Stage 3: decorate and fix as above

Exceptional Elephants

Time: allow 90 minutes
Materials: A1 or A2 card (probably 2 pieces each), scissors, staplers, masking tape, pens, paint, extra decorations
Organisation: working as individuals with everyone making their own masks but possibly working with a friend to help each other

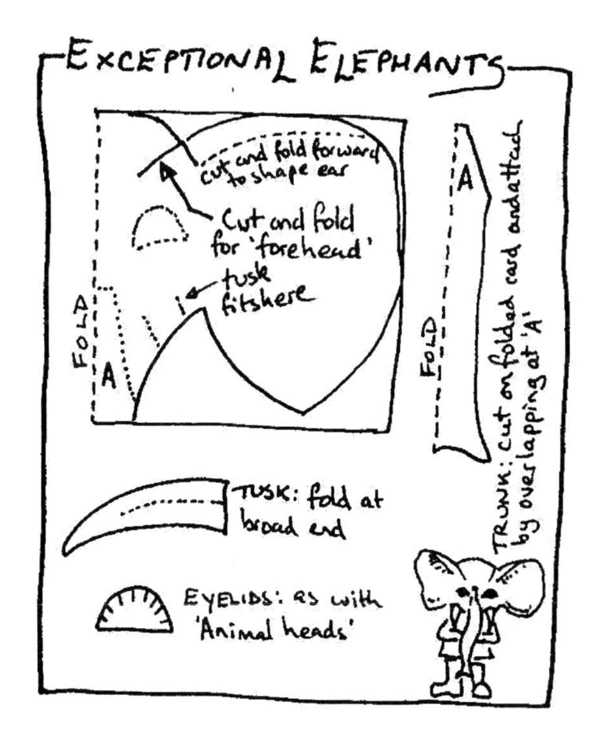

Preparation: card strips, again

A formidable variation on the above cutting and folding process, offered here as an example of what you can adventure towards. Look at the illustrations and try it for yourself.

On this scale, there is a precarious balance between cardboard thin enough to fold and fix with young people and too thin for the size of the mask. The best elephants we made used sheets of modelling foam (polyethylene foam, usually sold as "Plastazote" or "Crazy Foam"): shaped and fixed as with card and painted with sponged on acrylic paint.

Young Masks

Time: 30 - 45 minutes
Materials: A3 card, scissors, staplers, masking tape, pens, paint, extra decorations
Organisation: working as individuals with everyone making their own masks but possibly working with a friend to help each other
Preparation: card strips

A simpler version of the animal heads process, used with younger groups or where masses of people want results quickly

Stage 1: basic shape with ears attached (see illustration)

Stage 2: cut out, shape nose as above, fold ears forward, maybe small cut and fix to give them a bit of body

Stage 3: paint and fix as before

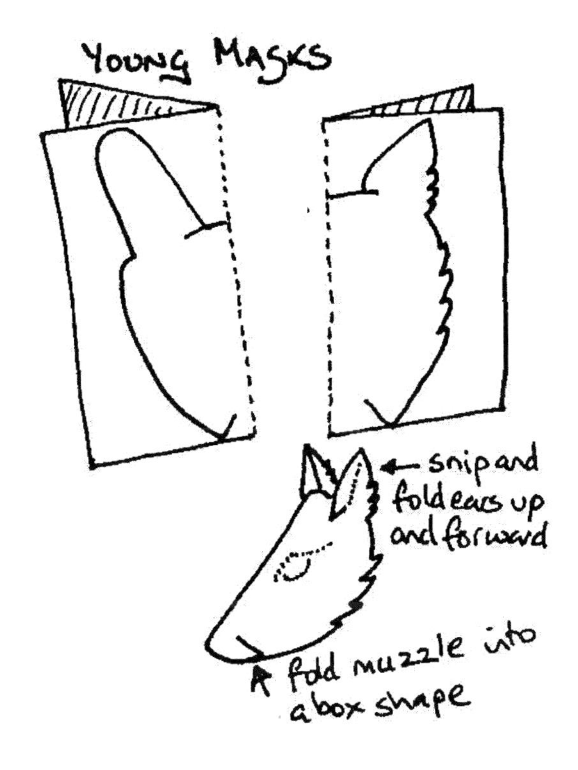

Habitat Hats

Time: anything from 40 to 90 minutes
Materials: A3 card, scissors, staplers, masking tape, pens, paint, extra decorations
Organisation: working as individuals with everyone making their own masks
Preparation: card strips

Another variation on the animal heads masks but starting with the "cap" and simply building a world around that: small model animals, plants, wisps of clouds to make miniature landscapes on top of your own or a friend's head.

You might vary this by becoming a landscape feature character by incorporating a "Human faces" mask.

Pole Masks

Time: anything from 40 to 90 minutes
Materials: A3 or A2 card, scissors, staplers, masking tape, pens, paint, extra decorations
Organisation: working as individuals with everyone making their own masks but often work with a friend to help each other

One of those things that hovers somewhere between mask and puppet. These are not really masks in the sense of something that sits on or straps to your head, but, mounted

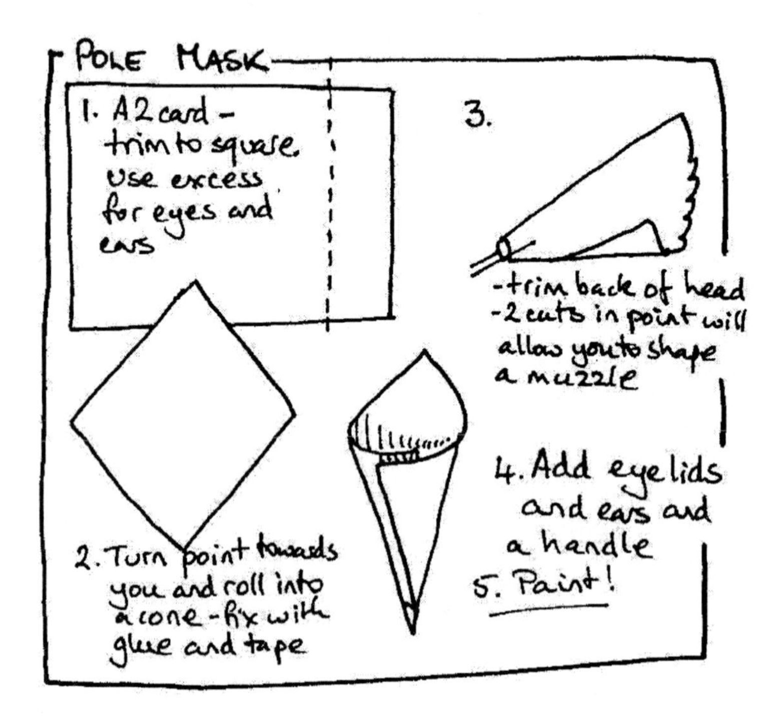

on sticks they can be held in front of faces or hefted aloft to become a procession of wavering long-necked creatures.

Stage 1: cut your card into a square (keep the extra strip for eyes and ears). Roll the square into a cone (hold card diagonally and pull the right and left hand corners together). Staple, glue and tape along the "seam". Cut the pointed back of this cone into a curve, or maybe cut into feathers and cut it ragged for a wolf's ruff.

Stage 2: shaping the nose: cut 2 slits in the side of the cone's nose, folding the small side and bottom bits of card inside the cone. Bend the wider upper section of card over to give a muzzle, tape into place. As with the animal heads, adjusting the width of the muzzle helps determine the nature of the animal's head.

Stage 3: add eyes and ears as with animal heads.

Stage 4: Paint!

Stage 5: (maybe do before stage 4): cut a small cross in the middle of the mask's "forehead' and slide a stick handle in. You might need a similar cut in the lower side of the head, but often the handle will sit against a notch formed where the cone "seam" lies. Tape strongly top and bottom. Add streamers to mask and handle. Wave

Pole mask

Variations: a) a good opportunity to play with other materials: we often add eyeballs rather than just eyelids, using chopped up bathroom sponges, table-tennis balls or even old Christmas baubles and cutting a cross to push the eyeball into, fitting the eyelid over this. Thin foam, leather or felt eyelids give very realistic folds as they crinkle around an eyeball. b) or cut out eyeholes and cut patterns through the card. Screen these holes with coloured plastic films and strap a torch to the pole to give glowing-eyed, lantern-like Beast masks.

c) If you insert a shorter stick sideways, instead of the main vertical pole, you get a handle that gives a very good animal head to hold on your hand. The start perhaps of a bigger puppet, often not needing anything other than that head to make it a potent, interactive character. At times, however, we have made these and covered all of the puppeteer with cloth so that only the mask/puppet/head can be seen and this strange lumpen creature can potter about with its head mobile on the end of a long "neck".

Parcel Tape Masks

Time: at least 2 sessions of 60 minutes with maybe a day between them
Materials: brown paper parcel tape, skin cream, scissors, thin wire, masking tape, carrier bags, paint, elastic
Organisation: individuals make their own mask, but for the first stage working in pairs is best
Preparation: cut parcel tape up into 5 cm lengths beforehand

Unlike most of the other activities in *Celebrating Nature*, this one takes several sessions and needs to be spread out over several days, unless you have good facilities for drying things quickly. It does give very effective masks and is included here because of its simplicity and that effectiveness. A good activity for school classes, groups who meet on a regular basis or who are on a residential course.

Session 1: making the basic mask
Carefully sit a carrier bag over mask-maker's hair, twisting it round at the back and tucking the twist under the edge of the bag to hold it in place. Apply a good layer of skin cream to protect the maker's face.

Start adding paper. The tape needs to be wet but not soggy, so dip it briefly in a bowl of water, or work it with wet fingers. We need to add at least three layers of sticky paper, like papier mache, to a face, working from chin to right up over the hair-line around to the ears. The first layer might go on sticky side out, being held against the skin by the cream. Go on adding layers, varying orientation of strips and maybe covering eyes (makes for a stronger masks but can be disturbing). Do not cover nostrils!

This part is most easily done by pairs of people, with A covering B, while C masks D. Then A can work on C, and so on. There will be a sort of diminishing pyramid of people until you as leader are doing the last one or two people.

When three full layers are on, the masked person needs to sit for perhaps 30 minutes until the tape is more or less dry. Play gentle music and relax. Tap the person's forehead gently: the mask should sound almost like eggshell.

Lift mask off gently and set aside to finish drying (may need to be overnight). Masks sometimes warp at this time so you could gently stuff the mask with balls of newspaper.

Wash face and if skin feels dry, apply a refreshing smear of skin cream.

Stage 2: adding features
At this stage, our mask looks like a death mask of the person concerned. We can leave it like this or develop it a bit more. The edges might need trimming to the size and extent you want to mask, eyes and mouth might need cutting out. Then we might work over existing features with tissue paper: rolling and glueing it to give simple extras like eyelids and more prominent nostrils. We might add textures, with bark, leaves, torn cardboard like bark, or stick on lentils and dry peas like scales and warts. String makes lovely textured spirals and lines. Paint. Varnish possibly. Punch holes and add elastic.

Stage 3: bigger features
For a more pronounced mask, we can use thin wire to shape features: beaks, ears, horns, antlers, and then use parcel tape again to cover those and integrate them with the main body of the mask. Then finish off with textures and paint as above

A slow process but giving wonderful, lightweight and surprisingly durable results. We could go through this whole process with plastercloth but I prefer the lightness of the tape and the paper is much less intrusive into skin pores and hair and easier to work with overall.

And now we have new faces to watch the world through. Hopefully, these might have grown out of earlier exploring, investigating and maybe even some story ideas. To develop things further, try some of the ideas in New characters or go back to the dance and drama activities in *Talking to the Earth* or try on your masks the improvisation ideas described in Puppets.

The Secret of the Ears

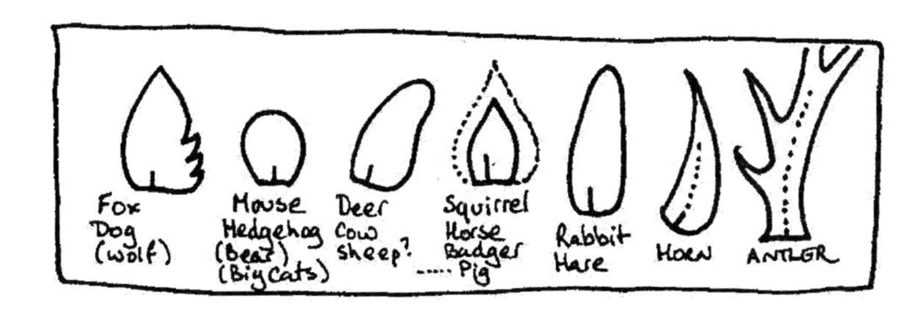

When working on mammal masks, or other models it is helpful to know that for most British mammals there are only 4 basic shapes of ears. These are drawn below and if you can remember them you will find that ears will fall into one of those forms. You will need to adjust scale and detail to suit: tuft ears for badgers and red squirrels, skew them a little for bats. This means that we can meet a group's needs quite easily (and get a lot of personal credibility for knowing so much about animals!) Being able to help people select "good" ears for their animal helps their sense of satisfaction and their confidence a lot.

If we then widen our range, we find similar shapes among mammals across the world. There are obvious exceptions (elephants have quite unique ears) but, again, most mammals will fit into those 4 forms. Hippos and rhinos could argue for a new form and monkeys and apes need round ones turned sideways but otherwise...

16

An interlude with flags

This is a short burst of textile work that did not quite fit in anywhere else. So here the flags can have their own moment of waving and shouting.

Two techniques are offered here for making simple but striking banners. Both processes work across a range of ages of makers and sizes of cloth. With younger groups, I have become quite firm about colours and ask groups to choose just 3 or 4 colours and ask them to be quite careful about applying paint. Do not let the need for some control discourage you: groups of 4 and 5 year olds can make banners that are just as delightful as those produced by older groups. Both these processes use cold water and paint rather than working with hot wax, Batik and dyes. These flags are very versatile: other processes might give subtler designs but these techniques work well with large groups, are fairly cheap and are very portable. Taped banners also work well outdoors on sunny days.

Size and shape of flags is very much dependant upon your situation. Small squares (30 x 30cm) are easy 1-person pieces, if not very exciting (they do patchwork together quite easily, however). Personal flags could, on the other hand, be triangles or long thin pennants, which offer more exciting shapes if with less space for images.

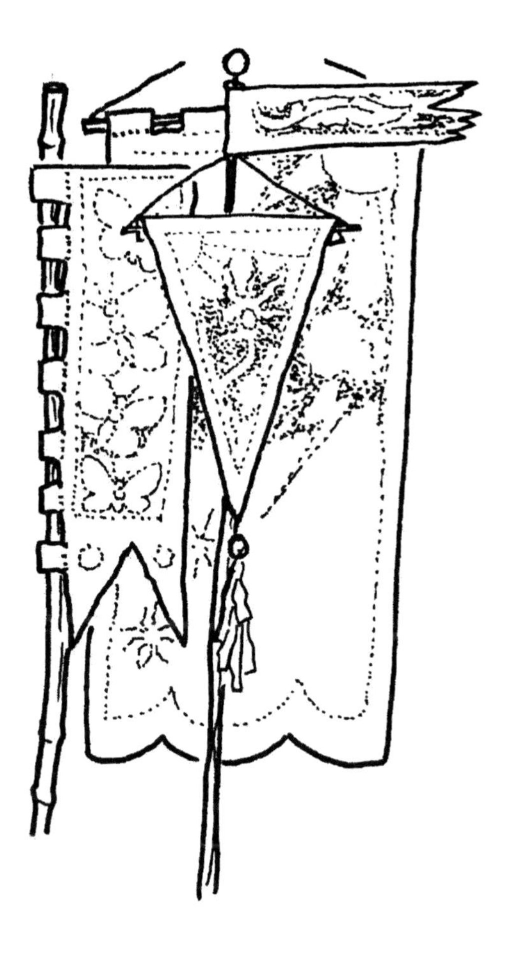

Timing in both of the processes below can be very unpredictable: I have spent whole days working with classes to make a few 1m x 2m flags (throwing in experimental individual pennants to start the process), while on other occasions groups of 3 or 4 children have made hanging triangles in 35 minutes. As with everything else, you need to experiment and think about what you are hoping to achieve. Preparing the image for painting is the slow bit. Painting can happen frighteningly fast!

Taped banners

Time: anything from 30 minutes to several hours depending upon the size of the cloth

Materials: cotton, fabric paint (or acrylic paint), chalk, masking tape (1cm and 2.5cm wide), paintbrushes, palettes, tubs for water

Organisation: small flags might be made by individuals: maybe allow an hour for a 30cm x 60cm piece, groups of 3 or 4 might work on a pieces a metre square and need maybe 90 minutes

Bold, simple patterns work well. Think about stained glass windows, about drawing outlines rather than detail and about drawing large. Experiment on paper first. Perhaps even settle upon some nice designs on paper and draw these in strong black pens which will show through the cloth.

Use wider tape to mark an edge to the print. Trace designs (or draw freehand) with faint chalk lines onto cloth. If the paper designs show easily through the cloth, maybe bypass the chalk bit and go straight onto taping. Apply tape along the chalk lines, folding tape (or sticking it down in lots of short pieces) round curves, tearing or cutting it to get thinner pieces. Tape and go on taping. This is the slowest and can be most frustrating part of the process. Finished? Now run a thumb over all the lines, making sure the tape is firmly stuck down. No other tape works as well as masking tape for this and even then if the tape is not firmly stuck down, paint seeps under the edges of the tape and loses the clarity of the image (this may be what you want, of course!). Use the palest chalk you can get away with as lines are left on the print: they do wear off with time but dark colours can rather spoil the stark contrast of white lines against the paint colours.

Now paint. Right up to and onto the edges of the tape. Bright, bold blocks of colour. Or perhaps more subtle gradations applied with sponges. Watch over-enthusiastic painters who

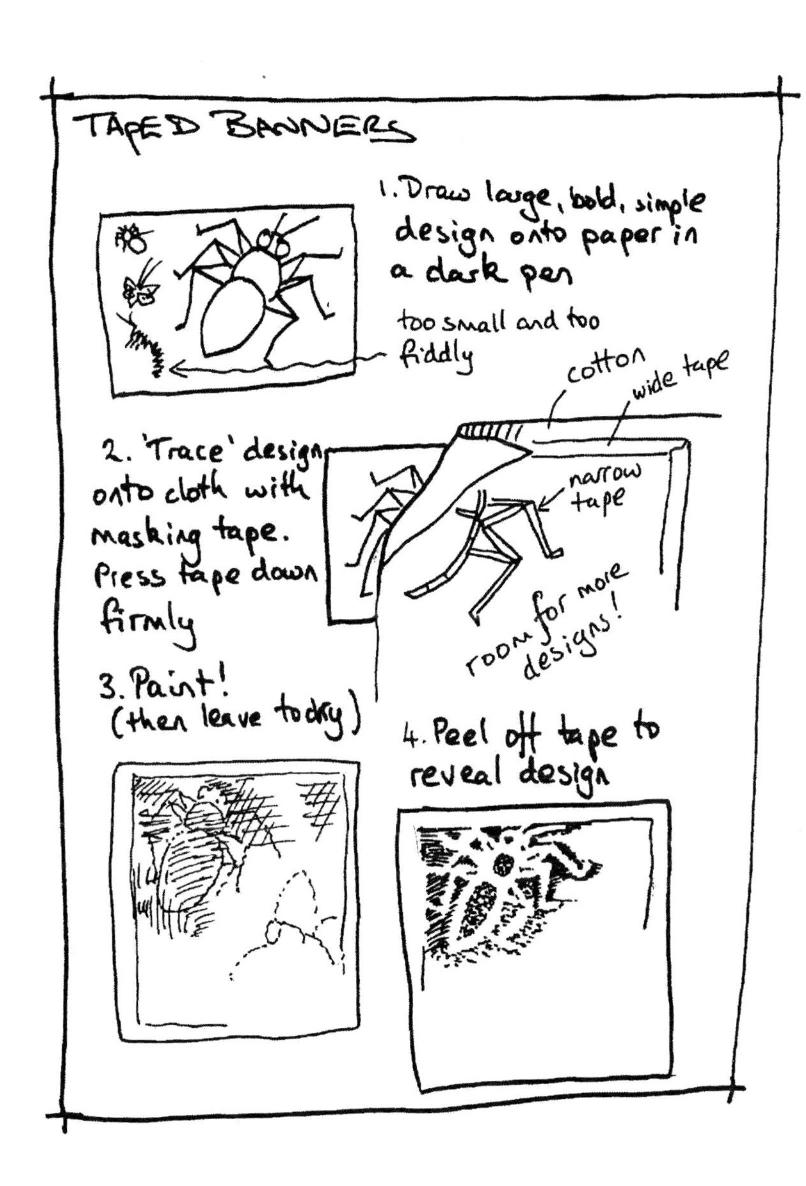
TAPED BANNERS
1. Draw large, bold, simple design onto paper in a dark pen
too small and too fiddly
cotton
wide tape
2. 'Trace' design onto cloth with masking tape. Press tape down firmly
narrow tape
room for more designs!
3. Paint! (then leave to dry)
4. Peel off tape to reveal design

pile on so much watery paint that the tape starts to curl off, or who pile one colour on top of another until everything is muddy brown. Leave it to dry. This might need to be overnight, but in warm settings an hour or so might be enough.

The most exciting part of the process comes with peeling the tape off. Think of the pleasure of picking scabs and removing plasters and you're on your way. Peel, pick, scrape off the tape and watch your picture be revealed. If you have used fabric paint, it now needs to be ironed (use a hot setting and iron with the flag under another cloth) to fix the colour. Acrylic paint should be waterproof when dry and no ironing is needed.

Flour and water flags

Time: variable again.
Materials: cotton, plain flour, wooden spoons, mixing bowl and small tubs, acrylic paint, paintbrushes, palettes. Hair drier, hot air gun or fan heater might be helpful. To apply paste see below.
Organisation: small flags might be made by individuals: maybe allow an hour for a 30cm x 60cm piece, groups of 3 or 4 might work on a pieces a metre square.

Now, we will use a flour and water paste as the resist that protects the cloth from the colouring. I met this first as a handy way of exploring some West African design processes where different muds are used both as the resist and as the dye on cloth. These Bogolanfini designs can make for interesting discussions to start the process: talking about language and stories contained within designs, rather than within letters or illustrations.

Again, work on paper first. Mix a runny flour and water mix. Then transfer the design onto cloth. Three techniques to consider:

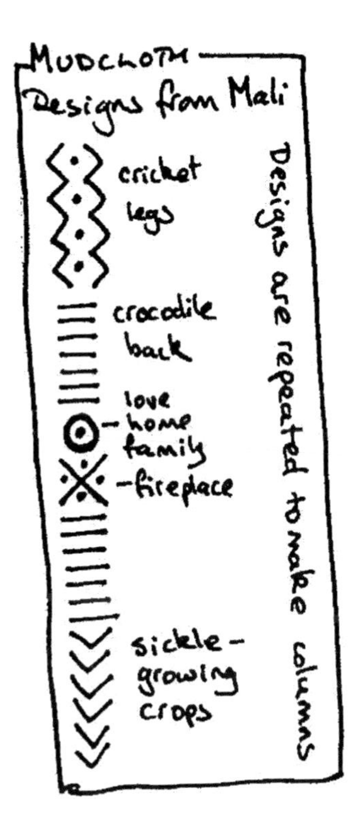

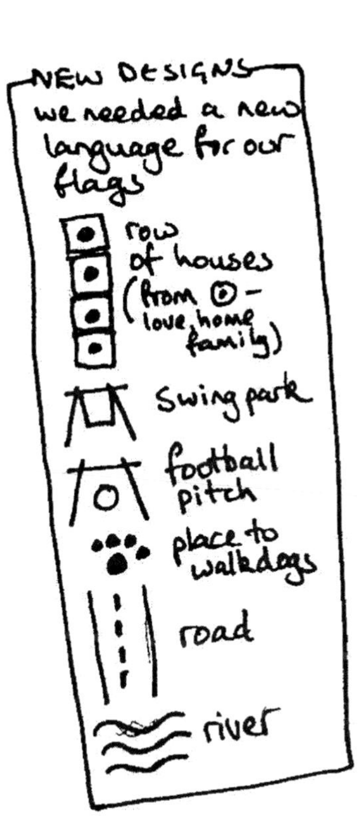

with paintbrushes: paint on the flour and water paste: most obvious technique but cleaning the brushes after is a nightmare

bottles: if you can get hold of enough, you might fill old plastic sauce bottles or something similar so that paste can be squeezed out along the lines of the design (these two techniques leaves white designs on coloured cloth)

"batik": spread a coat of paste over the whole cloth then scrape the design through the flour using plastic cutlery: either handle or working end. Experiment: you can "cut" designs with finger nails, false teeth, upturned cups, a bit of quivering of a pastry cutter.....If you let it dry, you could then crack the paste with a bit of careful crumpling and when it is stained it will have veins running through it. (Leaves coloured designs on white cloth)

Let the flour dry. It doesn't need to be bone dry, just dry enough to be tacky. An hour in a warm space is usually enough (or be vigourous with a hair dryer or hot air gun).

Paint with acrylic paint (not fabric paint). Leave to dry. Rinse. You might need to use a rough plastic pan-scourer to loosen flour but rinse it out and you should be left with exciting, slightly wobbly, designs. Fabric paint would need to be ironed before you could wash the flour out and ironing might bake the paste so hard you won't get it out easily (and it might burn and wreck the iron!). Acrylic paint is insoluble once it has dried. When you wash it, you will still get a bit of run-off from paint that was on top of the paste. It can look rather alarming but usually enough remains for good colours on the cloth!

Finishing off

Now you might want to:

hem flags

hang flags: either just fold over and staple a hem to slide a pole through or attach ribbon loops or sew tabs and slide a pole through these (recommend the last for permanent work)

add tassels: try the tassel making technique below

Tassels

Time: 10 minutes
Materials: shredded carrier bags, string, newspaper and tape or small balls
Organisation: usually make these as individuals - maybe have one person out of a flag team working on these

Cut a heap of carrier bags into strips: fold bags along their length (so you cut from side to side) and cut sections 1 -2 cm wide. These should come out as loops that need to be snipped and opened out when uses

Choose perhaps 8 of these streamers and 2 pieces of string about 10cm long. Take 3 streamers and tie a piece of string firmly round the middle of these. Lay them down with their ends pointing "north and south". Lay your other streamers across these first ones, fanning out around the compass. Sit your ball (or a ball of newspaper, tightly scrunched and maybe taped together) in the middle of all these. Gently fold the streamers round the ball then tie the streamers as tightly as you can where they meet on the upper side of the ball.

Hopefully you will now have a tassel with the first piece of string on one side to give you a loop to hang it up by and the streamers tied together under the ball and hanging down in a suitably tentacular jelly-fish fashion.

Often everything slides.

Try again.

Play with scale. You can make big tassels like this using shredded bin-bags and strange squidgy balls from toy-shops.

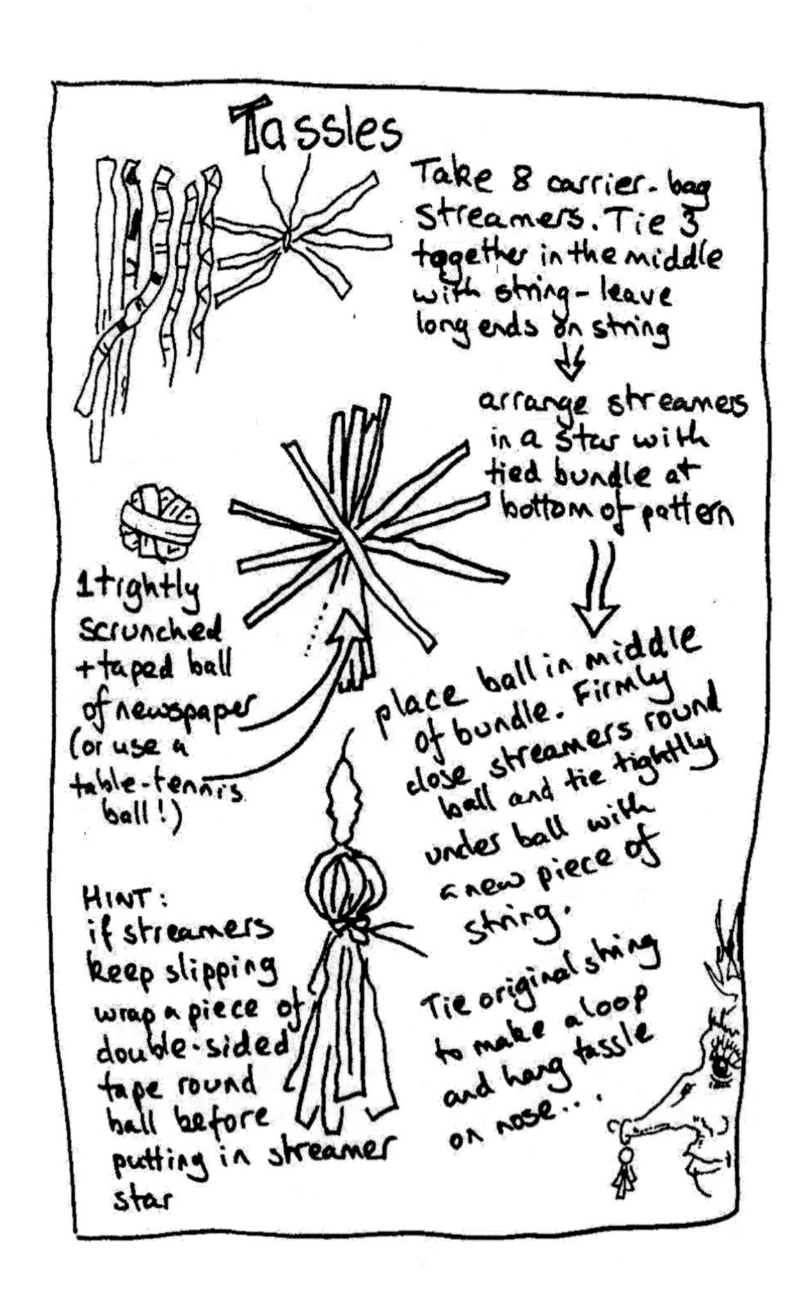
Tassles
Take 8 carrier-bag streamers. Tie 3 together in the middle with string - leave long ends on string
arrange streamers in a star with tied bundle at bottom of pattern
1 tightly scrunched + taped ball of newspaper (or use a table-tennis ball!)
place ball in middle of bundle. Firmly close streamers round ball and tie tightly under ball with a new piece of string.
HINT: if streamers keep slipping wrap a piece of double-sided tape round ball before putting in streamer star
Tie original string to make a loop and hang tassle on nose...

Mounting

Now they are done, you could hang your flags from poles, from cross pieces, on walls, from rafters. Carry them. Wave them. Whirl them, twirl them, wrap small children in them like cloaks. Wear tassels as ear-rings. Enjoy them.

17

New characters

Who comes first - the character or the story? In *Celebrating Nature*, we have looked for places where adventures might have happened, for objects that have participated in stories, for landscapes populated with characters who are clearly the stuff of epics. Other chapters have played with stories and landscapes, so here we can give ourselves time to play with people.

Here are a selection of ideas for developing characters. We might start this process from various points: from favourite places within a site, from items found on site or artefacts selected from a box, or just by slipping ourselves into the feel of a person and a place. Whatever process is used, as leaders we need to watch the pace of the activity. "Finding" a new character to play with needs time. That may mean quite structured time: a series of small offerings to keep the process moving, gradually accumulating ideas, one thought growing out of another, until there is a character there, waiting to be encountered, to tell their own story. Our balancing act lies in just how much input people will need. We need to have a selection of ideas to feed into the process but must watch and listen as, sometimes, it seems that our new characters are simply waiting to leap out and into action and the group will need relatively little input from us. At other times that constant feed is needed: as much to build up confidence as anything else.

Who else?

Time: 20 - 30 minutes
Materials: blank postcards, pencils
Organisation: probably working alone, or maybe in pairs

Simply sit down, take time to dream, to sit in some special place and soak up the atmosphere of that place. Think about what it might feel like at other times of day or night or season, or imagine across years and think what it might have been like last year, ten years ago, a hundred, a thousand years...

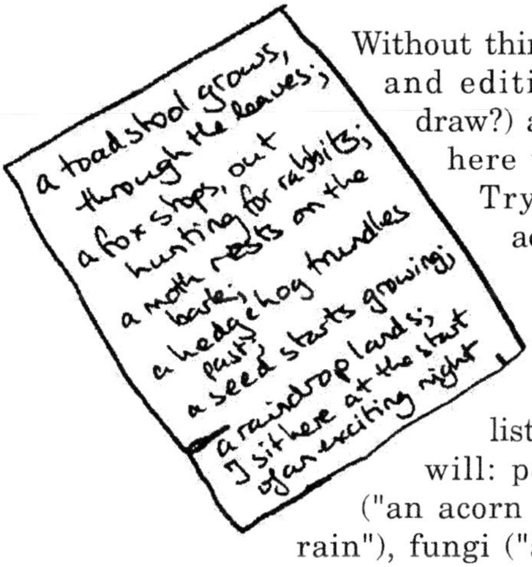

Without thinking too much about it and editing the list, write (or draw?) a list of "who else comes here when I'm not around". Try to make the list an active one, so that instead of just "fox", we might have: "fox hunting rabbits", or "fox under moon-light". The list can be as broad as you will: people, animals, plants ("an acorn waiting for spring and rain"), fungi ("a toadstool pushing up through the dead leaves"), the fabulous ("a unicorn breathing, silent as moonlight") and even weather ("a wind playing with falling leaves").

Afterwards, perhaps when we are all back together, jiggle that list around, like a cut-up poem. Try to find a sequence to your images: a sense of rhythm either with the words themselves or with the images: arranged now by time, maybe, or season, or century, or size. Maybe add a Stillness Poem to convey the atmosphere and with the two verses we have the opening of a story.

Feed back to everyone else.

Starting points: this activity works just about anywhere. You might need to adjust details to suit settings but you might try this while Disappearing, or simply by choosing an appealing place to rest. It also works well with built environments: castles, stately homes, formal gardens. You can try it on the move as well: dream along a woodland path or along a corridor in a ruined castle, up an old stairway. Even the act of opening a door might give you a set of "who else". The doorway could also move us into another activity.

The activities described below are largely written from the perspective of someone developing a human character. The same process might give us animal or fabulous characters. Be sensitive to possibilities and try to plan your words to keep possibilities open.

Diaries

Time: 15 minutes (or more)
Materials: postcards and pencils (or maybe small pieces of brown wrapping paper and something to lean on - more interesting than card). Objects as suggested in the variations.

"DIARY" entry: rather sad piece on brown paper, inspired by holding a wooden bowl and horn spoon

Organisation: again, essentially working on our own, maybe with a friend, but in the security of being with the whole company

More dreaming: Hold your chosen artefact. Close your eyes. Run our fingers over the surface, lightly, firmly. Sniff it. Hold it against your face. In the palms of your hands.

Know that somewhere, somewhen, someone (or something) else has held this thing, has sat and touched it just as you are doing. Through the eyes of your imagination, see the other hand that has held it, is holding it. See that hand. Feel the person behind the hand. Feel what they are feeling. (Don't worry too much about details of their lives yet - go for feelings).

What time of day is it? Where are they sitting - or what else are they doing?

Quietly pick up your pencil and write that person's diary for the day when they were holding that object.

This is a lovely, dreamy, activity that can gives some deliciously unexpected results. it often works best if we can encourage a sense of connection to the ordinary people of a place: to the servants, farmers and soldiers of a castle rather than kings and queens and to the numerous small animals or a woodland rather than its one and only dragon.

But don't be too prescriptive.

Variations: You can write Diaries in so many contexts that it is up to you to think through the best language for your situation. Having an object to hold makes all the difference. You might try one of the following:

Found objects: treasures found during earlier activities and maybe already storied in a Lying session.

Natural objects (or representations): I have various bundles of bits that we use in indoor sessions. There is a water life box: shells of different sizes, plastic model polar bears and seals, life-size fish, crab and lobster models, a seal skull, dried seaweed. For more challenging activities, we might open the stone box and tap into the memories of stones, minerals and fossils, producing not diaries but snippets recalled from ancient lives.

Historic artefacts: try offering a selection of small, everyday items out of the past of a place or a people. On the whole, keep these simple with maybe a few "high status" items. It is unlikely that a group will all go for the "golden goblet": people work from all sorts of things...

My history box holds several wooden bowls, pewter tankards, stoppered glass bottles, a horn spoon, pewter and brass goblets, a leather cup, a falconry hood, small wooden box with iridescent glass marbles, some rings, a mortar and pestle.

After writing our Diaries, it is good to share at least some of those entries with a partner and with the whole company. We might go on to try Responses or Meeting People, below, or jump straight to Character Sheets.

After diaries

Responses
Time: 10 - 15 minutes, or maybe a bit more
Materials: diary entries, strips of paper to write on
Organisation: pairs and small groups ending as a whole company maybe

As people finish their diary entries, they might pair up and quietly read their entries to each other. As a whole company we might then hear several entries.

Responses: invite people (either in the whole company, or maybe in small groups, or pairs) to listen to diaries and feed back:

> how you think that character felt when they wrote their diary
>
> is their any advice you would give them?
>
> is there a gift you think would help them?

These responses might be spoken but, especially if working in groups, people might write their responses down on scraps of paper. Now, take it in turns to read your own diary entry, gather response slips, but do not look at them until everyone in the group has read their diaries and collected responses.

Thoughts arising from these responses might feed into Character Sheets below.

Meeting People

Time: 10 - 20 minutes
Materials: diary entries, maybe bits of costume
Organisation: work in pairs or groups to start, gradually building up to a whole company - or maybe half a company, while others observe.

Now, hold your starting object again. Read your diary entry again, quietly to yourself. Take a few minutes to feel that character again. Sit on your chair they way they would. Feel the shape of them around you. Their height. Their build. On the whole, let them speak your language.

Look around.

As you catch someone else's eye, start reading your diary entry, as that character, to them. Speak as that person and listen as your partner responds with their character's diary. Have a conversation as those two people, meeting across time (and species) perhaps. Stand up, walk around. With your new friend (?), meet other characters out of other diaries.

This often works well only for a few minutes and then can lose momentum. Those few minutes may be enough: they let us taste more of the personality behind our characters and we can move onto Character Sheets. At other times, a group gets caught up in their characters and whole new stories unfold through their interactions.

You might go back to Responses again after this, but don't overdo it.

Character Sheets

Time: 30 minutes
Materials: diary entries, sheet of A3 paper each, pens, glue, tape or staplers
Organisation: working as for Diaries

Now, in our heads we have all sorts of bits about a character, so take time to assemble the information. Stick your diary entry onto a big sheet of paper and start working round it. Ask yourself questions: sometimes you won't know answers, which is fine, just keep moving. And, as with so much story work, take the first thoughts that bounce into the front of your mind: the unplanned response often gives the most exciting results!

As a company, you, as leader, might want to read a set of questions out but this activity usually works best with a short opening discussion along the lines of "what would you like to find out about this person?", encouraging people to give themselves their own list of questions (maybe briefly scribbled on the back of the sheet). Then, as your group works, you can circulate and support.

Look for:

- name, age, sex, marital status
- where do they live
- what do they do for a living
- what do they look like (do a drawing)

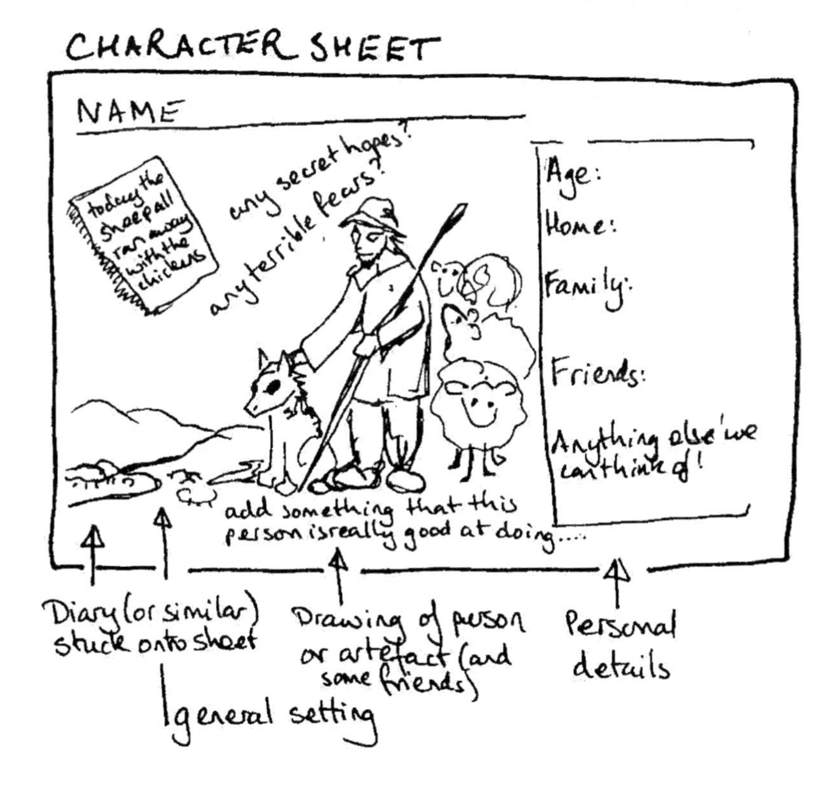

any special ambitions?

anything they are very good at doing?

anything they are terrible at doing?

secret loves?

hidden fears?

Answers might be single words, scribbled notes, drawings or even lines spoken/written in character.

By the end of this time we should have a whole collection of personalities to play with.

The value of information

Without overloading people, these activities benefit from and offer an excellent opportunity to use existing knowledge. Input might come in two phases: initially we could spend time building up general background information: about a place, a situation or whatever. We might look for water supplies, sources of firewood, main occupations, building materials, food. Then, after we have started developing characters we might go back and look for more specific information that might relate to the sorts of people we have been writing about: how did they carry the water? names? money? who did the cooking? what did children do? could we play football? could girls play football? did we ever have baths?

Artefact Sheets

A variation on character sheets, might be slipped in here although perhaps it would fit better into Stories . Instead of taking an artefact and distilling a person from it, we might take an object and draw its own story from it, not going so much for characters and personalities as adventures and journeys and "how did it get here".

The process is very similar: go for memories, little scraps of ideas, of experiences scribbled down. Where did it come from? Who worked with it? Who shaped it? How did it travel? How did it get here? Where would it like to be? Where will it go next? Does it have an overall plan for its adventures?

To keep it engaging, encourage people to tell a personal story. Let the object itself tell its story.

Variation for small groups

Share one object between 5 or 6 people and, in a familiar story-making activity, take it in turns to tell fragments of its story. People may give whole sections of the adventure, taking a sentence or two to say : "This journey began a long time ago and far, far away, when this wooden bowl was a tree growing in a forest at the edge of the sea, until...." and then pass the item on to the next person who will pick up the tale.

Or, more erratically, offer snippets of memory that don't necessarily slide smoothly into one another: "sunlight, warmth, roots digging deep into the ground", "fear, pain, shavings falling!", "a warm, firm hand, holding me close, hugging me", "the pond-mud feel of being full of porridge".

The latter session might precede the more complete story making.

So, now we have some characters to work with. This work might inform, or be informed by puppets, masks or other stories. "Knowing" about the personalities behind our ideas and activities gives the whole process depth and offers our participants a strong feeling of personal connection, even if their character is completely fictitious.

Celebrating Nature has not given much space to drama work and now we are running out of space! Essentially, now we can take our characters and play with them. Use your own ideas to explore the interactions between these characters, to see how they relate to the world around them and generally to get to know them better. Try applying the stages described in Waking your puppet to these characters and use that to start some improvisations.

Here is a seed

A little story-poem-dance for use with younger groups

start sitting down, hands on knees, one hand relaxed, the other curled into a ball -this is the hand that begins. If you say the words and do the actions, ask the group to copy you. Speak:

here is a seed lying on the ground
(seed-hand is still)

here is a root growing into the earth
(other hand slides out and wriggles downwards)

and here is a shoot growing into the air
(seed-hand opens and waivers upwards, wrist first)

Here is a branch
(raise seed-hand elbow up and out)

and here is a twig
(unfold arm, hand still closed, bud-like now)

and here is the leaf that opens in the sun
(open fingers wide)

Here is the sun that warms the tree
(stand up, lifting both hands together above your head, fingers splayed, slowly opening arms sideways, describing a big sun-circle)

and here is the rain that feeds the tree
(hands back above head, fingers wiggling, crouch down, raining down to ground and drum fingers on floor)

Here is the bud
(both hands cupped in big bud, stand slowly, maybe twisting through a spiral to grow upwards)

that opens into a flower
(hands in front of face, open out into big flower)

Here is the bee that visits the flower
(one hand keeps flower shape, other comes out from behind back, one finger leading, buzzing in a wandering path to the flower)

And flies away again
(buzz off)

Now the flower becomes a fruit
(both hands in flower shape now curl up into round "apple" shape)

Here is the child that picks the fruit
(stretch right up above your head to pick fruit. You might need to jump for it)

and eats it
(munch, munch, loudly)

and throws away the core
(throw it away, following its flight with a finger, sitting back down as the seed lands)

Here is a seed that lies on the ground
(start again)

Try this 3 times: once with you leading, second time with everyone joining in - and shouting out the sort of fruit their tree grows! In a final run through, try it without words.....and before you know it, we have a dance. Add music. Add new elements. Tell the story of a garden.

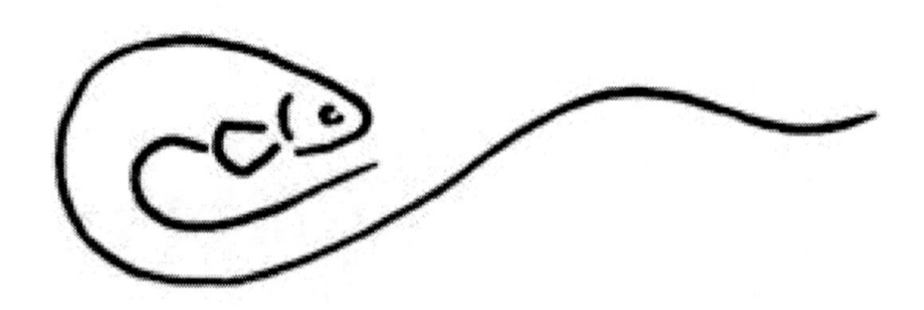

18

Holding onto words

Holding onto words? Surely you just have to write them down? Yes, maybe, perhaps: but how do you write them? What else could we do with them? How can we make the writing process itself more exciting?

And of course, to hold onto our words, to remember our stories we do not need to write them down. Perhaps we just need something to jog our memories of the shape, the pace, the action, the characters of our stories. If we do want to write things down, remember how crushing "putting it in an exercise book" can be: how easily that can rob an activity of its enchantment.

No, it need not be like that and some people will enjoy formally writing or word-processing their work. But in keeping with our general wave of rampant creativity in *Celebrating Nature*, here are some alternative ideas for recording our words and stories.

Without writing

Mapsticks - story sticks
See Mapsticks in Personal moments and now use them as storysticks: coding your story as colours and incidents along your stick.

Storyscopes

Time: 30 minutes
Equipment: A4 card squares (see below) or cardboard tubes, pens, pencils, decorative bits, glue, tracing paper or acetate film, permanent pens
Organisation: everyone can make their own Storyscope

A Storyscope offers a simple, colourful visual conclusion to a word-session. On a Storyscope we can record in words or pictures the essence of a story, or other experience. Working first on the cardboard body of the 'scope, we might disguise it with leaves, bark and earth. We might draw and write key

moments from a story. We might simply draw our dreams and ambitions onto it. Then on one end we stick a disc of tracing paper (acetate sheets possibly gives a sharper finish) with a drawing in fine permanent pens that is the essence of everything else: your hopes for the flowerbed that has decorated the body of the 'scope, the main character from your story, a portrait of the dreaming person. Completed, a Storyscope is held up to the light and looked down so that the disc is seen illuminated at the end of the tube.

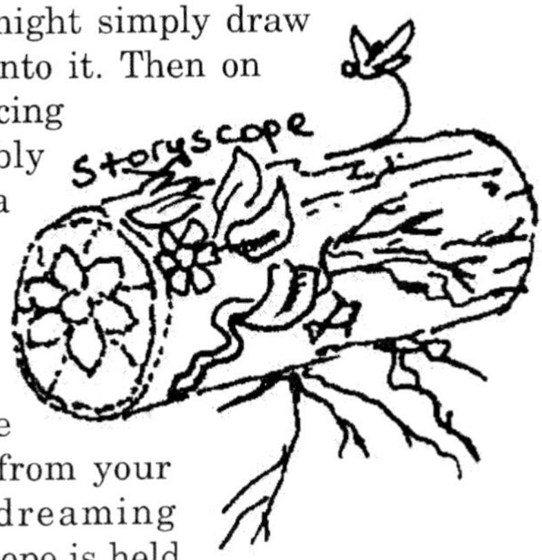

The simplest Storyscopes use cardboard tubes and simply require a disc sticking over one end. If tubes are in short supply, you can work with cardboard. Cut card squares (about 20cm is good), run a narrow line of double-sided tape down on side and on an adjacent edge cut tabs that can be folded out to give points of attachment for the picture disc. Decorate the card while still flat and only rolled and taped and the picture glued on at the end of the process.

Water Pictures

Time: 30 minutes (but getting ready takes as long)
Equipment: strong white tissue paper, other tissue, delicate found materials (thin leaves, petals, feathers), plastic to work on (cut up bin-bags are good), PVA glue, bowls and sponges, food colouring, permanent pens
Organisation: ideally, everyone should make their own picture, but this can be a messy process: maybe work a group at a time at the sticky stage

Here we can work with words and, or images: writing stories and poems onto tissue paper to incorporate into the bigger water picture, or turning our story (or ideas and impressions) into pictures or collages.

Lay down a piece of plastic big enough to hold a sheet of tissue the size of your finished picture. Sponge some PVA and water (c 50:50 mix) onto this and lay a sheet of tissue onto it. Sponge some more glue onto the tissue (it needs to be wet but not dripping!). Now compose your picture on the wet tissue. Lay out leaves and feathers, add torn bits of coloured tissue, add words written in permanent pen on tissue (some people

could be preparing this while others do the wet bits). When completed, lie another sheet of white tissue on top and sponge it so the whole composition is a sort of damp tissue paper sandwich with the "filling" firmly sealed in. As a last touch drip some food colouring onto the surface and let it run and stain the picture. When the picture is quite dry, peel it off the plastic sheet and hang picture in a window to let the light shine through!

To transport these, gently fold or roll the wet sheet so that plastic lies on tissue (don't let tissue touch tissue or they'll stick) and take it away. As soon as possible, unfold the picture and let it dry.

More words

Parchments

Time: anything from 15 - 45 minutes (gauge by your group)
Materials: sheets of A3 sized paper (square sheets are often nice) - maybe cartridge or brown paper, range of pens and other drawing materials, ribbons, glue
Organisation: everyone working no their own parchment, maybe in groups to share resources

A simple activity: fold your sheet of paper into a "package": folding sides in, then folding main body over to make a package, or roll it up to make a scroll. The options here are limited only by what your group can do with your sheet of paper. Have a couple of examples and let your group experiment for themselves. Something that unfolds in sections offer good spaces for breaking up text and boxes for illustrations, while scrolls invite the addition of willow spars to hold top and bottom.....

Then write. Make it interesting. Look at illuminated letters. Add borders. Leaf print onto paper first and write over this.

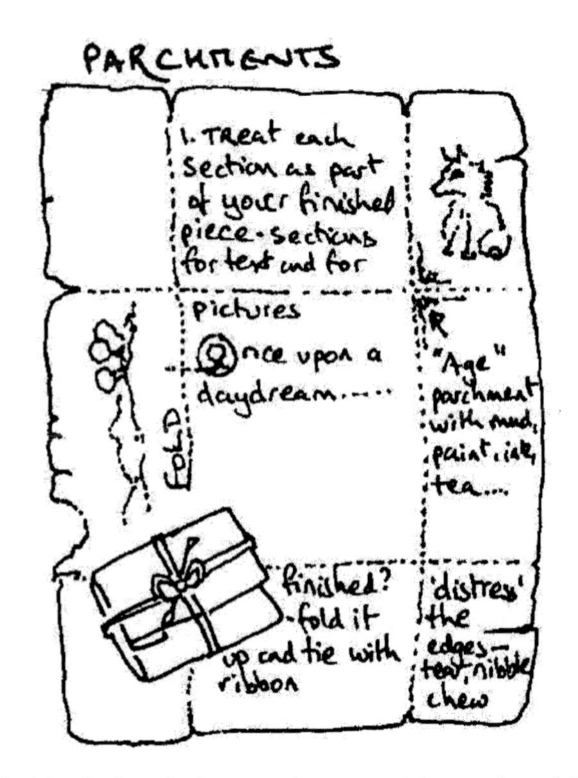

When finished, "age" the parchment with earth rubbed into creases, stain with old tea bags, singe (carefully) with matches, smear with almost-dry paint.

Then fold it tight and crease firmly. Add a ribbon (glue at one point on the ribbon) to tie it all closed.

Cut-up Poems

Time: 20 - 30 minutes
Materials: scraps of sugar paper, (A3) sheets of paper or card, box of scrap tissue, etc, glue sticks, scissors, pens
Organisation: everyone working no their own sheet, maybe in groups to share resources

An easy development from some of our earlier poetry ideas. Take, perhaps a Stillness Poem and write it out again on sugar paper, tearing the paper into strips with one line on each strip.

Stick these down on a sheet of card or paper (black card looks good), add appropriate decoration round it

This should be a very quick activity but people can become very engrossed in working with their words again and it might end up taking much longer than you expect

Variation: instead of working with a ready-made poem, try starting with images that have turned up elsewhere, maybe in Walking and talking. Write these onto strips of paper and shuffle the strips around until you find a sequence that you like: arranged by sense perhaps? Or size of experience. Or place - maybe your words become a journey into a moment. Then stick this new poem down on the main sheet (do you need to add some linking words to help it flow?).

Decoration: working with your paper "sideways" (landscape format), often opens up a sweep of space for picture, or the opportunity to play with the arrangement of your word, or to feed your words into a pattern rather than a picture that holds the essence of the experience you describe with your words.....a winter journey in words and a wintry swirl of colour and shapes.

Books

Now we have two bigger activities. Adventure Books works very well with younger groups, giving us quite structured stories but with lots of space for the group's own ideas. Wild Books is one of those deceptively simple ideas that become completely absorbing and swallow groups, producing a wonderful variety of ideas from that single, straightforward starting point.

Adventure books

Time: build over several activities

Equipment: book blanks, pencils and crayons, hole punches, wool

Organisation: with younger classes, you might work these in groups of 4 or 5 children (or do individual ones) with an adult with each group to do the writing perhaps?

8 pages, 8 questions......prepare some books for your group: photocopy a set of question sheets and staple them together or lace them up (as in Wild Books below). We usually have postcard sized pages and A5 sized book covers.

Then go exploring using those questions to set things in motion.

Title page: "Our Adventure, by...": stick paper onto a card cover for the book

Page one: "What did we wear?" use getting ready for adventures

Page two: "what did we take with us?" again, use getting ready for adventures

Page three: "How did we move?" set off creeping into the wilderness: collect as many words about the movement as possible

Page four: "What did we hear?" pause, settle in silence, listen to the world around us

Page five: "How did we feel?" - excited? scared? brave? - did we need to help each other through these feelings?

Page six: "Who (or what) did we meet?" at this point, we often sidetrack into making little creatures out of clay who we could then take home with us, or draw into our books. We also went on might also make houses for them out of natural materials

Page seven: "What happened after that?" and...?

Page eight: "And at the end of our adventure..." who knows!

Wild Books

Time: 45 - 60 minutes or more (or just 15 minutes at the end of each workshop over a number of sessions)

Materials: basic kit, range of small pages (A6 - postcard size), hole punches, wool, beads, pens: permanent, italic and gel are all useful. Stronger card for covers

Organisation: usually working alone or in pairs but sometimes, especially where time is short, you might work in larger groups and make collective volumes

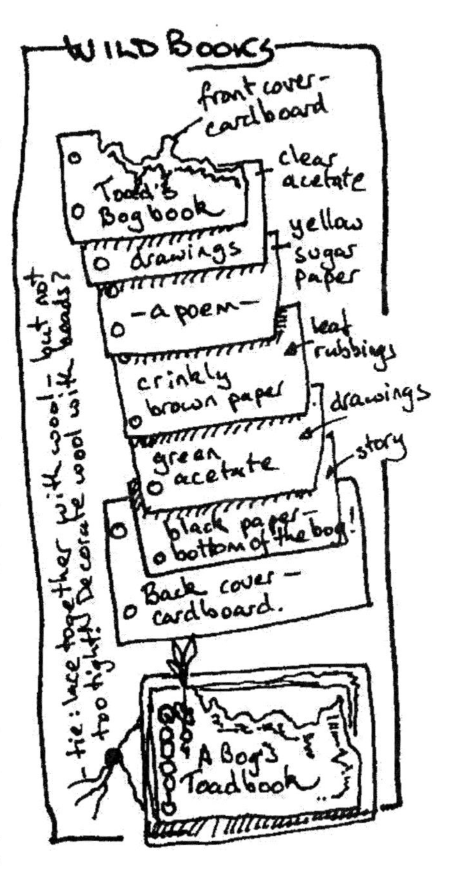

The novelty of this simple book-building activity comes with offering a range of different materials to make the book from. Cartridge or sugar

paper provides a solid foundation, but add to this tissue, acetate (coloured cover sheets for presentation booklets), brown paper, scraps of wrapping paper, maybe even some smart parchment type sheets, big leaves. As with so many of these activities the very personal nature of the resulting volume holds a lot of its attraction and charm for a group.

Basic: write on maybe 8 pages, punch 2 (? or 1 or more) holes in these and in the cover cards, lace them together with a piece of wool, adding beads to wool as you go, and tie it off to finish.

Extra excitement: encourage people to work with a variety of materials. Try not to treat this as some formal writing exercise....the book can be described in any way that awakens enthusiasm and can incorporate everything from poetry to formal descriptions and sketches of animals and plants seen during a walk to adventures that might, or might not have befallen the authors. We have had Bogbooks: building the layers of a peat bog as a book, Pond Books: "the story of our pond" and "the adventures of a pond skater", Tree Books:

describing the life and adventures of a particular chosen tree. There has even been A Wizard's Secret Spellbook.

Use the variety of page papers: look at the way images may be seen: acetate illustrations can lie on top of words, colours may change to suit depth of water or time of day, the sound of the pages may change with the age that is being described.

Overall, however, these are "My Own Book" books: make sure people have freedom to build the book that is right for them. Sometimes, a Wild Book is the centre of a whole workshop, building books as we explore a site: adding drawings, poems, spells, maps, secrets told at Disappearing points. This work is all done on site, carrying the minimal equipment needed with us. On longer projects we may build Wild Books as personal journals. Not as formal 'project journals' but as unfolding stories. We have seen "explorers" recording their latest rainforest experiences, describing meeting their first rainforest beetles, their journey to the jungle, an unexpected page where a tribal child got hold of the journal and wrote about seeing these strange people...

19

Pulling it all together

AND THEN YOU JUST HAVE TO DO IT!

Now, we are nearly there. We have told stories, had wild ideas, gone exploring, made things, danced, wriggled, squirmed and changed all our ideas several times. But at last we are reaching the end of this adventure and the prospect of a finale looms.

As we said right back at the beginning of all this, a final, approximately formal, celebration might not be essential. The process itself may be celebration enough, but a finale of some sort brings the process to a close. Hopefully, any celebration at this point will just mark the close of this phase of a process that will run on much longer than our immediate activities. For participants, however, a finale is often important: a chance to celebrate themselves and their own achievements and to show all their friends and relatives just what it is they have been doing during these strange workshops. You will probably find that the interest spreads wider than the immediate associates of your participants. There may be the morning dog-walkers who have seen you all out rummaging curiously in the undergrowth. There may be the people from the shop where you've been buying sandwiches while covered in paint and leaves...who knows who has been touched by your activities. A final celebration opens up a possibility of connection to lots more people.

Planning this final celebration needs its own time and preparation. Try to give yourself that time: don't just drop everything and do it. Plan it. Preferably with the participants themselves so they own as much of the whole process as possible (and could go on to plan their own celebrations later). This chapter assumes that we are working towards an active, participatory celebration: something falling somewhere between performance and ceremony, but your final celebration might take other forms. Hopefully, the ideas here, and in A shape for celebrations, might still give you some principles to adapt to your own situation.

Review and plan

Step back and look at what you have got to work with and what you hope to achieve.

Be realistic. It is good to go through this planning phase with your group, but is there time and opportunity to do so? Is it appropriate to your group, or groups, and situation? In the end, would it be better if you and your team sit down and plan it out yourselves? With big groups, it might be easier to have a few representatives joining in the planning process rather than everyone. With smaller groups but shorter periods of time, you might need to have planned most of this before and bring that celebratory structure, well advanced, for your group to spend just a few minutes fine tuning to accommodate their ideas. Ideally, however, try and do as much of the following with as many people as possible. It can be a tricky balancing act and may call upon all your skills as a workshop leader but it is worth doing and builds skills and a sense of final ownership in these closing stages that are valuable in completing the whole process with groups who have been involved all the way down the line already

The following ideas will be presented as if you are working through the stages with a group. If I find myself planning more or less on my own, I still make myself go through this sort of process. The discipline helps make sure that I miss out as little as possible.

We need to:

check what we've got now against our initial ideas

think about the audience this celebration is for

check out practical issues

what sort of celebration are we having anyway?

plan what will happen during our celebration

do it

Starting points

As a company, think about:

what have we done so far: what have we got to work with? This need not be just physical things we have made, it might be ideas, observations, stories and dances. Reflect on special moments in the process you have gone through that you feel visitors should also encounter: feelings, atmospheres or even just things we have seen: where fish gather in the pond, the bush where butterflies hover.

go back to the beginning: what were our first ideas? What were we trying to do? Is that story or storyline still valid or have we grown into something else along the way? Try to distil this into a single sentence that sums up what we are hoping visitors will experience in our celebration. It need not make much sense outside of its story context, "We want visitors to meet the inhabitants that we would like to find in our local woodland" was the summary line for an "Enchanted Woodland" finale.

Audience

Who is the celebration for? Is this an event that is just for ourselves with no-one else around? (In that case still go through the process but try to keep different elements of it secret, each managed by a different small team so that the final event becomes a series of surprises). Or do we hope that other people will come along. Will this still be a closed event: maybe just for other members of a school or college, or will we plan something open to anyone who turns up (might that raise issues about people management)?.

Usually we plan a celebration so the "audience" become involved in the "performance". We need to remember that while we should have some understanding of what is going on, our audience probably will not, so plan for clarity and simplicity. These are also maybe not the best words to describe people attending the event: audience? performers? Try celebration (rather than "performance"), "guests" or visitors for the "audience" who will join in the event and, for our company, "celebrants" (perpetrators of celebration).

Look at the best ways of letting people know when and where all this is happening. By now it may be a bit late for a new publicity campaign but

> **posters**: quick ones in shop windows and the like can help
>
> **fliers, or invitations**: something for all participants to take home to make it clear who else is invited to join us is helpful. You will need to send some information home with groups anyway: do not rely on people remembering what is said at a meeting about dates and times. Make sure people have a piece of paper to remind them where and when they are needed and, if possible, how long it is going to last

local news: local papers, radio and TV might all offer good last minute opportunities.

What sort of celebration

By now, we probably all have some assumption of what form our final celebration will take, but it might still be worth just pausing to consider options:

indoors or outdoors (I'm writing this as if we are working in a park or somewhere similar)

no live action: a series of installations to look at or experience but no celebrants actually in performance? There will still be questions about siting such experiences: in one place like a gallery or more of a wandering trail across a site. With the latter, pursue the process below to consider a sequence to the experiences if that seems appropriate

live action: again, in one place or spread out so that we use all of a site (not always appropriate to have large numbers of people traipsing around)

procession: slightly different from the above where perhaps the act of movement is the heart of the experience and often involves more people than other celebrations

Mapping the action

Here is the single most important stage in this process, so take it easy and keep it focussed but light

a) start by working in small groups each with a shared idea or planned bit of "action" and write characters/ incidents on postcards. Maybe look at up to 10 such encounters through a celebration. If possible, working

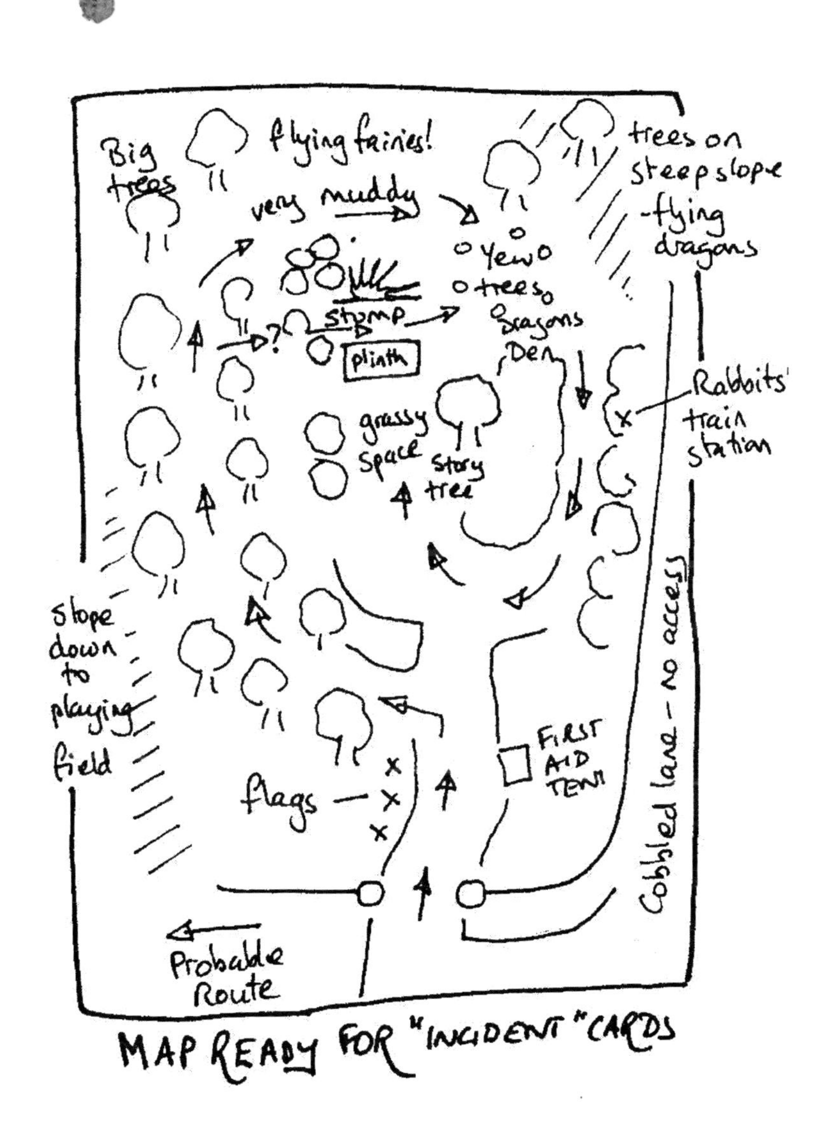
Big trees
flying fairies!
trees on steep slope
very muddy
-flying dragons
Yew trees
stump
?
plinth
Dragons Den
Rabbits' train station
grassy space
Story tree
slope down to playing field
FIRST AID TENT
flags
Cobbled lane - NO ACCESS
Probable Route
MAP READY FOR "INCIDENT" CARDS

on site is good. Let groups discuss: where their incident should happen, how they would like visitors to feel as they enter the scene and how the visitors will feel when they leave, is there anything visitors can do as they meet your moment?

b) on site, give people time to wander across the site again, looking at possible places for their precious moment and think about the practicalities of what they are proposing.

c) when you gather together again, remind yourselves of the celebratory structure and see if your planned sequence does tell your story or unfold your storyline

d) spread out a big map of the site. Check out that people know where they hope their encounter will take place, then start to work through the story or storyline with those cards being placed on the map as we go. Negotiate changes to venue to keep a sense of flow through story and site. You role here is both storyteller and mediator.

This stage is important and often rather chaotic. Hopefully, there is lots of laughter as we find we've just turned all our visitors into frogs in one moment when in the next they are meant to be flying like eagles round a tree...

So, stop and check out the story again: does it work?

Grab your cards, map, props perhaps and walk, hop, scramble and snigger your way round the site and through the whole story several times.

Try to find time to collect masks, puppets or other "perform-ance' pieces and rehearse again.

OK, done that.

Is it looking good?

Can we add any special effects? A bit of this or that, extra decoration?

Music? Live music helps a lot. It can hold people in one place, or keep them moving onwards. It can add depth to the simplest of scenes. It can get us all dancing. And, inevitably, it can all go horribly wrong! If you have access to some local musicians who'll join in, consider:

> are they a group, community or professional, who can be relied on to fill one space in the celebration (we've had a school recorder group serenading trees and an impromptu choir singing tones to dispel grief)? Should they have been part of the earlier workshop process?
>
> are they good for keeping people moving: Samba, brass and silver bands?
>
> should we hold them back as part of a single climatic moment?
>
> are they good at improvising? Could they join these final mapping sessions, watching and listening, and be relied

upon to add background and rhythm to the final celebratory activities

Of course, if you are very lucky, you might have had musicians involved all the way down the line, working as one strand in your storyline and perhaps creating music with workshop participants for this final celebration as well as adding their own experience and expertise to the occasion.

Final preparations

This is a section for you and your team of workers, usually without lots of young celebrants running around expecting attention and support for their sudden last minute nerves.

Give yourself time to get static things in place. Remember that once you have set things on site you might not be able to leave the area unattended. Toadstools left in glades may end up wandering away into neighbouring gardens if not watched carefully. So plan your time carefully.

Before the celebration you need to:

give yourselves time to "rig the site" - put everything in place

talk through the final storyline: checking roles, cues, points of delicate timing or especial concern

have time to get dressed up, painted or whatever for yourselves

Rigging

As ever, you have to establish safety protocols to suit yourself and any site managers involved. Then:

for suspending things in trees, we usually use clothes-lines lobbed up and over a branch and tied off at ground level (a 4 m bamboo pole can be very helpful here)

use short bamboos as supports and stakes for more grounded items, or fix sections of plastic drainpipe in place and at the last minute slip items on longer poles into these

flags and banners and other things on long poles might be best on strong bamboos cable-tied to fence posts, established trees, gate-posts and the like

lanterns, etc can have penlight torches in them that are switched on at the last minute. I would be reluctant to leave even nightlights burning unattended. Torches are safer but more likely to be "liberated" when your back is turned

After the event, arm your team with secateurs and craft knives and clear the site in sections.

Celebrants

For the final event, make sure you have a team of people to support you. These might be your original working team or perhaps teachers, group leaders or other reliable people involved with the development of the event. They will probably not be "performers" themselves, as we need these folk to be:

stage managers: getting groups into action at the right moment

stand-ins: someone who can pick up the action and improvise if our celebrants are too shy at the last minute to do their stuff

a ring-master or two: maybe needed to lead the visitors through the celebration process: maybe a costumed character who is part of the strangeness or a very sensible character leading people through the strangeness: both scenarios work, or a combination of both might suit your storyline better

stewards: managing the audience: keeping visitors together, welcoming people, showing them where to park, where to wait, keeping a mindful eye on things generally

Of course these roles tend to overlap and we may well find our "ring-masters" are also the main stewards and visitor "hosts" while stage managers tend to become stand-ins and everyone helps with clearing up afterwards.

At the celebration itself; try to get your celebrants there earlier (not always easy), give them time, if needed, for face painting, costuming, emergency repairs (have a couple of sets of staplers, scissors, cable ties and strong tape on hand), and the like. Expect various forms of panic: be confident and supportive, smile encouragingly.

After the celebration: if it is possible, provide refreshments for celebrants, and maybe the audience as well: time to applaud and appreciate. Appreciation will, hopefully,also have been built into the Master of Ceremonies' closing words, but over a glass of juice and a slice of cake we can be more personal and salute the individuals who have sailed over their own reservations and achieved wonderful moments all of their own.

Processions

Planning a procession might need a few words of its own. A Procession might simply be an exciting way of moving people from one point to another, perhaps from a meeting point through the woods, up the hill and over the bridge (watch out for trolls) to where a main celebration will take place. A Procession might, however, be the final celebration itself: the movement will contain the specialness of the occasion.

Consider, now, what you are doing. Check out the practical stuff (see Appendix 1). Consider especially what will happen during the procession

a) processors: who is in the procession: visitors who have little previous exposure to our activities? Or perhaps people who have visited some workshops and have come dressed and excited: primed as it were and ready for action but still not aware of the whole picture...the description of "In Pursuit of Love and Passion" at the end of this chapter might help with thoughts of activity here

b) music: helps the movement and creates atmosphere and gives the whole event pace and excitement. Will you use the same music or band through out or will there be changing points? Encourage people to respond to the music: dance, wave flags, stamp, sing or plunge into a funereal gloom (and enjoy it!)

c) silence: you might work with absolute silence. Throughout? In one stretch? Very effective and dramatic if you can get the message across to the whole company! Communicating ideas within a large procession becomes difficult! Even if you have announcers stationed at different points, declaring perhaps "Hush! Hush! Here is silence and a time to dream..." as the company passes, some will still be nattering away to their neighbours!

d) incidents: will your procession encounter scenarios along the route? They might see lantern boats floating on a pool, a choir singing as they pass, go under the arched flowers of giant plants. Are these passive installations to observe or active incidents that communicate with the parade? If the encounter is active, remind performers that they may need to repeat activities several times as the parade passes by, or have a "holding" activity to repeat until the whole company has gathered and are ready to watch and respond to the performing group's main action

e) beginning and ending: it helps a lot (again) to have someone or several people who can welcome visitors and set the scene and who will keep reappearing throughout the procession to mark changes and encourage responses where appropriate. End your procession with a collective moment, if possible. Plan for a place where everyone can gather, a place to pause and thank and celebrate collectively. Here the whole company can join in a set of actions that will help that sense of communal awareness and purpose. A walking spiral usually works well, with flags waving and lanterns glowing, or maybe a simple circle dance. Laugh a lot. Call for silence, lower flags, bow to each other. Try one of the Closing Moments below.

Just Do It

This chapter isn't over yet, but at some point, we need to interrupt the planning and worrying and preparing. Relax. Step into your role as "leader of celebrations" - whether you are out front as a ringmaster or behind the scenes. Let that tide of celebratory excitement sweep you up, and go with it. Stop talking. Stop worrying. Stop panicking. Watch the people arriving, full of anticipation and curiosity. Then take a deep breath. A celebration is an occasion of wonder and delight. Smile. And just celebrate.

Behind the scenes

In preparing for these final sessions, there are practical issues you will need to address. These may be those you have already dealt with in the process of reaching this point, but your celebration may bring more people into your site and may call for extra thought generally.

Rather than filling the rest of this chapter with lists of things you might need to consider, we have filled an appendix instead! In Appendix 1 there are checklists of "practical points to consider" and, hopefully, they will help you plan so that your celebration runs smoothly.

There are a few other points you could think about and set up to help ease the planning process.

The observant among you will have noticed that the usual "time", "materials", and "organisation" notes are missing in this chapter. This is largely because these are not clearly defined activities as such and their organisation will vary from one situation to another. Preparations you could take, however, include:

> **map the site**: have maps in several scales of the site (working on A2 or A1 paper is good for showing to a whole company). Maps do not need to be highly detailed: go rather for simple and clear. Often graphic (drawings and names) are more accessible than cartographic (lines and numbers) ones. Include major landmarks and access points but do not crowd the map: that will happen when we start positioning people's activity cards on it
>
> **postcards**: have a plentiful supply of blank bits of card for groups to draw and write on

so, add pencils and maybe double-sided sticky tape to the bag so that as final decisions are reached, cards can be stuck onto their chosen place

do a final version: in your own time, go over that main map and do your own final, smaller version that can be photocopied and circulated among your team

Closing moments

Here are a few ideas for a final ending action. This might come right at the very end of things, but you will need to gauge things by your own situation. If a group is holding together well, we might do some straightforward "thank-yous": to the place, to celebrants, to visitors, to funders and so on and then do one of these activities. We need to try to catch the last moment of cohesion before people simply, decide "it's over" and start to trickle away on their own.

It can be quite good after one of the following to have your band strike up a lively tune and people can dance "informally" if they wish or simply leave with a light heart...

Walking spiral

Time: depends upon groups, allow 10 minutes for about 100 people
Materials: none. Music or musicians help a lot: something light and "walkable" rather than very lively and dancy is probably best
Organisation: start with everyone holding hands, preferably in a circle. If not in a circle to begin with, when you start walking, aim to draw people into something approximately circular before you spiral inwards

Walking in a circle, anticlockwise, break hands with the person on your right and start spiralling inwards (everyone else hold on tight to each other!). Keep the spiral quite loose, going for maybe 2 turns before reaching the middle where you simply turn round and start walking back outwards, passing everyone else on the way. The whole company, if they stay linked, will then follow the spiral path inwards and outwards. As you reach the outer rim again, you might need to add another turn so that the company ends in a circle facing inwards again.

Walking clockwise: same pattern but, in theory, you should come out of the spiral with yourselves facing inwards.

Spirals are lovely, lots of fun and rather unpredictable! They are fun whatever the situation and look especially good with lanterns and flags

Simple Circle Dance

Time: as long or as short as you make it, but probably about 10 minutes
Materials: none. Again music helps. If no musicians are available try stamping feet to set a rhythm (using the words for the steps often sets the beat). If you have musicians, again look for something bouncy but not too lively. Too much energy with a large joined together company tends to invite falling overs and trippings and flat on our faces!
Organisation: large circle holding hands: or maybe several concentric circles who could try the following steps in different directions

Walk/skip round the circle clockwise for 8 steps ("Round for 8"). Turn and go the other way for another 8 steps ("Back for 8") - or you could do this just by walking backwards. Face the centre and take 8 steps in - or 4 steps if a smaller group - (crouching down as you go? lifting arms up as you go? : "in for 8"). Back out again for 8 (bounce up and back from centre?, lower arms and bow? "Back for 8").

Start again.

Add variations: drop hands and turn round at the end of the sequence, add a kick , or a stamp at step 8, hop or skip instead of steps 1 and 2.....play with it

This may not seem like much of a dance, especially when compared to the huge repertoire of folk circle dances that we might do. But here we are trying to get a large company of people simply doing something together. To spend 10 minutes teaching anything more complex could wreck the moment completely!

You might call in a company of practised people to do a more complicated dance in the centre of the company first and then get everyone else to join in with something simpler.

Thank you

Time: 1 minute
Materials: none
Organisation: circle holding hands

Take a moment for everyone to:
"Turn to the person on the right of you and thank them for being brave and joining in our celebration to-day" . Bow to them or even kiss their hand.

Do the same to the person to the left of you.

"Kiss your own hand to thank yourself for being brave..."

This tends to mean we could bow to someone's back, but generally, everyone spins back and forward to give and receive thanks. Kissing hands is a nice touch, but for some groups bowing is enough.

Salute

Time: 1 minute
Materials: none
Organisation: circle holding hands

Follow one of the above activities by pausing. Stand in silence, hands joined. Then bow to the circle of people we are part of. Slowly walk backwards. Keep walking until our hands slide apart and our circle opens. If space precludes this, simply step back a few paces and drop hands but using the gradual separation is nice. Then stop.

"Now our celebration is ended but we leave this special space waiting for the next people who want to come here and have a celebration of their own." Repeat the bow inwards, turn and bow outwards to thank the world. Then, stamp a foot or raise a shout to mark the end of it all......(Most groups then cheer or applaud).

In Pursuit of Love and Passion

Without going into all the background details, here is a description of a procession from Buxton in Derbyshire.

In February, a series of free, open-access, drop-in workshops sets the scene for the final Pursuit (5 years old in 2006). Everything that happens in this main celebration grows out of these workshops. It is dark, and at the top of the hill outside the Town Hall, we can watch little groups of pirates, people in ball gowns, wild hats, occasional dinosaurs, clutching lanterns, come trickling up to our lamp-post meeting point.

The Conductor of Despair meets everyone and sets the scene....on this cold, dark night when it seems as if winter will never end, we will set off in pursuit of love and passion to warm us through the cold and into the summer beyond. But to find love and enter passion, we need to recognise the fear, grief and woe that hold us back. So we start in gloom, choosing for ourselves 5 despairs: dreams unfulfilled, loves lost, woes we would be rid of. The local High Peak Samba Band strikes up a mournful beat and, with a sway and a moan, we set off, slowly, down the hill....and into the Victorian Pavilion Gardens where strange small creatures with glowing eyes run through the yew trees, pacing us, stalking us....in the distance a procession of veiled figures are seen, small lanterns glowing faintly.....the Beasts slip in among us as we reach the Wailing Women and we sing one of our Despairs away with the choir and to the howling of the Beasts. Fire gleams, reflected in the pool and a saxophone draws us on so that we can let another Despair burn away in a flaming pirate ship or float a third away in the little nightlight boats that go drifting off across the pond. Then, silence. Smoke and mist coil out of a tunnel. Green and red flashes of fire light the way as we whisper another Despair to the stones. Now, light! Bubbles! Cascades of petals! Laughter! Scarlet women dancing! And out of the trees the Pirates of Despair come to steal away the last grief that we hoard like treasure in our pockets. Tiny pirates inevitably appear among the children of our company and they pillage our woe like bandits. (Useful delay while the Samba run round to get in position...) The Band strikes up a lively tune. The Conductor is replaced by the Lady of Love and Passion and we go dancing into the world of excitement. We see birds of paradise whirling on long poles. Waving flags and lanterns, we dance round the beautiful rose spiral. Beyond the Bandstand, we gather as a whole company to celebrate: sometimes there will be fire jugglers, sometimes giant lanterns of our favourite buildings in town, sometimes just all of us, exploding into laughter.

We end with a blessing,a poem celebrating ourselves as people of the High Peak, of the stones, the hills, the rain and the dark winter nights. People of imagination, friendship, creativity. People of love and passion.

20

And afterwards

Now it is done. The debris is sorted. Drifts of stray animal masks clutter up your house. Lost puppets are seen roaming school corridors and are found loitering in community centre cupboards. Essentially it is "over" but is it "over, done and finished with" or might this work we have done together spark a new fire of excitement and inspiration? We can hope, and much of *Celebrating Nature* is based on the hope, that more will follow, and these few, last words are to set some thoughts in motion

Evaluation: turn back to How are we doing? Try some of those activities now to review how you feel it all went and start thinking about ideas and issues arising. You might also consider that while the event is over, we hope that the process continues, so:

how do you feel? Exhausted? Tired, but satisfied? Try to be objective in that post-event euphoria. Who would do this again?

what have you learnt: think, reflect discuss this as an individual and as a team and both personally (how are you as a team member? team leader?) and professionally (what new skills have you added to your repertoire?). How can you use what comes out of such a discussion?

using materials:

could some of those left over bits and pieces go to make up a stylish and impressive exhibition? Try the local library, community centre, school, museum – set out to inspire other people

encourage participants to take things home and try activities for themselves: go on inspiring other people

can you share left-over materials – or just your skills with other people, groups or projects?: even more inspiring other people

what comes next? Do we have a list of people interested in being involved next time? Organise a social evening soon! Maybe try the Calenders activity with them. Send a report and images into local press. Invite interest. Invite participation. Decide before any such meeting what you hope might come from it. Do you and your team want to do this particular celebration again? Do you want to hand it over to someone else? Will you be receptive if someone wants to do that? Would support something "similar but different" growing out of your efforts? Listen to people. Encourage a sense of ownership

give yourselves time to recover! While you may feel that you need to gallop on and into the next celebration while there is still a surge of public excitement to work with, doing that might leave you so shattered that you don't enjoy the project and leave the final product feeing just as tired and rushed as you do. Give yourselves time: time for you to relax and feel ready again, time for new workers to take hold of an idea and grow it into their own event, time for the site you worked on to breathe again don't rush. Respect yourselves and your public, and if you have done and, are doing, an effective (and relevant) job, the people will come back and join in again. Sometimes support works on a sort of 2 year cycle. People come back to you after a break, so sometimes a second "go" at an idea feels like you are mostly working with completely new people and you are left wondering what happened to all that enthusiasm from last time. Sometimes, you may find that people have gone off and started organising their own little celebrations, inspired and en-skilled by their sessions with you

Perhaps those are some of the best measures of immediate success: inspired, people act: with you or on their own. Long term success? A world that begins to feel as valued and as cherished as the communities we have celebrated with?

"we live in a world worthy of celebration"

Appendix 1

Planning an event

Here are some practical points to check out when planning a workshop or a celebration within a project.

This list is not, and will never be, exhaustive: every situation will call for new perspectives to be considered, but hopefully this may give you some pointers to start your own checklists...

site: conservation issues, carrying capacity (how many people will it take?)

site safety: physical - dangerous areas
social - dangerous people
natural - dangerous animals and plants
First Aid: who? access points for ambulance or fire brigade

communication system: walkie-talkies/ mobile phones? nearest public telephone, access to site for ambulance, name of access road/car park?

access: physical - can people get around the site - pushchairs, etc?
social - cars, public transport, bikes, publicity
numbers - how many people can you cope with?

access to event: open-access - anyone who turns up (within a specified age group?)

first come, first served: queue for tickets on the day
prior booking

staff:
how many have you got
how many would you like - for planned activities?
how many should you have for expected numbers?
Police clearance/voluntary disclosure forms
what training do people have - what can you offer?
ratio of experienced group leaders to inexperienced helpers
admin people/lunchtime leaders/gopher

legal
what are you doing?
where are you doing it?
who are you doing it to?
insurance - public liability at £2 -£5 million?

budget
costs/income
will you charge for the event?
volunteers expenses (travel and provide lunch?)
outside groups (funds for musicians?)
funds for specific themes: environmental or social sponsorship/ grant aid

Publicity

In advance: events programme for a 6 month period?

Within a month of the event:

posters: A4 or A3 - keep them clear and simple - basic information and maybe an eyecatching image
fliers: A5 - as poster
Press Release - again keep it clear and simple but

now you can include a couple of paragraphs explaining what the event will contain, why you are doing it and a little bit of background to your group and the project

Week or two before:

arrange silly photo opportunity for local press
large numbers of fliers to local schools and youth centres, etc
display in local shopping centre + leaflet distribution

Distribution:

posters/fliers to anywhere where people gather and hang around long enough to read something: local shops, libraries, doctor/dentist waiting room, community centre, tourist office, schools...

press releases: all local papers, local radio, regional BBC/ITV, free newspapers, several months in advance might be worth trying regional magazines

Basic information

Be clear:

title - short, snappy; "A Spring Feast"
sub-title (tells a bit more) - "wild foods in the Mersey Valley"
date
time - starting and approximate finishing times
meeting place
cost - will there be a charge?
who is this for - "for all the family", "not suitable for young children", etc
what it is - a short walk, a family event, a picnic
public transport to site/ car parking
further information: contact name and number is advance booking needed?

Appendix 2

Materials and equipment

This is a list of the basic materials I buy on a regular basis for work on projects, going usually for a balance between effectiveness and cheapness in money spent. This selection is not in any way exhaustive! Other things are bought or hunted out as impulse or inspiration suggests. Prices given are approximate, 2003, using mainly scrap stores or school suppliers, but will vary a lot depending upon area and the suppliers you have access to.

Glue
PVA - 5 litre bottles - strong and essential - dilute for most uses. Give it time to dry - it washes out when wet but is waterproof when dry.
Rubber Solution Glue - carpet glue - available from DIY stores or carpet warehouses- can be diluted and used with paper or cloth to skin frames. Use neat for faster bonding than PVA
Copydex: a bit less pungent than Carpet Glue but tends to be more expensive.

Tape
Gaffer (or Jumbo or Duck) Tape- "waterproof cloth tape" - expensive but invaluable. Be mean with it and make its use count. Scrapstores tend to be cheapest supplier or try theatrical or industrial suppliers
Masking tape - basic tape for most work. Use 19 or 25mm widths for most work and buy in bulk. Try scrapstore or industrial sources.
Double-sided sticky tape - expensive but has its moments (stationary or arts suppliers)

Brown-paper parcel tape - gummed - use for close-fitting face masks or instant papier mache

Fasteners
Staplers: standard school ones should do, taking 6mm staples
Staple-gun - useful but sometimes perilous - often has to be "adults only"
Paper-fasteners/split pins - 12, 25 and 35mm lengths are all useful.
String - parcel string, baler twine, rope, gardening jute - have a number of balls or different types
Thread - "carpet thread" and "button twine" both come on 100m and 50m reels - tough and fine, very useful for more delicate constructions

Sticks
Peasticks - plain or green 30 - 45cm stakes. Buy by the hundred from scrapstores (or willow suppliers maybe) if possible. Garden Centres another, but more expensive source
Bamboo canes - a range of sizes is always useful. Buy 3m ones whenever you see them and make sure you retrieve them at the end of an event! Prices are very variable. Try scrapstores, garden centres and willow suppliers
Withies - slender 1 - 2m stripped willow canes. Obtain dry in bulk from specialist suppliers or maybe a scrapstore. Fresh, green willow does not keep as well but can often be obtained free from local countryside rangers, etc with willow coppices on their sites.

Paper
Sugar paper - packs of 250 A2 coloured, recycled.
Newsprint - plain, unbleached, A2
Lining paper - buy by the roll in DIY stores - excellent for communal drawing or planning projects - rolls vary in price depending on length
White Tissue - buy good quality paper from a packing supplier (check that you are getting crisp, white paper and not a very

thin newsprint.). "Wet-strength tissue" paper is much stronger but much more expensive!
Coloured tissue - can be hard to get in bulk - most places only sell in packs of 20 or so sheets.
Cardboard - packs of A3 coloured, recycled available, watch thickness: black and white tend to be heavier than coloured and better for construction. Otherwise, "cereal packet" weight is good for working with

Drawing & Other Materials
Wax crayons, coloured and graphite pencils, felt-tip pens, charcoal, pastel crayons are all useful and don't forget the pencil sharpeners
Paints - ready-mix bottles often easiest - c80p - £1.60 for 1 litre bottle (mix with a little PVA for water proofing), metallic powder paints are good on damp surfaces (dust or blow them over) and lustre (slightly) and
glitter paints are worth investment if feeling rich. Acrylic Paints are also good but expensive: give strong colours and good coverage
Paintbrushes - go for a variety of cheap ones with broad or fat heads rather than lots of delicate ones - some will inevitably get used for glue, lost in the mud and so on: short-handled hoghair, 25 brush selection £9.00 from school supplier
Scissors: get children's round-tipped ones. You will need some stronger ones: try to avoid things that are very long, slender and deadly. Remember to bring in left-handed ones as well
Tufkut scissors: designed for cutting plaster casts off limbs, these are strong, oddly shaped scissors: good for work on willow (and plaster cloth)
Hole-punch pliers: generally make single holes through paper or thin card, very useful
Craft knives - metal-bodied "Stanley" knives with retractable blades are best - keep on a length of string to slip onto a belt-loop
Plaster cloth - "mod-roc": sheets of scrim impregnated with plaster of paris, dip in water and wrap round moulds, where

plaster will set quickly, conforming to shape of mould. Great stuff and wonderfully messy. Mix PVA into water first for a stronger and slightly more flexible finish

Sources

Scrapstore: "play resource centres" : many local ones. Most work with a membership scheme: annual subscription allowing access to low cost materials and lots of exciting, safe, scrap material for use by groups. Often have parachutes, earthballs, etc for hire. Finding your nearest scrapstore: try web search under the "Scrap Store Network" or contact your local council: child services, leisure or libraries might all be able to help, or speak to local youth group leaders

Withy: regional suppliers in Somerset, Yorkshire and East Anglia. I often get a bale from my scrapstore at about the same cost as buying wholesale and adding delivery charge. Useful supplier: P H Coate & Son, Mear Green Court, Stoke Street, Gregory, Taunton, TA3 6AY - ask for "six foot, buff willow". Another supplier: Jacobs, Young & Westbury, Bridge Rd, Haywards Heath, W Sussex, RH16 1UA. Tel: 01444 412411 (also sell bamboo by the bale)

School suppliers: many areas have "county suppliers" of materials for schools - ask local education advisers or a teacher for a contact. A national supplier with an excellent range is NES Arnold Ltd, Novara House, Excelsior Rd, Ashby Park, Ashby-de-la-Zouche, Leics, LE65 1NG Tel: 0870 600 0192

Wet-strength tissue paper: the only UK supplier I know is: Richards & Appleby, Heads of the Valleys Industrial Park, Rhymney, Gwent, NP22 5RL Tel: 01685 843384

Bibliography

Creeping Toad books

MacLellan, Gordon: *Talking to the Earth*, Capall Bann, 1995, ISBN 1 898307 43 1

MacLellan, Gordon: *Sacred Animals*, Capall Bann, 1997, ISBN 1 89830 769 5

Brown, MacLellan, Mason and Vis: *StarMatter*, StillWell, 2005, ISBN 0 9550345 0 7: astronomy, geology and creative education

Art examples and inspiration

The Hundred Languages of Children, Unipol 1996. ISBN 88 87960 08 9

Carson, Rachel: *The Sense of Wonder*, HarperCollins, 1998: ISBN 0 06 757520 X

Coult, B & Kershaw T: *Engineers of the Imagination*, Methuen 1983 - excellent source of street theatre and celebration inspiration and guidance, ISBN 0 413 52800 6

Drury, Chris: *Silent Spaces*, Thames & Hudson, 1998, ISBN 0 500 09276 1

Finlay, Victoria: *Colour, travels through the paintbox*, Sceptre, 2002, ISBN 0 340 73329 2

Goldsworthy, Andy: Parkland, Yorkshire Sculpture Park, 1988 (1 871480 000)- but also look out for *Wood*, *Stone* or any of Andy Goldsworthy's other books!

Gooding, M & Furlong, W: *Song of the Earth*, Thames & Hudson, 2002 (0 500 51016 4): draws together images and interviews from a range of modern environment and landscape artists

Matthews, S: With Animals, *Pedalling Arts*, 1994. ISBN 1 899281 00 2

Murphy & Neill: *By Nature's Design*, Chronicle Books, 1993. ISBN 0 8118 0329 5

Wyatt, G: *Spirit Faces*, Thames & Hudson, 1994. ISBN 0 500 2 7800 8

Celebrations

Brafford and Thom, *Dancing Colors* (paths of Native American women), Chronicle, 1992, ISBN 0 8118 0165 9 (part of a whole, exciting series)

Franklin & Mason, *Lammas: celebrating the fruits of the first harvest*, Llewellyn, 2001, ISBN 0 73870 094 0

Frazer & Oestreicher: *The Art of Remembering*, Carcanet, 1998. ISBN 1 85754 377 7

Hole, Christina, *British Folk Customs*, Paladin 1978, ISBN 0-586-08293-X one of the best sources of info on folk traditions. Now out of print but often turns up in secondhand stores in hardback editions

Jones & Deer: *Cattern Cakes and Lace*, Dorling Kindersley, 1987 ISBN 9 78086 318252 5
Kindred, G: *Sacred Celebrations*, Gothic Image 2001
Matthews, J: *The Winter Solstice*, Quest Books, 1998, ISBN 0 8356 0769 0: also look out for the companion volume "The Summer Solstice" (1 84181 134 3)
Teish, Luisah, *Carnival of the Spirit*, seasonal celebrations and rites of passage, Harper Collins, 1994. ISBN 0 06 250868 7

Anecdotal information

Good sources of snippets...

Briggs, Katherine: *An Encyclopedia of Fairies*, Pantheon, ISBN 0-394-73467-X, another wonderful source of material from KB. An earlier edition came out as "*The Dictionary of Fairies*"
Darwin, Tessa: *The Scots Herbal*, Mercat Press 1996, ISBN 1 873644 60 4
Froud, B & Lee A: *Faeries*, Pan 1978, ISBN 0-330-25756-0 (various editions and reprints)
Hull, Robin, *Scottish Birds, culture and tradition*, Mercat Press 2001, ISBN 1-841-83025-9
Mabey, Richard: *Flora Britannica*, Sinclair Stevenson, 1996, ISBN 1-85619-377-2. The original edition is amazing.
Mac Coitir, Niall: *Irish Trees, myths, legends and folklore*, The Collins Press, 2003, ISBN 1 90346 433 1
Miles, Archie: *Silva: the tree in Britain*, Ebury Press, 1999, ISBN 0-091-86788-6
Pakenham. T: *Meetings with Remarkable Trees,* Phoenix 1996, ISBN 0 75380 237 6
The Common Ground Book of Orchards, Common Ground 2000, ISBN 1 870364 21 X

Environmental awareness

Baker, Nick: *Nick Baker's Bug Book*, New Holland, 2002, ISBN 1859748953
Cooper, G: *Outdoors with Young People*, RHP, 1998, ISBN 1 898924 24 4
Cornell, J B: *Sharing Nature with Children*, Exley, ISBN 0 905521 37 4
Hodgson, J & Dyer, A: *Let Your Children Go Back to Nature*, Capall Bann, 2003 ISBN 1861631723
Packham, Chris: *Wild Side of Town*, New Holland, 2003, ISBN 1843303558
Sample, Geoff: *Nature Safari, imaginative things for you and your children to do outdoors* : Collins 2003, ISBN 0007138393
van Matre, S et al: *Acclimatisation*, ISBN 0 87603 007 X

Sunship Earth (0 87603 007 X)...and others - earth-changing concepts,
Look for the series of books published by WHITTET: a whole range of books on specific animals ("Hedgehogs", "Foxes", etc) and habitats ("Pond Life")

Art techniques

Warnes, Jon: *Living Willow Sculpture*, Search Press, 2000, ISBN 0 855 32834 7
Hunt, W Ben: *The Complete How-to Book of Indiancraft*, Collier, 1972, ISBN 0 02 011690 X
Kilby, Morgenthal & Taylor: *The Book of Wizardcraft*, Brimax 2001. ISBN 1 8585 4421 1
Maguire, Mary: *Magic Lanterns*, Collins & Brown, 2002, ISBN 1 843 40138 X,
Petrash, Carol: *Earthwise*, Floris 1993. ISBN 0 86315 158 2
Schneebeli-Morrell, D: *The Pumpkin Carving Book*, Lorenz Books, 1996, ISBN 1 85967 305 8
Shepherd, Rob: *Hand-made Books*, Search Press, 1994, ISBN 0 855 32754 5
Watson, David, *Creative Handmade Paper*, Search Press, 1991, ISBN 0 85532 730 8

Storytelling activities and techniques

Caduto & Bruchac: *Keepers of the Earth*, Fulcrum, 1989, ISBN 1 55591 027 0. Watch also for *Keepers of the Animals* and others
Colwell, Eileen, *Storytelling*, Thimble Press, 1995, ISBN 0 903355 35 3
Gersie, Alida, *Earthtales: storytelling in times of change*, Greenprint 1992, ISBN 1 85425 065 5
le Guin, Ursula: *Steering the Craft*, Eighth Mountain Press, 1998, ISBN 0-933377-46-0 Exciting stuff; more about writing than storytelling but still useful
Johnstone, Keith: *Impro for Storytellers*, Faber & Faber, 1999, ISBN 0-571-19099-5
Maddern, Eric: *Storytelling at Historic Sites*, English Heritage, ISBN 1 859 743789: very useful
Nanson, Anthony: *Storytelling and Ecology*, University of Glamorgan Press, 2005, ISBN 1 84054 125 3
Scottish Storytelling Centre: *Telling Stories, the resource pack for storytelling in Scotland* Contact: The Netherbow 43 - 45 High St, Edinburgh, EH1 1SR Tel: 0131 557 5724
Zipes, Jack: *Creative Storytelling*, Routledge, 1995, ISBN 0-415-91272-5

Collections of stories

There are increasing numbers of story collections, gathered by country, theme, or just by what the editor likes! Choosing from such a range is a very personal thing. The list below contains a few of the ones that I have found particularly valuable. As a rule, I go for books that have lots of stories for me to sift through rather than relying on a small selection with lovely illustrations. Second-hand bookshops and charity shops are excellent places to go a'foraging

Briggs, Katherine: *A Sampler of British Folk Tales*, Routledge, 1977, ISBN 0 7100 8553 More recent imprints are available. Briggs is always worth watching for: wonderful resources to draw upon

East, Helen: *The Singing Sack*, Black 1989, ISBN 0 7136 3115 5. Stories with songs and music. One of an extensive series

Erdoes & Ortiz: American Indian Myths and Legends, Pantheon 1984, ISBN 0 394 74018 1: wonderful extensive collection: still in print

Karas, Sheryl Ann: *The Solstice Evergreen*, Aslan 1991, ISBN 0 944031 26 9, mixed collection of stories about trees - not all Christmas trees!

Miller, Moira; *A Kist o'Whistles*, Andre Deutsch, 1990 ISBN 0 233 98537 9: a lovely collection of tales

Crossley-Holland, Kevin: *The Old Stories*, Dolphin, 1997, ISBN 1 85881 753 6 Also try "*British Folk Tales*", Orchard, 1987, 1-85213-021-0

Riordan, James: *Songs My Paddle Sings*, Pavilion 1997, ISBN 1 86205 076 7. Beautiful collection of native American legends

Drama, dance, masks and puppets

The Eco-puppets Handbook, The Broads Authority, 1999. ISBN 0 948199 48 9

Evans & Powell: *Inspirations for Dance And Movement*, Scholastic, 1994 - part of a whole series of useful "inspirations" books ISBN 0 590 53089 5

Flower & Fortney: *Puppets: methods and materials*, Davis Publications, 1983, ISBN 0 87192 142 1

Foreman, J: *Maskwork*, Lutterworth, 1999, ISBN 0 7188 2948 4

Fraser, P: *Puppets and Puppetry*, Batsford, 1980, ISBN 0 7134 2073 1

Hamblin, K: *Mime: a playbook of silent fantasy*, Lutterworth Press, 1978, ISBN 7 188 2461 X

Jackson, A: *Instruments Around The World*, Longman 1988, ISBN 0 582 2244 0

Sivin, Carole: *Maskmaking*, Davis Publications, Inc, ISBN 0871921782

INDEX

Talking to the Earth by Gordon MacLellan

This book welcomes the reader onto an adventure of creativity into the wild that hides in the corners of park and city: a chance to explore the world around us and express discoveries in exciting ways. "Talking" is a collection of activities to let the artist out in everyone:- using natural, recycled or cheap materials, here are chances to explore new ways of expressing the relationship between ourselves and the natural world. Ranging from the dramatic potency of "Masks" to banners and story boards, activities are presented with easy to follow guidelines, practical notes for teachers, parents and group leaders and handy hints for a smoother run. Designed for use by children of all ages from infant to ancient, "*Talking to the Earth*" is an invaluable manual for anyone working in environmental art - from the experienced art-worker to the cautious beginner. ISBN 1898307 43 1 £10.00

Let Your Children Go Back To Nature by John Hodgson & Alan Dyer

'Its a book and an idea and an educational at a deep and true level' The Times Educational Supplement.

This ground-breaking book by two long-experienced educationalists challenges the current orthodoxies about the upbringing of younger children. It offers parents and teachers an attractive means to ameliorate the deadening demands of the National Curriculum. It is crammed with new and stimulating ideas, games and creative activities that have already delighted thousands of children of all abilities. The ideas and adventures in this book started as a two year experiment with 24 Devon children; the concept proved so popular that is grew to encompass many more activities and thousands of children across southern England. The aim is to provide not only enjoyment, but also 'real' education too with a great deal of 'required' information - strongly reinforced by direct experience, games and creative activities. Activities include story-telling, costumes, poetry, music and dances, drama, games for fun and enchantment, traditional country activities, and much more - an 'Enchanters' Brew' of ideas and activities with plenty of nourishment for young minds and bodies - for the children *and* you! ISBN 186163 1723£12.95

Gardening For Wildlife by Ron Wilson

"If you have only one wildlife book, this is the one to have. The information contained in this book is invaluable. A very interesting read for young and old alike, to which you will always refer." The Professional Gardener ***"..a real delight...a fascinating read...all of the methods I have tried so far have gleaned superb results"*** *Touchstone* ***"lively, colloquial style...quick and easy to read...inspiring and full of helpful tips'*** *Place*

"..a nice book...lively drawings which clearly illustrate techniques...covers everything...a good starter book" *Permaculture*

A few 'modifications' and additions could enhance the value of most gardens for wildlife. That is what this book is all about. It offers practical advice and ideas for improvements and where possible suggests the inclusion of 'extra' features which will support and encourage a rich diversity of plant, insect, bird and animal life. Plants, foods and features are all described in plain English. Everything in this book is explained in straightforward terms to enable anyone to help their local wildlife. ISBN 1 86163 011 5 £10.95

Magical Guardians - Exploring the Spirit and Nature of Trees

by Philip Heselton

"..shows us that the trees in our gardens, parks and woods have a spiritual nature ...magical guardians of the wildwood, healers and entrances to the Otherworld.. Highly recommended." *Prediction* ***"straightforward, unpretentious account of how to build up a personal relationship with your favourite tree - memorable pictures"*** *3RD Stone*

This is a book about trees, but a book with a difference, for it acknowledges trees to be wise beings who can teach us much if we approach them in the right way. This book shows how to go about it, revealing the origins of our awakening interest in - and love for - trees. Trees have a spiritual nature, and opening up to this spirit has been a constant feature in human society. Through practical guidance, this book gives hints on how we can make that contact for ourselves. The personalities of the ancient trees - our Magical Guardians - are explored, and the book reveals how we can start to acquire some of their deeper meanings. ISBN 1 86163 057 3 £12.95

The Enchanted Forest - The Magical Lore of Trees by Yvonne Aburrow

"..wonderful insight...easy to read...very informative, a lovely enchanting book". *Touchstone*

Fascinating & truly unique - a comprehensive guide to the magical, medicinal & craft uses, mythology, folklore, symbolism & weatherlore of trees. There are chapters on trees in myth & legend, tree spirits, trees in ritual magic, trees & alphabets (runes & Ogham) & weather lore. These chapters are followed by a comprehensive 'herbal index' with in-depth coverage of individual trees from acacia to aspen, wayfaring tree to willow. Profusely illustrated. ISBN 1898307 083 £11.95

Music and the Earth Spirit by Bob Dickinson

This is a book about music and sound; a multi-cultural exploration from pre-history to the present day, revealing how man has used these forms to commune with nature and the environment. Underlying this communion is an acknowledgement of the spiritual powers of Mother Earth herself. The author shows how music and sound can be used to enable a 'tuning' into this spirit. The book includes sound workings enabling the reader to sing his/her own Earth spirit song. ISBN 186163 1170 £9.95

Sacred Welsh Waters by Chris J Thomas

"many years of research and actual walking in the Welsh hills....recommended" *The Cauldron*

The result of years of intensive research, hundreds of conversations and a great deal of time spent walking and clambouring around the Welsh countryside. This is a treasury of information on sacred and healing wells and springs in Wales. Authentic local stories, legends and beliefs are related. All but a very few of the wells and springs described here have been personally visited by the author - they really exist and can be found using the excellent directions provided. ISBN 186163 1510 £12.95

The Magic and Mystery of Holy Wells by Edna Whelan

Drawing on her own extensive field work, augmented and enhanced with research into ancient history, geology, archaeology and natural history, Edna shares the magic, mystery and sanctity surrounding Holy Wells. There is a certain atmosphere surrounding a Holy Well, particularly the secret ones which are hidden away in our ancient landscape. Here, beside the ageless, ever-running water, it seems that time stands still and the quietness and serenity abiding there seeps into one's heart and soul, bringing a calmness and tranquillity which is surely the cure for debilitating stress and unease. The text is further brought to life with numerous illustrations. A source of knowledge, calm and inspiration from the ancient magical waters. ISBN 186163 1359 £8.95